ALEXANDRIA

CITY OF THE
WESTERN MIND

THEODORE VRETTOS

THE FREE PRESS

NEW YORK • LONDON • TORONTO • SINGAPORE • SYDNEY

*f*P

THE FREE PRESS
A division of Simon & Schuster Inc.
1230 Avenue of the Americas
New York, New York 10020

THE FREE PRESS and colophon are
registered trademarks of Simon & Schuster Inc.

For information about special discounts and bulk purchases,
please contact Simon & Schuster Special Sales:
1-800-456-6798 or business@simonandschuster.com

DESIGNED BY KEVIN HANEK

Manufactured in the United States of America

1   3   5   7   9   10   8   6   4   2

Library of Congress Cataloging-in-Publication Data
Vrettos, Theodore.
Alexandria : city of the western mind / Theodore Vrettos.
p.   cm.
Includes bibliographical references (p.) and index.
1.   Alexandria (Egypt)—History.   2. History, Ancient.   I. Title.
DT73.A4 V73   2001   2001040891
932—dc21

ISBN 0-7432-0569-3 (alk. paper)

To the memory of Lawrence Durrell

CONTENTS

N

PHAROS LIGHT

GREAT
HARBOR

PORT of
PIRATES

present-day coastline

HEPHAISTION
GATE

HEPTASTADION

PHAROS
TOWN

Docks

The ISLE of PHAROS

present-day coastline

Docks

PORT of
EUNOSTOS

MOON GATE

R
H
A
K
O
T
I
S

PORT of KIBOTOS

ALEXANDRIA

in Cleopatra's Time

Canop

City Walls

Navigable
Canal

NECROPOLIS

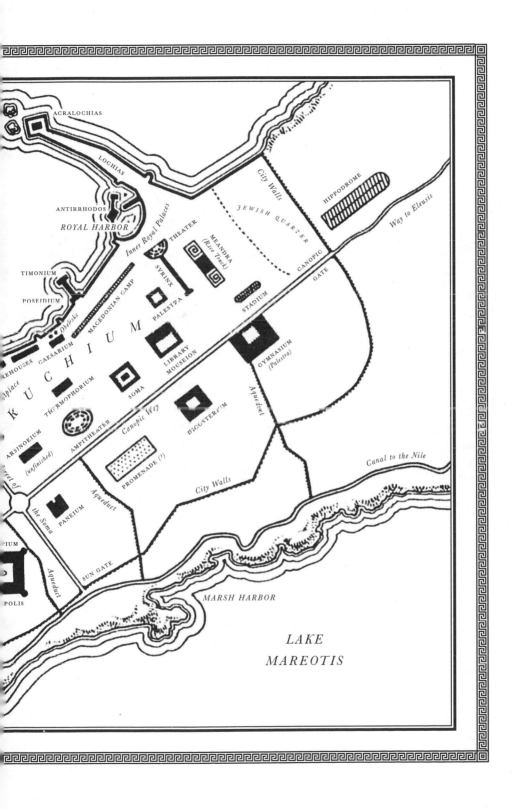

ACRALOCHIAS

LOCHIAS

City Walls

JEWISH QUARTER

HIPPODROME

ANTIRRHODOS

Way to Eleusis

ROYAL HARBOR

Inner Royal Palaces

THEATER

MEANDRA
(Race Track)

TIMONIUM

SYRINX

CANOPIC

GATE

POSEIDIUM

MACEDONIAN CAMP

PALESTRA

STADIUM

Obelisks

B R U C H I U M

CAESARIUM

LIBRARY
MOUSEION

GYMNASIUM
(Palestra)

REHOUSES

SOMA

Aqueduct

alplace

THERMOPHORIUM

ARSINOEIUM

AMPHITHEATER

Canopic Way

DICOSTERION

(unfinished)

PROMENADE (?)

City Walls

Canal to the Nile

reet of

the Soma

Aqueduct

PANEIUM

PIUM

Aqueduct

SUN GATE

POLIS

MARSH HARBOR

LAKE
MAREOTIS

PROLOGUE

I N THE *Odyssey*, Homer describes "an island in the surging sea which they call *Pharos*, lying off Egypt. It has a harbor with good anchorage, and hence they put out to sea after drawing water."

When Alexander the Great came upon this site in 332 B.C., a settlement named Rhakotis sprawled along the shore and was a haven for fishermen and pirates. Behind it, five native villages were scattered along the strip between Lake Mareotis and the Mediterranean Sea. Just off the coast lay the island of Pharos, where Alexander stayed before setting out to find the oracle of Zeus Ammon in the Siwa Oasis.

Diodorus Siculus, writing in the first century B.C., furnished detailed information about Alexander's deciding to found a great city in Egypt and issuing orders to his architects that they build the city between the marsh (Lake Mareotis) and the sea. "He himself," stated the Greek historian, "laid out the site and traced the streets skillfully and ordered that the city should be called after him, *Alexandria*. It was conveniently situated near the harbor of Pharos, and by selecting the right angle of the streets, Alexander made the city breathe with the Etesian winds [the northwestern winds of summer], so that as these blew across a great expanse of sea, they cooled the air of the city and thus provided its inhabitants with a moderate climate and good health. Alexander's architects also laid out the walls so that they were large and very strong. Lying between the great marsh and the sea, the city thus afforded two approaches by land, both narrow and easily protected in case of war."

Since the Nile was only twenty miles away, Alexander realized that wherever this great river poured itself into the sea, so much silt and mud would collect at the Delta it would be impossible to have a sound harbor there. But at Pharos, silt posed no problem. His new city would have two clear harbors: one on the Mediterranean, the other facing Lake Mareotis to the south. Furthermore, he would construct a canal from the lake to the Nile, connecting Alexandria with all the river ports of southern Egypt. Thus the city would be able to accept trade ships from the Mediterranean as well as from the Nile without danger of being clogged by the accumulation of sediment.

Because Alexander had defeated the Persians at the Dardanelles and at Asia Minor, and because Egypt clung to its bitter hatred of the Persians, the country fell willingly into his hands. He was twenty-five when he entered Memphis, the ancient capital of Egypt (modern Cairo). From there, he traveled by barge down the Nile, all the way to the clay-bound coast facing Pharos Island. The place apparently fascinated him, and he ordered his architect Deinocrates to build a magnificent city on the site. The Greek biographer Plutarch wrote that Alexander knelt down and sliced out the streets of this proposed city with strokes of his finger in the sand—streets wide enough for eight chariots to travel side by side, each leading diagonally to the sea.

To maintain control of his newly acquired Egyptian territory, Alexander needed a capital on the coast to serve as a supply link with Macedonia. At Pharos, he had found the ideal site: secure harbor, mild climate, with ample fresh water, and easy access to the Nile and the Lower Kingdom. Alexander hoped that the genius of Hellenism would be perpetuated here, a metropolis of culture to benefit the entire world.

When Alexander departed for the Siwa Oasis, Deinocrates, a renowned architect of the time, carried out Alexander's instructions, laying out the new capital of Egypt: crossing the streets at right angles and lining them on both sides with columns the full length of the city, east to west. Along with spacious parks and gardens, slaves constructed lavish buildings and palaces, including a university called the Mouseion (home of the Muses), and a magnificent library, which would attract the best scientists, philosophers, mathematicians, physicians, teachers, and scholars of the age.

Amazingly, Alexander's grand dream would find its way into the mind and soul of the city, and produce a profound influence on western culture, art, politics, and religion to this day.

ACKNOWLEDGMENTS

I AM GRATEFUL TO Dr. Hassan I. Ismail, curator of the Greco-Roman Museum in Alexandria, for his cooperation and help. I am also indebted to Dr. Djanane Batanouni of Alexandria for her assistance in tracking down elusive documents, manuscripts, and maps of ancient Alexandria.

I received invaluable support and encouragement from John Updike, from my esteemed fellow Joyceans, and from Dr. Francis Blessington of Northeastern University.

Many libraries and museums throughout the world offered necessary information and material. Among these are Harvard University's Widener Library, the Vatican Museums in Rome, the Archbishop Iakovos Library and Learning Resource Center at Hellenic College in Brookline, Massachusetts, the Harvard Divinity School Library, the Archeological Museum of Pella in Macedonia, the National Archeological Museum of Naples, the National Gallery of Art and the Library of Congress in Washington, the Metropolitan Museum in New York, the Boston Public Library, the Goddard Library of the Gordon-Conwell Theological Seminary in Hamilton, Massachusetts, and the Peabody Institute Library in Danvers, Massachusetts, particularly its competent researchers: Nick McAuliffe, Suzanne MacLeod, and Donna Maturi.

I owe utmost thanks to my astute editor, Stephen Morrow, at The Free Press, also to his assistant Beth Haymaker for her support, and to Fred Wiemer, for his excellent copyediting of the manuscript. My most sincere thanks are reserved for my agent, John Taylor "Ike" Williams, for nurturing the book with his many valuable suggestions and for his devoted work throughout.

Acknowledgments

My heartfelt love to my family under the sun—Bess and Peter—and to those in the shade—my parents Zacharoúla and Leonídas, sister Mary, and brothers Charles and Louis.

As always, my greatest debt of gratitude is to my wife, Vas, for her dedicated labor and love.

Principal Characters

Aeschylus (525–456 B.C.), Greek poet and tragedian.

Agrippa, Marcus Vipsanius (63–12 B.C.), Roman general and statesman.

Alexander the Great (356–323 B.C.), king of Macedon; conqueror of the Persian Empire and Egypt.

Antony, Mark (83–44 B.C.), Roman general and statesman; Cleopatra's lover.

Apelles, contemporary of Alexander the Great; the greatest painter of antiquity; court painter of the kings of Macedon.

Apis, the sacred bull of ancient Egyptians.

Apollonius [of Perga] (c. 262 B.C.), Greek geometer of Alexandria.

Apollonius [of Rhodes] (c. 222–212 B.C.), Greek epic poet of Alexandria.

Appian (c. 2nd cent. A.D.), Roman historian, native of Alexandria.

Archimedes (c. 287–212 B.C.), Greek mathematician and inventor.

Aristarchus [of Samos] (c. 3rd cent. B.C.), Greek astronomer.

Aristarchus [of Samothrace] (c. 170 B.C.), the greatest editor among Homeric scholars in Alexandria.

Aristophanes of Byzantium (c. 200 B.C.), Homeric scholar.

Aristotle (384–322 B.C.), Greek philosopher; pupil of Plato; tutor of Alexander the Great.

Arius (died A.D. 336), Greek theologian of Alexandria; condemned as a heretic.

Arrian (A.D. 96[?]–180), Roman historian.

Artemis, Greek goddess of the hunt.

Athanasius (A.D. 293–373), patriarch of Alexandria; opponent of Arius.

Athena, Greek goddess of wisdom and the arts.

Augustine (A.D. 354–430), Early Christian Church Father and author; born in Numidia.

Brutus, Marcus Junius (85–42 B.C.), Roman political and military leader; one of Caesar's assassins.

Bucephalus, the beloved horse of Alexander the Great.

Caesar, Julius (100–44 B.C.), Roman statesman, general, historian, and dictator; father of Cleopatra's son Caesarion.

Callimachus (3rd cent. B.C.), poet and grammarian; librarian of the Alexandrian Library until his death in 240 B.C.

Caracalla (A.D. 188–217), emperor of Rome.

Cicero (106–43 B.C.), Roman statesman and orator.

Cleitus, black officer and close companion of Alexander the Great.

Clement of Alexandria (born c. A.D. 150), theologian, author, and esteemed teacher of Origen.

Cleopatra (69–30 B.C.), queen of Egypt.

Constantine the Great (A.D. 280–337), Roman emperor, first to adopt Christianity as the state religion; his capital was transferred from Rome to Byzantium, renamed Constantinople in A.D. 330.

Darius III, king of Persia, defeated by Alexander the Great and died in July 330 B.C.

Erasistratus (c. 3rd cent. B.C.), physician and anatomist of Alexandria.

Eratosthenes (c. 3rd cent. B.C.), mathematician and astronomer of Alexandria; he accurately estimated the circumference of the earth.

Euclid (c. 3rd cent. B.C.), Greek mathematician, author of *Elements.*

Galen (A.D. 130–201), anatomist, physician, and physiologist.

Herodotus (5th cent. B.C.), Greek historian, "the Father of History."

Herophilus (3rd cent. B.C.), Alexandrian surgeon and anatomist.

Hippocrates (460–377[?] B.C.), Greek physician, "the Father of Medicine."

Homer (c. 8th cent. B.C.), Greek epic poet; author of the *Iliad* and the *Odyssey.*

Hypatia (A.D. 370–415), mathematician and philosopher; daughter of Theon (author of scholia on Euclid's work); murdered by a mob of fanatic Christian monks in Alexandria.

Lysippus, famous Greek sculptor who lived in the time of Alexander the Great; his works are said to have numbered over 1,500.

Napoleon Bonaparte (1769–1821), emperor of France.

Nelson, Horatio Viscount (1758–1805), British admiral; hero of the Battle of Trafalgar, during which he died; lover of Lady Hamilton.

Octavian [Augustus Gaius Octavius] (63 B.C.–A.D. 14), Roman emperor; adopted son of Julius Caesar; victor over Mark Antony in the Battle of Actium.

Olympias, mother of Alexander the Great.

Origen (A.D. 185–254), renowned Alexandrian teacher, theologian, and author; he castrated himself at the age of eighteen.

Philip II (382–336 B.C.), king of Macedon, father of Alexander the Great.

Philo Judaeus (c. 20 B.C.), Hellenistic Jewish philosopher and author.

Pompey the Great [Gnaeus Pompeius Magnus] (106–48 B.C.), Roman statesman and general.

Ptolemies, a dynasty of Macedonian kings and queens who ruled in Egypt from 323 to 30 B.C.

Ptolemy [Claudius Ptolemaeus] (2nd cent. A.D.), Greek astronomer, mathematician, and geographer; lifelong resident of Alexandria.

Theocritus (316–246 B.C.), Alexandrian bucolic poet.

Zenodotus (3rd cent. B.C.), the first director of the Alexandrian Library; chief editor of Homer.

Zeus, the presiding god of the Greek pantheon; ruler of the heavens; father of gods and of mortal heroes.

ALEXANDRIA

PART ONE

THE BIRTH

OF THE CITY

ᏕᎢᎢᏦᏓᎯᏉ

WITHIN A CENTURY after Alexandria was built, it was larger
than Carthage and growing so swiftly that it acknowledged no
superior, even Rome. It had already become the center not
only of Hellenism, but also of Judaism. Its Mouscion was the leading university of its time—the finest teachers, philosophers, and scientists flourishing within its walls. Here ancient scholars produced the Septuagint (Greek
translation of the Hebrew Old Testament), and on these streets Julius
Caesar would stroll with Cleopatra to the wild cheers of the populace.

For the thousand years after its foundation, Alexandria served as the
cultural, political, and religious center of Egypt. In addition to its reputation for learning, its architecture was famous. The Royal Palaces were
spread out along the northeast angle and occupied the promontory of
Lochias, which locked in the harbor on the east. The Great Theater, together with the gigantic temple to Poseidon, stood on an imposing hill,
while below, the docks of the Emporium accepted ships from all over the
world, their marble arms stretching out toward the sea, all the way to the
Caesarium, which was protected on each side by two gigantic obelisks,
Cleopatra's Needles. The Gymnasium and Palestra were situated in the
eastern half of the city, whereas the Mausoleum of Alexander the Great
lay at the point of intersection of the city's two main thoroughfares:
Canopic Way and Street of the Soma (body of Alexander). The Serapium, the most famous of all Alexandrian temples, stood toward the
western border of the city near Rhakotis Hill and occupied the highest
spot in Alexandria. Later excavations revealed that its basement contained a series of long subterranean galleries and burial chambers carved
in the rock and lined with limestone.

Many descriptions of this extraordinary city survive. The ancients liked to compare places with objects. A map of Piraeus resembled a vase; the island of Rhodes looked like a theater and its rounded port an orchestra. Of Alexandria, the Roman scholar Pliny wrote: "The city is made in the image of a Macedonian chlamys [a short oblong cloak worn by horsemen], circular in shape, notched along the edges, and jutting out to left and right."

The shape of the city indeed resembled a chlamys. Moreover, it was approximately bisected by Canopic Way, which ran from the Sun Gate to the Moon Gate, a distance of 40 furlongs (8,000 yards). Its width was a plethron (100 feet). Both sides of the lengthy street were bordered with endless rows of magnificent columns and rich facades of houses and temples. Finally, before embarking for the Siwa Oasis, Alexander instructed his architects to build royal palaces that would be notable for their size and massiveness. Those who were to rule Egypt after him would repeatedly enlarge these already lavish palaces.

By the early part of the first century B.C., the city had grown so rapidly that travelers and historians overwhelmingly agreed she was the greatest city of the civilized world and surpassed all others in size, elegance, and luxury. She was at the height of her fascination and beauty when the geographer Strabo visited her in 25 B.C. and remained there for several years, consulting the works of historians, geographers, and astronomers at Alexandria's famous Library. Both the long sides of the city were washed by the waters of the Mediterranean and Lake Mareotis, with a diameter of some 30 stadia (approximately 606 feet), while the short sides were the isthmuses, each 7 or 8 stadia wide and pinched in—one by the sea, and the other by the lake. For administrative purposes, the city was cut into five sections, each called after a letter: Alpha, Beta, Gamma, Delta, Epsilon.

Beta included the Royal Palaces, the Mouseion, and other buildings; Delta was the Jewish Quarter. The city was intersected by streets ideal for horse-riding and chariot-driving; two in particular, Canopic Way and Street of the Soma, extended to more than a plethron in breadth (a stadion was 6 plethra), cutting one another into two parts and at right angles. There was building on building here, all linked with one another and the harbor—even those that lay outside the harbor on the Lochias promontory.

The Mouseion was part of the palaces. It had a public walk, an exedra (a hall or arcade with seats or recesses suitable for lectures and discussions), and a large building to house the scholars who resided there. They not only held property in common, but also had a leader in charge of the Mouseion, formerly appointed by the kings, and later by the caesars. In addition, there were many spacious exedras with porticoes and seats where philosophers, rhetoricians, physicians, scientists, and poets studied and debated new theories. Part of the palace area (the Mausoleum) provided the enclosure where Alexander the Great and the Ptolemaic kings were buried. Across the Great Harbor, on Pharos Island, the imposing Lighthouse, one of the Seven Wonders of the World, warned ships of the approaching coast.

The first sight to catch the traveler's eye as he sailed into Alexandria's waters were the Royal Palaces, which ran contiguous with the Royal Palaces on Lochias. Along its serene coast rolled groves of lush trees and shrubs. But it was what lay inside Alexandria that attracted visitors: the countless temples, a magnificent Theater, Cleopatra's Needles standing guard over the port, the Poseidium, and particularly the Emporium, with its busy bazaars and warehouses extending as far as the Heptastadion, the great mole that connected Pharos Island to the mainland.

Further on, a navigable canal led to Lake Mareotis; and beyond the canal, the Necropolis (Western Cemetery), with abundant gardens, graves, and halting stations for corpse-embalming. Along both sides of the canal, as far as the Serapium, there were more buildings. The most beautiful of all, however, was the University, whose rows of porticoes extended more than a hundred meters in length. At the heart of the city stood the imposing Court of Justice. Here too was the Paneium (temple to Pan, the Greek god of shepherds and goatherds), reached by a winding spiral road, and from whose commanding summit the whole city could be viewed below.

☙❧

After the conquest of Egypt, Cleomenes was appointed collector of revenues by Alexander. He was greatly despised. Demosthenes called him "Ruler of Egypt and dishonest manipulator of the country's lucrative grain trade." Aristotle concurred, citing Cleomenes' numerous incidents of fraudulent conduct with merchants, priests of the temple, and government officials. The Roman historian Arrian added his own assessment: "He was an evil man who committed many grievous wrongs in Egypt."

Although Deinocrates had drawn up the original plans for the new city, it was Cleomenes who began Alexandria's construction. During his two-year tenure as collector of revenues, Cleomenes had amassed a huge fortune through bribes and corruption. Soon after the death of Alexander, however, General Ptolemy took control of Egypt and one of his first functions was to have Cleomenes put to death. Deinocrates then proceeded to lay out the city and to erect some of its principal buildings. Alexandria grew so rapidly, first under Ptolemy Soter, then under his son Ptolemy II, that in 270 B.C. the city had to be divided into three governable districts.

Rhakotis was the native Egyptian quarter, within which was erected the Serapium. Here also was Pompey's Shrine, the Catacombs, and the Race Course.

Bruchium, the royal Greek-Macedonian quarter, occupied the entire front of the Great Harbor from the promontory of Lochias to the long causeway that connected Alexandria to the island of Pharos. Together with the large population of Greek-Macedonians, many other Europeans and Asians dwelt in this quarter. It was the most thriving section of the city, with its elaborate government offices, trade marts, and imposing public buildings. Of these, the Mausoleum, or Soma, stood out, as did the great Mouseion with its famous Library and Theater, both of which were adorned with colonnades of rare Egyptian marble. Toward the slender promontory of Lochias, among exotic gardens and groves of unusual trees and flowers, rose the beautiful and stately palaces of the Ptolemaic kings and the Temple of Isis.

The Jewish Quarter was almost as large as the Greek. It had its own sturdy walls and was governed by an ethnarch (Greek for "leader of the people") under a Jewish council and laws. In essence, the Alexandrian Jews had a city of their own. Occasionally, quarrels broke out between them and the Greeks or the Romans, and with every change of political wind their privileges were periodically abolished. According to the historian Josephus, Jews settled in Alexandria shortly after the death of Alexander the Great. At first, they dwelt in the eastern sector of the city, near the sea; but during the Roman era, two of the city's five quarters (particularly the fourth, or Delta) were inhabited by Jews, whose synagogues spread over almost every part of the city. The Jews of Alexandria engaged in various crafts and commerce. Though some were extremely wealthy (merchants and moneylenders), the vast majority worked as artisans. Together they formed an autonomous community governed by respected leaders, ethnarchs, and a council of seventy-one elders. The ethnarch was responsible for the general conduct of Jewish affairs in the city, especially in matters of law and the drawing up of documents.

During the Ptolemaic period, relations between the Jews and the government were good, and many of the Jews acquired citizenship in the city. Only twice (in 145 and 88 B.C.) did insignificant clashes break out, both over political disagreements. In 38 B.C., during the tumultuous reign of Caligula, a serious riot erupted against the Jews, instigated largely by the anti-Semitic attitude of the Roman governor, Flaccus. As a result, many Jews were murdered, their leaders publicly scourged, synagogues defiled, and all the Jewish population confined to one quarter of the city. On Caligula's death, the emperor Claudius restored their religious and national rights.

Within the three main districts of the city, the Greek, Egyptian, and Jewish quarters, an enormous population of many other groups and classes coexisted: Asian tradesmen; Greeks from the mainland and the Aegean Islands, Afrasians from Cyrene; people from Syria, Asia Minor, Arabia, Babylonia, Assyria, Media, Persia, Carthaginia, Italy, Gaul, Iberia, and India. In truth, the city was a universal nurse, or *pantotrophus*, nurturing each race that settled there.

Alexandria was cut into these distinct parts by two large avenues: Canopic Way stretched from the Moon Gate in the Western Harbor and extended through the heart of the city, all the way to the Sun Gate at the eastern outskirts, beyond the Jewish Quarter. The Street of the Soma began on the shore of the Great Harbor and traversed the city, crossing Canopic Way from north to south, on to the shore of Lake Mareotis. These two magnificent streets were more than 100 feet wide and flanked on both sides with marble colonnades, statues, monuments, and sphinxes. Most of the other streets ran parallel to Canopic Way or braced the Street of the Soma.

Every cistern in Alexandria connected to the Nile, carrying water clear of silt for domestic use. Like the cisterns, all the buildings in the city were built of stone—even the ordinary dwellings—without wooden floorings and timbers. Their foundations were of masonry and adorned with vaulted arches. The absence of wood construction made Alexandria the only fireproof city in the world. Sprawled over the mainland and Pharos Island, this superb metropolis boasted a wide variety of shops, industrial factories, institutions of learning, centers of culture, and magnificent works of art. Almost daily, ships from every corner of the globe docked on each side of the Heptastadion, a thin strip of land connecting Pharos with mainland Alexandria. The workers loaded and unloaded their wares: silk and rice from the Orient, grain and corn from the fertile valley of the Nile bound for Greece and Rome, ivory from deep in Africa. For bathers, massive marble steps descended from the shore into the salty waters of the Mediterranean.

Within the confines of the city were military camps for the Macedonian and mercenary soldiers, barracks and arsenals, a huge Gymnasium and Stadium for athletic events, halls for lectures, theaters for drama and comedy, where spectators could look up beyond the stage and see the eternal flame of the Pharos Light.

Entering Alexandria by land was an unforgettable experience, according to ancient accounts. The Greek historian Achilles Tatius traveled to the city from Ephesus in the fourth century A.D. and, after a journey of eight days, he reached Alexandria, entering it by the Sun Gate, just to the east of the Jewish Quarter. A straight, double row of columns led all the way from the Sun Gate to the Moon Gate near the Necropolis. From this vantage point, two things struck him as especially strange and extraordinary: it was impossible to decide which was the greater—the aura of the place and its beauty, or the city itself and its inhabitants. So deep was the impression, he later wondered "whether any other city in the world could be found large enough to hold such a population." It so happened that he arrived in Alexandria during the combined sacred festival of the Greek god Zeus and the Egyptian Serapis. There was a long procession of torches. Although it was late evening and the sun had gone down, "it seemed as though another sun had arisen, vying indeed with the sky for beauty."

Strabo, the Greek geographer, visited Egypt in the days of Augustus and was so enthralled with Alexandria's beauty, he decided to remain there for an extensive period of time. He claimed the best approach to the city was from the sea, sailing along the right hand of the Great Harbor, past the Pharos Light. On the left hand, along the reefs and promontory of Lochias, stood the Royal Palaces; and within the harbor, just in front of the Royal Docks, rose the smaller island of Antirrhodus, with its plush gardens and multicolored lodges. "It is indeed quite fitting," he remarked, "that

Alexandria, with her two excellent harbors and easy access to the fertile valleys of the Nile, should be called the greatest emporium in the world!"

Son of Philip II and the Epirote princess Olympias, Alexander was born in 356 B.C., on the sixth day of the month Hecatombaeon (near the end of July), the same day that the famous Temple of Artemis at Ephesus was burned. This coincidence inspired Hegesias of Magnesia, a Greek rhetorician and historian, to construct a ponderous joke, "frigid and dull enough," according to Plutarch, to have put out the fire. "It was no wonder," jested Hegesias, "that the glorious temple of Artemis was burned, since she was away from it, attending to the birth of Alexander the Great."

All the Persian soothsayers and magi in Ephesus imagined that the destruction of the temple was but the forerunner of an even greater disaster, so they ran through the streets of the city beating their faces and shouting, "On this day is born the destroyer of Asia!"

Philip, who had just captured the city of Potidaea, received at this time three messengers. The first announced that his general Parmenion had overthrown the Illyrians in a great battle; the second, that Philip's superb racehorse had won a victory at the Olympic Games; and the third, that his son Alexander was born. As expected, Philip was delighted with such good news, but he was particularly overjoyed when the soothsayers told him that his son, whose birth coincided with these victories, would surely be the greatest king in the world.

Alexander's personal appearance was best depicted by the sculptor Lysippus, the only artist whom he allowed to represent him, and in whose works can be clearly traced the slight droop of his head toward the left and the piercing glance of his eyes that formed his chief characteristic, later imitated by his friends and successors. The Greek artist Apelles, in the celebrated painting of Alexander wielding a thunderbolt, did not catch the fresh tint of Alexander's flesh, but instead made it darker and swarthier than it was reputed to be. According to Aristoxenes, one of Aristotle's pupils, Alexander's skin was quite fair, even inclining to a reddish hue around the face and breast. In addition, "his body diffused a rich perfume,

9

which scented his clothes and even made his breath remarkably sweet." Theophrastus, Aristotle's successor at the Peripatetic school in Athens, explained that the sweet scents emanating from Alexander's body were caused by his hot and fiery temperament, an assertion supported by the popular belief of the time that sweet aromas were caused by heat acting on moisture. Theophrastus's logic suggested that "the hottest and driest regions of the earth produce the most aromatic perfumes, because the sun dries up that moisture which causes moist substances to decay and putrefy." Therefore, Alexander's body would do the same.

Even as a child, Alexander showed unusual self-control, abstaining from all sensual pleasures despite his passionate nature. While Philip prided himself on his oratorical prowess and even minted his victories in the chariot races at Olympia on his coins, Alexander rarely chose to pursue glories of this type. To test him, his friends, knowing that he was a swift runner, asked him one day if he would be willing to compete in the foot race at Olympia. "Yes," he replied, "but only if I compete against kings."

He disliked athletic competition, particularly boxing and the pancratium, which included the footrace, leaping, throwing the quoit, hurling the javelin, and wrestling. In this contest, no one received the prize unless he was victorious in all five events.

Disdaining professed athletes, as a young man Alexander instead awarded prizes to dramatists, musicians, and rhapsodists, and enjoyed only hunting and cudgel-playing. Around this time, his father invited Aristotle to be his tutor. From the great philosopher, Alexander learned that moderation alone could hold a kingdom together. In contrast, his mother Olympias was a proud and exceedingly passionate woman, a fervent disciple of the orgiastic rituals practiced in Thrace and Macedonia, all of which greatly offended her husband. Despite her sensual nature, Alexander revered her all his life, and while he acquired from his father the strong qualities of leadership in both government and military affairs, his true character and nature were largely hers.

From a young age, Alexander possessed an inquisitive mind. When several Persian envoys visited his father at the Royal Palaces, Alexander drew them aside and questioned them about the routes across Asia. Throughout his life, he nourished a deep love for poetry, and always kept a copy of the *Iliad* (which Aristotle had revised for him) under his pillow. Everywhere he went, even into battle, he carried the *Iliad* with him. His heroes were Achilles and Heracles.

Aristotle also taught him logic, ethics, metaphysics, politics, and was responsible for stimulating Alexander's deep interest in scientific investigation, geography, hydrography, ethnology, zoology, botany, and medicine.

When Philonicus the Thessalian offered a champion horse named Bucephalus to Philip for the huge sum of thirteen gold talents, the king and several of his friends went to a level area of ground to test the horse's speed. Plutarch wrote that Bucephalus was so unmanageable, he allowed no one to mount him or even draw near. With this, Philip became incensed and harshly told Philonicus to take the vicious animal away. Alexander witnessed the episode and, edging toward his father, said, "Let me tame the horse." "And if you can't tame him," Philip smirkingly replied, "what penalty will you offer for your impudence?" "I will pay the entire price of the horse," said Alexander.

While Philip laughed and proceeded to take bets with his guests, Alexander approached the horse, took it by the bridle, and turned it toward the sun. Apparently, its shadow dancing on the ground had alarmed the animal and made it skittish. Speaking gently to the horse, Alexander patted it on the rump several times, then, flinging off his cloak, leaped on Bucephalus's back and reined it steadily in without violence or blows. Immediately, the horse showed its willingness to gallop. Alexander calmly urged it to full speed with his voice and heel.

At first, Philip and his guests remained silent, but when Alexander wheeled the horse around and rode up to them, they all burst into applause. The historian Diodorus wrote that Philip so wept for joy that as soon as Alexander dismounted, he kissed him and said, "My son, seek a kingdom worthy of yourself. Macedonia is not large enough for you!"

From then on, Philip was careful in his relationship with his son, never issuing orders or making him do anything by force, always realizing that Alexander required, as Sophocles said of a ship, "Stout ropes to check him, and stout oars to guide."

It was more from guilt perhaps that Philip decided to pay Aristotle a handsome fee to be his son's tutor. He had just captured and destroyed Aristotle's native city of Stagira; and now he decided to rebuild and repeople it, ransoming the citizens who had been sold for slaves and bringing back those who were living in exile. He appointed the temple and grove of the nymphs near the city of Mieza as a schoolhouse and residence for both Aristotle and Alexander. The stone seat where Aristotle sat and the shady avenues where he daily walked were preserved for centuries. Alexander was taught not only Aristotle's doctrines of ethics and politics here, but also those abstruse mysteries that could only be communicated orally and kept secret from the public. After Alexander had invaded Asia, he heard that Aristotle had published some treatises on these mysteries and became so greatly upset he wrote his tutor a sharp letter:

> Alexander wishes health to Aristotle: You have not done well in publishing abroad these sciences which should only be taught by word of mouth, otherwise how shall we be distinguished from other men if the knowledge we have acquired is made the common property of all?

To pacify him, Aristotle wrote back and assured him that these doctrines were published only for those who had been instructed in philosophy by himself and would be quite useless in other hands.

Alexander's own memoirs disclosed that above all else, Aristotle implanted a love of medicine in him. Not only was Alexander fond of discussing it but even prescribed for his friends when they were sick, ordering them to follow special courses of treatment and diet. Not surprisingly, he loved and admired Aristotle even more than he did his father. "The latter," he said, "has taught me to live, but the former has taught me to live well."

At sixteen, Alexander governed Macedonia in Philip's absence, and even put down a Thracian uprising; at eighteen, he commanded the left flank of Philip's army at Chaeronea. During these early years, the relations between his mother and father were strained, chiefly because the headstrong Olympias did not tolerate Philip's concubines. The situation reached the breaking point when Philip married the niece of his general, Attalus. Philip had always been unsure that Alexander was his real son (the rumor was first spread by Attalus) and this suspicion was augmented at the wedding feast, when Attalus requested everyone present to pray for a *legitimate* heir to the throne. Alexander flung his cup into Attalus's face and shouted, "Then what am I, a bastard?"

Philip supported Attalus and would have run his sword through Alexander, but he was drunk with wine, and as he went to stand up, his feet slipped and he fell down on the floor. Still fuming, Alexander insulted him: "See there," he said, "the man who wants to pass through Europe into Asia, and he can't even stand on his feet!"

Alexander took his mother and fled to Illyria.

The next year Philip was assassinated. The greatest blame was placed on Olympias, while additional suspicion was attached to Alexander himself. However, Alexander's complicity seems unlikely, since he went to great lengths to seek out and punish the conspirators.

⚬⚬⚬

Alexander was twenty when he succeeded his father to the throne of Macedonia. Soon after, he was chosen by the Greeks to be their leader in an invasion of Persia, and subsequently many statesmen and philosophers paid him visits to offer their good wishes and congratulations. Only the eccentric philosopher Diogenes failed to make an appearance. He was at that time living quietly in the small village of Craneium near Corinth, and Alexander, anxious to visit with him, rode there on horseback from Athens. He found Diogenes lying full length on the grass, basking in the sun. "Is there anything I can do for you?" Alexander asked him. "Yes," replied Diogenes, "you can stand a little to the side. You're blocking the sun's rays from my body."

Shocked at the philosopher's insolence, the accompanying crowd jeered and scoffed, and Alexander raised his hand and silenced them. "I tell you this," he said. "If I were not Alexander, I would prefer to be Diogenes."

Before embarking on his Persian campaign, Alexander decided to consult the oracle of Apollo at Delphi. By chance, he arrived there on one of the days when the oracular responses could not be obtained. At once, he sent for the chief priestess, but she refused to officiate, saying she was forbidden to do so by law. Not to be denied, Alexander entered the temple and dragged her to the prophetic tripod. She had no choice but to yield to his persistence. "You are invincible, my son," she said. This was all Alexander wanted to hear.

He reached Egypt late in November 332 B.C. and went upstream on the Nile to Memphis, where he sacrificed to the Egyptian god Apis and was accepted as pharaoh. From there he traveled to the coast, and on the Mediterranean shore near the village of Rhakotis, he knelt on the sand and with his finger traced out the lines of what was to become Alexandria.

After instructing his architect to build the city, he set out across the western desert, accompanied by a few followers, including the historian and philosopher Callisthenes (nephew of Aristotle), to find the oracle of Zeus Ammon in the Siwa Oasis. The oracle of Ammon had for centuries ranked, along with Delphi and Dodona, as one of the three great shrines of the Greek world. Pindar had written a hymn to Zeus Ammon, and the Athenians had only recently consecrated a temple, naming it Salaminia Ammonias.

Alexander did not take the regular route directly to the oracle. Instead he chose to travel along the coast to the city of Paraetonium, where he accepted Cyrene's offer of alliance for a second invasion of Persia. From there, he headed across the desert, and when his guides lost the way, he was led the remaining distance by two vigilant crows on their own search for the oasis.

He entered the shrine alone and later refused to disclose what the oracle had told him, except that Ammon was pleased to see him. In his memoirs, he admitted that Ammon had told him to sacrifice to certain gods when in trouble (as Apollo told Xenophon). Afterward, the priest greeted him as the son of Zeus Ammon, granting him dominion over the whole world. Armed with the conviction that he was now a god, Alexander headed east again to face the Persians in battle. This time it would be with an entirely different goal: to harmonize the whole world, not to Hellenize it.

King Darius of Persia had meanwhile collected a huge army and posted it at the passage of the Granicus River, forcing Alexander to engage the Persians at a strategic yet well-fortified location. Alexander's generals were alarmed at the depth and coarse bed of the river, and especially at the rugged and uneven ground on the nearest bank where they would have to mount their attack. Several raised a religious issue, warning that the Macedonian kings never made war during the month of Daisius. In response, Alexander decreed that the second month in the Macedonian calendar would henceforth be called Artemisium. Everyone except General Parmenion accepted the decree. The general beseeched Alexander not to risk a battle at this time of the year because the region was noted for its storms and torrential rains during autumn.

Alexander paid no heed. "The Hellespont would blush for shame," he said, "if I crossed it, and then feared to cross the Granicus." He then plunged into the stream with thirteen squadrons of cavalry, leaving the bulk of his army behind. To them, it seemed the act of a madman rather than of a general. It would be riding through a swift river under a storm of arrows and missiles, toward a steep bank, where every advantageous position was occupied by the enemy. Nevertheless, Alexander and his cavalry gained the opposite shore and established a sound footing, despite the steep slope slippery with mud.

The Persians immediately met Alexander's assault with shouts and spears. Many of the Persians pressed around Alexander himself, a conspicuous figure with his shield and long white plumes hanging on each side of his helmet. At one point, a javelin struck him in the joint of his corselet, but the sharp thrust did not find his chest. Then two of the Persian generals, Rhoesakes and Spithridates, attacked him simultaneously. He avoided the charge of the latter, but broke his spear against the breastplate of Rhoesakes and was forced to engage him with his sword. As they battled, Spithridates rode up behind Alexander and, standing in his stirrups, dealt him a blow with his battle-ax, cutting off one side of Alexander's plume and piercing his helmet to the scalp. Preparing to strike another blow, Spithridates was run through with a lance by one of Alexander's soldiers, an African cavalryman name Cleitus. At the same moment, Alexander spun around and slew Rhoesakes with his sword.

During this fierce cavalry encounter, the Macedonian phalanx successfully crossed the river and attacked the enemy's infantry force, none of which offered much resistance except for a body of mercenary Greeks under the hire of Darius. These troops fled to a ridge above the river and begged for mercy, but Alexander, riding up to them himself, attacked them. Unfortunately, his horse (not Bucephalus) was slain by a sword thrust into the stomach from one of the mercenaries lying wounded on the ground.

The Persians lost 20,000 infantry and 2,500 cavalry in the Battle of Granicus. Aristobulus, the Greek historian who accompanied Alexander on his campaigns, wrote that the total loss of Alexander's army was 34 men, 9 of whom were foot soldiers. For each of these heroes, Alexander decreed that statues be made in bronze by the sculptor Lysippus; in addition, to satisfy his allies in Greece, particularly the Athenians, he sent them three hundred captured shields. On the remaining plunder he placed the following inscription: "Alexander, the son of Philip, and the Greeks—all but the Lacedaemonians—won these spoils from the barbarians of Asia." To his mother, he sent golden drinking cups, purple drapes, curtains, vases, and urns. Overall, Alexander kept little for himself.

The victory at Granicus brought further rewards. Many of the neighboring states of Asia Minor submitted to Alexander without a struggle, including Sardis itself, which was the capital of Lydia and the main fortress of the Persians in that region. The only cities that resisted him, Halicarnassus and Miletus, he took by storm, and eventually conquered all the adjacent territories.

All this time, Alexander deliberated about King Darius of Persia— whether to attack him at once and risk all that he had won, or to consolidate and organize his gains on the Asia Minor coast and thus gather new strength for the final battle. He finally chose the latter course and forthwith extended his conquests along the entire coast of Asia Minor as far as Phoenicia and Cilicia. After this, he put down a revolt among the Pisidians and conquered the whole of Phrygia.

On his arrival at Gordium, King Midas's ancient capital in central Asia Minor, he was shown his celebrated chariot that was tied up with a knot of cornel-tree bark, and learned from the natives that whoever untied the knot was destined to become ruler of the entire world. Most historians contend that the knot was so secure it was impossible to untie, so Alexander drew his sword and cut it in two: his personal historian Aristobulus, however, who was present at the scene, reported that Alexander untied the knot by simply pulling out of the pole the pin to which the strap was fastened, and then drawing off the yoke itself from the pole.

A few days later, Alexander received an intelligence report that Memnon, the brilliant general to whom Darius had entrusted the defense of the Asia Minor seacoast, had suddenly died. Meanwhile, Darius had amassed an army of 600,000 men and was encouraged by a dream in which he saw the Macedonian phalanx engulfed in flames as well as Alexander wearing a courier's cloak and acting as his servant. Plutarch wrote that the king of Persia was further inspired by the long inaction of Alexander in Cilicia, caused in all probability by an illness that resulted from the physical and emotional hardships he had undergone during his arduous conquests. However, those close to him maintained it was the consequence of bathing in the icy waters of the Cydnus River. Local physicians dared not attend him because they felt he was beyond the help of medicine, and if they tried to cure him and failed, they dreaded the displeasure of the Macedonians.

At last, an Akarnanian physician named Philip decided to run the risk of treating him. He compounded a mixture and persuaded Alexander to drink it, saying it would give him strength and enable him to take the field. When General Parmenion heard about the supposed cure, he immediately dispatched a letter from his camp, warning Alexander to beware of Philip because he had been bribed by Darius to poison him. Alexander read the letter and placed it under his pillow. At the appointed hour, Philip entered the room, carrying the medicine in a cup. Alexander took the cup, handed him the letter from Parmenion, and proceeded to drink the compound. After reading the letter, Philip fell on his knees beside the bed, professing his innocence. Alexander ignored him. Instead, he smiled and drank the cup dry. At first, the drug produced extreme fatigue, and Alexander lay back on the bed speechless and insensible. Within a short time, however, under Philip's constant watch, he slowly recovered his strength, and eventually showed himself to his army, healthy and eager for battle.

Although outnumbered by Darius's forces at Cilicia, Alexander not only avoided being surrounded by them, but was able to outflank their left with his own right wing of Macedonians. By this clever maneuver, he soundly defeated the Persians, slaying more than a 100,000. Amid the clashes, Darius abandoned his army and Alexander sped after him. But the Persian king had gained a start of more than a mile and managed to escape. Nevertheless, Alexander captured the Persian king's chariot, along with his bow and arrows. When he returned to camp, he found the Macedonians reveling in the newly captured riches. The royal pavilion of Darius, full of beautiful slaves and finely crafted furniture, was reserved for Alexander himself. According to legend, Alexander pulled off his armor, proceeded to the bath, and said, "Let me wash off the sweat of battle in the bath of Darius." "No," one of his soldiers laughed, "in the bath of Alexander!"

After he entered the bath and saw that all the vessels for water, the bath itself, and the boxes of unguents were made of pure gold, he passed from the bath into a spacious and lofty salon, where a sumptuous banquet awaited him. Addressing his officers, he boasted, "This indeed is what it means to be a king!"

While he was dining, he was told that the mother, wife, and two daughters of Darius, among the many captives, had seen the chariot and bow of the Persian king and were mourning for him, assuming he had died. So Alexander sent a messenger to inform them that they should neither mourn for Darius nor fear Alexander. This message to the captive family preceded other acts of generosity permitting them to both bury any of the slain Persians they wished and to take back all their clothing and furniture that had been seized by the soldiers as plunder. Alexander also allowed them to retain their royal titles and state, and even increased their revenues. But in perhaps the noblest gesture of all, he protected them from vulgar language and the idea that they might suffer any form of violence while under his jurisdiction. Thus they lived relatively unharmed, "as though they were in some sacred retreat of holy virgins rather than in a camp."

Like the famous Helen, the wife of Darius was said to be the most beautiful woman of her time. Her match, Darius himself was the tallest and handsomest man in Asia; his daughters resembled the parents in grace and charm. With his signature restraint, Alexander never touched any of them, though he once exclaimed to his officers that "these Persian women make men's eyes sore to behold them." Despite their magnetism, he was determined that his self-control should be as much admired as their beauty, "and he passed by them as if they were images cut from stone."

Plutarch reported that when Philoxenus, the commander of Alexander's fleet, informed him that Theodorus, a slave merchant of Tarentum, had two lovely slaves for sale and desired to know if he wished to buy them, Alexander reprimanded Philoxenus, ordering him to send Theodorus and his merchandise to hell. On another occasion, when he learned that two Macedonians of General Parmenion's regiment had raped the wives of some mercenary soldiers, he wrote to Parmenion and ordered him "to put them to death like brute beasts that prey on mankind." In that same letter, he confessed, "I have never seen, or desired to see the wife of Darius; and have not even allowed her beauty to be spoken of in my presence." If Alexander could tame his lust, so would his men.

While preparing to march in pursuit of Darius, Alexander attended a banquet among his officers, several of whom brought along their mistresses. One of these, the celebrated Thaïs, was of Greek parentage and later became the mistress of General Ptolemy in Egypt. At first, she amused Alexander with her intelligent conversation, then flattered him until at last, when he was drunk, she bragged of her Greek patriotism. She declared that after suffering the hardships of the Asia campaign with the Macedonian army, she wanted nothing more than to burn down the famous palace of Xerxes, because he had burned her native Athens. She explained that she wanted to apply the torch with her own hand in the presence of Alexander, so that it would be remembered by history that a woman, who shared Alexander's conquest of Asia, had now taken revenge on the Persians for the wrongs they committed in Greece.

Applauded by all the officers, her speech convinced them and Alexander to execute her wish. Plutarch wrote that Alexander was so captivated by her spirit that he leaped from his couch and headed for Xerxes' palace with a garland of flowers on his head and a torch in his hand. His officers and their mistresses followed close behind, all erupting with cheers when Thaïs stepped forward and applied the torch to the palace. Deep down, these officers had another reason for their pleasure, since the destruction of Xerxes' palace signaled that Alexander would at last leave Persia and return home.

The rest of the army, however, was not that anxious to depart from Persia. They had found extreme luxury and extravagance there. Many of the soldiers even had their sandals fastened with silver nails, while others confiscated camels, nets for hunting, rich perfumes, manservants and chambermaids.

Alexander admonished them, warning, "Our great conquests will come to an end on the day when we learn to live like those whom we have vanquished." To stress this point even further, he set an example for them, exposing himself to even greater hardships and danger, not only in battle but also in his hunting expeditions. When he killed a lion one day, an old officer ran up to him and said, "Alexander, you have now conquered the kingdom of lions." This hunting scene of Alexander fighting with the lion was later depicted in bronze at Delphi—some of the figures executed by the sculptor Lysippus, and others by Leochares. Alexander risked his life in these endeavors to teach his army to live with simplicity and fortitude. It was not an easy task, for they had now become rich and important persons, desiring only to enjoy themselves and never again embark on perilous campaigns and long marches across arid territory unknown to them. It was only natural that they would begin to murmur against Alexander, even plan to revolt, but he bore all this with typical calm and self-assurance, never speaking badly of them. Despite repeated warnings by his closest friends, he joked, "It is the fate of a king to do good for his subjects, and to be ill-spoken of by them in return."

While in Persia, Alexander proved himself to be a voracious reader and avid letter writer. As commander of all the forces fighting under him, he had to listen to and settle the quarrels of his subjects. Often, in an effort to show his impartiality, he would cover one ear with his hand while the prosecutor was speaking, so that he might remain unbiased when the accused spoke out in his defense. But the charges and trials soon became so numerous that Alexander soured of arbitrating and judged all of the accused were guilty. The one act he never tolerated or forgave was a slur against his reputation, for he valued this more than his life or his crown.

Meanwhile, with every nation he conquered, kings endeavored to marry off their daughters to him, which he respectfully declined. However, when he beheld a certain Roxana dancing in a chorus after a feast, he was so struck by her beauty he made immediate arrangements to marry her. Though Roxana was to become the only woman he had ever loved, it was said that he never approached or touched her until he was lawfully married to her. Focused on his military campaign, Alexander had little time for anything else.

After conquering all the countries on the higher bank of the Euphrates, he finally marched to attack Darius, who was advancing toward him with an army a million strong. The decisive battle was fought, not at Arbela, as most historians believed, but at Gaugamela, "the House of the Camel." During the month of Boedromion, which coincided with the celebration of the Eleusinian mysteries, there was an eclipse of the moon. On the eleventh day after the eclipse, the two armies came within sight of each other. As Darius kept his troops under arms and inspected their ranks by torchlight, Alexander allowed his soldiers to rest, while he himself, along with his soothsayer Aristander, performed mystical ceremonies in front of his tent and offered sacrifice to Apollo.

When General Parmenion and Alexander's senior officers saw the entire plain between Mt. Niphates and Gordium blanketed with the campfires of the Persians, and heard the din of the army, they all agreed that it would be too difficult to fight the mass of soldiers in pitched battle by daylight. They waited until Alexander had finished his sacrifice, then went to him and tried to persuade him to attack the Persians at night, to prevent their army from seeing the sheer size of the opposing forces. Alexander's response was swift and sharp: "I will not steal a victory."

Waiting until his officers left, he retired to his tent and slept through the night. At dawn, while his officers and army waited to launch their attack, he still slept. With mounting agitation, Parmenion stepped up to his tent and called out his name several times, and when at last Alexander awoke, Parmenion asked him how he could sleep so well before such an important battle. "Now that we no longer have to chase Darius over this wasted land," replied Alexander calmly, "we have already gained the victory."

When Alexander finally walked out of his tent, he was fully armed, wearing a Sicilian tunic tightly around his waist, covered by a double-woven linen corselet from the Granicus spoils. His polished steel helmet, bright as silver, had been forged by Theophilus, a famous craftsman of the time. Around his neck, he wore a steel collar inlaid with precious stones. His sword, extraordinarily light and well-tempered, had been presented to him by the king of Citium in Cyprus. But above these things, the cloak hanging from his shoulders distinguished itself through the artistry of the maker, Helikon, and because it was given to him by the capital city of Rhodes, of the same name.

In the final inspection of his Macedonian soldiers, Alexander rode another horse, to spare the seasoned Bucephalus. But as soon as he was ready to launch the attack, he rallied the Thessalians and the other Greek troops, mounted Bucephalus, then led the charge toward the Persians, shifting his lance into his left hand and raising his right hand to heaven. Plutarch writes that at this moment Alexander prayed to the gods that since he was the true son of Zeus, they would assist and encourage the Greeks to victory. The soothsayer Aristander, riding by his side in a white robe and wearing a crown of gold, pointed to an eagle that rose directly over Alexander's head and was arching its flight straight for the enemy lines. Because the omen so heartened Alexander and his cavalry, they spurred their horses and rushed at the Persians, shadowed by the Macedonian phalanx. As the cavalry engaged the enemy, the Persian line gave way and Alexander drove toward the center where Darius had stationed himself, hidden among a cluster of soldiers. But Alexander had spotted the striking figure of the tall, handsome king standing in his chariot, surrounded by the royal bodyguard behind the deep ranks of the Persian army, a glittering mass of well-armed horsemen.

The onslaught of Alexander's army caused a general rout among the Persians and drove them into hasty retreat. Confronting disaster, Darius tried to turn his chariot to flee, but the wheels, so encumbered by the mounds of corpses, refused to rotate, and the charioteer was unable to manage the alarmed horses. Darius then leaped from the chariot, mounted a mare that had recently foaled, and rode away. Had several mounted messengers from General Parmenion not arrived just then to beg Alexander for assistance in a flanking operation that was challenged by a Persian counterattack, Darius's escape might not have succeeded. Alexander was incensed at the request; nevertheless he ordered the trumpets to sound the recall, allowing Darius to elude him.

The Battle of Gaugamela brought about the complete destruction of the Persian empire. Alexander was immediately saluted as king of Asia, and after making a ceremonious sacrifice to the gods, he distributed Darius's sizable treasures and provinces among his friends and officers. Then he wrote to the Greeks in Athens, informing them that he had driven all the tyrants and despots out of the conquered nations of Asia and that each city would govern itself independently with a constitutional government.

Tragedy soon accompanied Alexander's triumph. His beloved horse Bucephalus was found dead one morning in the military stables. It was first believed that the horse died of wounds received in the battle, but it was later confirmed that Bucephalus died of old age and overwork. Alexander grieved over the loss of his faithful horse and mourned as if he had lost one of his best friends. He founded a city as a memorial for him on the banks of the river Hydaspes, and named it Bucephalia. Known for his affection for animals, Alexander had also commemorated his favorite dog, Peritas, raised from a puppy, by founding a city deep in Asia, adorning it with magnificent buildings, and naming it Peritas.

After further victories at Issus and Tyre, Alexander proceded toward India, traveling down the Indus River and its tributaries all the way to the Arabian Sea. The march required seven full months. Ordering his fleet to follow the line of the coast, he led his army through a desolate landscape. Of his original 120,000 foot soldiers and 15,000 cavalry, he lost one-fourth to sickness, contaminated meat, and excessive heat. Another sixty days' march brought them at last to Gedrosia, where the exhausted army was rewarded with abundant supplies of food, clothing, and women.

Then a greater tragedy befell Alexander. While in the city of Ecbatana, he busied himself making plans to explore the Caspian Sea in hope of discovering a northeast passage to India. For an evening's recreation, he invited his usual friends and artists, and held competitions, gala banquets, and athletic games. During these festivities, his most beloved general, Hephaestion, fell ill with fever and Alexander rushed out of the stadium to be at his side. Their relationship was often compared to that of Achilles and Patroclus. Alexander entrusted his "Patroclus" with the task of founding cities and colonies. Hephaestion also built the fleet that was intended to sail down the Indus, and Alexander rewarded him with a golden crown and the hand of Drypetis, the younger daughter of King Darius.

Plutarch writes that in that same year, Hephaestion died suddenly, so Alexander ordered a general mourning throughout the conquered lands in Asia. In Babylon, the inhabitants erected a gigantic funeral pyre at enormous cost. For three days and nights, Alexander lay upon the decaying body of Hephaestion and wept until his officers had to drag him away by force. He refused food and water, and withdrew to his tent alone. When he finally showed himself to his army, he had sheared all his hair as Achilles had for Patroclus, then ordered the manes and tails of the cavalry horses be clipped as well. Lastly, he dispatched an embassy to the oracle of Zeus Ammon at Siwa, requesting that Hephaestion be granted the same divine honors as he.

It was the least he could do for Hephaestion. Alexander could not even find the strength to attend the funeral games of his friend, for the competitions among his artist friends who had gathered at the stadium in mourning. At last, heavy with grief and restless for some action that could assuage his pain, Alexander lay siege to and defeated the Cosseans, who had controlled the road between Susa and Babylon for many years. Though the kings of Persia had tried and failed to subdue the Cosseans despite years of effort, Alexander defeated them quickly and decisively, forcing them to surrender. Still, it was not without a price. During the battle, Alexander suffered a chest wound from a sword thrust by an enemy foot soldier who in turn was beheaded by one of Alexander's men with one blow of the ax.

Alexander was no stranger to calamity during his extensive military campaigns. Nevertheless, both Arrian and Plutarch attest to his uncanny ability to weather the violence and the risk of battle. Purportedly, on one occasion during a fierce storm, General Parmenion glanced at Alexander and noticed that he was smiling at the feverish retreat of the enemy. He radiated a serene ecstasy characteristic of his attitude in battle, a sense of unshakeable calm and decisiveness, quite unlike the attitude of his father, who reveled in the suffering of others and, far worse, was enthralled by the destruction that he had wrought.

✺

Alexander the Great was thirty-two years and eight months old when he died in Babylon during the 114th Olympiad (June 10, 323 B.C.). The accounts of his death differ. One source, Ephippus (a noted gossip), claimed that the young king died of excessive drinking. Another writer living in this period, named Nicobule, maintained that Alexander's death did not result from debauchery but occurred shortly after a formal dinner with Medius, a companion from Thessaly. At this final dinner, Alexander recited an extract from Euripides' play *Andromeda*, which he had memorized; later, he drank to the health, in undiluted wine, of all twenty guests in attendance. They, in turn, drank to him in equal amount, and when he left the party, it was not long afterward that he was seized with severe stomach cramps.

A document, never entered in any history, and part of a work called *Romance,* which was compiled five hundred years after Alexander's death, gives a more elaborate account, listing the names of the twenty guests at Medius's dinner, with comprehensive explanations of their motives. Among these were Philip the royal physician, another Philip who was a Greek engineer, Nearchus the admiral, and General Peucestas. Each had a reason to attend the banquet given by Medius on the night of May 29, 323 B.C. Excluding General Ptolemy, Perdiccas, and Eumenes, the royal secretary, all the others were implicated in the plot to poison Alexander.

On the night of the banquet, everything went as planned. Alexander drank from his cup, then suddenly shouted "as if struck through the liver with an arrow." After a few minutes, still obviously in pain, he told the guests to continue drinking and he rushed to his bedchamber.

One of Alexander's generals, the royal secretary Eumenes, added more mystery to the details of Alexander's death in his diaries: "The last days of Alexander's life." he wrote, "were taken up with hunting birds and foxes, banqueting and playing dice."

These royal diaries of Alexander's general referred mostly to Alexander's alleged drinking parties and all-day sleeping periods to recover from the nocturnal episodes. "Five such orgies occurred in that last month alone," Eumenes recalls, "each of which required thirty-six hours of sleep before Alexander could begin to hunt, play dice, or drink again."

Did Eumenes speak the truth about these incidents? Alexander certainly refused to censure such accounts of his behavior. As for the theory of being poisoned, this too lacks credibility because the poisons of herbalists in that day were typically swift, without antidote. Why then did twelve whole days elapse before Alexander breathed his last? And did Parmenion see the smile on his king's face as he confronted the most fearful eyes of Charon, the ferryman of Hades?

When Alexander's death was announced, it was said that an ominous darkness fell on the streets of Babylon. People stumbled through the city, afraid to kindle a light because the great Alexander had departed from life among men and thus deprived them of light when his soul ascended to its eternal home among the sun, moon, and stars.

While the body lay exposed in the halls of Nebuchadnezzar's palace, and his soldiers wondered about their future, the officers revealed their human weakness by arguing with one another over the throne. Alexander had, in part, created this problem. When the officers had gathered together to visit Alexander on that last day, they asked him: "To whom have you left your kingdom?" He was terse: "To the strongest."

The officers, nevertheless, picked over Alexander's meaning: Did he say "strongest" or "stronger"? His words implied a choice between his two dearest friends: Craterus or Perdiccas. Since Alexander was in the throes of delirium, he could have mumbled one when he meant the other.

Fate would choose another recipient. The eventual heir to the throne was Heracles, born to Alexander's Persian mistress Barsine, daughter of King Artabazus. At three, the child so lacked the expected intelligence of one that age, the royal physician Philip pronounced him an idiot and half-wit. Still, a choice had to be made. General Perdiccas convinced Alexander's bodyguards and cavalry to favor Roxana's unborn child, but the foot soldiers banded around their brigadier Meleager, and a heated fight ensued. Perdiccas and General Ptolemy hurried to the chamber where the king's body lay in state, and found that the door had been smashed in by Meleager's soldiers, who began throwing spears at them. Perdiccas summoned his cavalry and retreated to an area on the outskirts of Babylon and ordered that all food be blocked from reaching the city. In time, Meleager and his soldiers were forced to accept an agreement in which Philip's bastard son Archedaeus would share the throne with the expected child of Roxana if it was a boy. Both armies then performed a ritual purification of Alexander's death by marching between two halves of a disemboweled dog according to an ancient Macedonian custom. When Meleager's soldiers' attention suddenly turned elsewhere, Perdiccas and his soldiers seized Meleager's men, threw them to the elephants to be trampled. Realizing that his cause was now hopeless, Meleager took his own life. Subsequently, Perdiccas became guardian of Roxana's baby, a son, only to be stabbed by his soldiers after he ordered them to cross a place in the Nile that was infested with crocodiles. Craterus, the other likely successor to the throne, was trampled and killed by his horse during a battle in the same month.

Archedaeus was now given the task of bringing Alexander's body back west, and when at last he completed the great carriage on which it would be carried, he began making preparations for the long journey. First, a coffin of the proper size was constructed of hammered gold, after which skilled Egyptian craftsmen and Chaldean embalmers bound it in malleable plates of gold and filled the space around the body with spices to make it sweet-smelling as well as less corruptible. On the coffin itself, they placed a cover of gold, matching it exactly and fitting it over the upper rim. Above this was laid a magnificent purple robe embroidered in gold, beside which the royal arms were placed.

When everything was near completion, they set up the vehicle to carry Alexander's body, placing on it a vault of gold 8 cubics wide and 12 long, and covering it with overlapping scales and precious stones. Beneath the roof, cloaking the entire chamber, rested a rectangular cornice of gold from which heads of goat stags in high relief projected. Gold rings, two palms broad, were hung from these, while through the rings ran a garland decorated in bright colors. Tassels of large bells were then attached to both ends so that people could hear the sound of the approaching carriage from a great distance away. On the corners of the vault, at each of the four sides, stood the golden figure of Victory holding a trophy.

The gold colonnade supporting the vault was adorned with Ionic capitals. Within it, a golden net carrying a series of tablets was spread out on each side. One tablet depicted Alexander in the chariot, holding a sceptre in his hands, while around him stood groups of armed Macedonian and Persian attendants. A second tablet showed an army of elephants arrayed for battle, carrying their Indian drivers. These in turn were followed by Macedonian soldiers fully armed. The third tablet displayed troops of cavalry in battle formation; and the fourth, ships ready for naval combat.

Squatting alongside the entrance to the chamber were two golden lions, their fierce eyes staring upon those who dared to enter. A golden acanthus stretched along the center of each column toward the capital; and above the chamber, under the open sky, was a purple banner blazoned with a golden olive wreath which, when the sun cast down its eyes, set forth such a vibrant gleam that from a distance, it was said, it flashed like lightning.

The wheels of the funeral carriage were shod with Persian iron and equipped with special devices to protect them from the poor condition of the Asian roads. Still, the spokes were overlaid with gold. Sixty-four selected mules were strapped to the carriage, each with gilded crowns and bells. The carriage was accompanied by a trained staff of road-menders, mechanics, architects, and engineers, along with a select body of Macedonian soldiers.

Multitudes from surrounding cities and villages flocked to Babylon to witness the dazzling spectacle, whose preparation alone required two full years. When the time finally came for the long journey to begin, the funeral procession set out from Babylon, first to Mesopotamia, then into Syria and Lydia. It was about to advance into its final lap toward the capital city of Argae in Macedonia when impassable roads forced it to swerve toward the west and head for Egypt. In Memphis, however, the high priest refused to allow the body to enter the city. "Do not settle him here," he cried, "but at the city he has built, for wherever his body lies, that city will be plagued with wars."

At this point, Ptolemy Soter intervened and arranged to have a massive mausoleum constructed in Alexandria. It was respectfully given the name Soma and erected in the Bruchium, the royal Greek section of the city, where the city's principal streets crossed at right angles. The area was set apart and protected by massive walls. Hellenic craftsmen, master builders, and architects wrought this imposing memorial from the rarest Greek and Egyptian marble. Within its spacious courtyard, lined by an array of columns, a flight of marble steps led down to the sepulchral ante-room, the Place of Lamentation. At the farthest end of the enclosure, alongside a full-length sculpture of the king, Alexander was at last laid to rest in the city he built but never saw.

For centuries this mausoleum would be the revered place of the Roman and Greek world: Julius Caesar, Mark Antony, Augustus, Severus, Caracalla, Vespasian, Hadrian, Aurelian—each would come here to pay his respects to Alexander, and although each passing generation would never know him, it would admire him as if he were still alive. "As for the exact thoughts he nourished throughout his brief life," Arrian wrote, "no one was either able or concerned to know them. Nevertheless, it can be stated emphatically that his intentions were neither common nor mean, and that Alexander never remained content with any of his achievements. He always searched for something unknown, and if he found no other competition, he competed against himself."

Quite remarkably, this also would prove true for his city. Alexandria would never remain content with her great accomplishments, and even after surpassing all the cities of the ancient world in science, literature, government, religion, and the arts, she would turn within, and compete with herself.

PART TWO

THE MIND
OF THE CITY

THE MOST LEGENDARY BUILDING of Alexandria, and perhaps of all antiquity, was the huge Lighthouse, standing on the eastern point of Pharos Island. Ptolemy Soter began its construction in 290 B.C. yet it was still unfinished at his death in 285. During the reign of his son Ptolemy Philadelphus, it was finally completed, at a staggering cost, using a considerable amount of slave labor. The architect was Sostratos, a Greek from the Asia Minor city of Cnidus. The kings of ancient times forbade any other name but their own from being carved on buildings during their reign, and Ptolemy Philadelphus was no exception. However, Sostratos devised a plan to get around this: without Ptolemy's knowledge, he chiseled his own name and dedication on the foundation stone of the building, then covered it with a layer of plaster, upon which he carved the consecration in honor of Ptolemy. In time, the plaster peeled away, obscuring Ptolemy's dedication completely and leaving only the deeply carved inscription of the architect:

Sostratos of Cnidus, son of Dexiphanes, to the savior gods, for sailors.

Yet Pharos was more than a lighthouse. Every day it was crowded with visitors, Alexandrians as well as travelers from every corner of the world. It was approached first through the Heptastadion at the entrance to Alexandria's excellent harbor, a wall of solid granite that extended the length of seven stadiums and connected the city with Pharos Island. The Lighthouse consisted of three sections. The base (about 100 feet) was of square construction, the middle portion octagonal, and the top cylindrical. Its site was on the easternmost point of the island. One of the greatest achievements of the Egyptian mind, it was dedicated in 279 B.C., when Ptolemy Philadelphus held a festival to honor his parents.

This towering structure was to be the prototype of all lighthouses in the world, and for centuries it withstood the storms of tide and time. In the year A.D. 1115, Idrisi, a Moorish geographer from Spain, traveled to Alexandria and was so astounded by the enormous edifice, he proceeded to number all of its stairs, and to measure the height of its balconies, bazaars, and majestic tower.

Fifty years later, another Moorish scholar from Spain, Yusuf Ibn al-Shaikh, undertook an even more elaborate examination, confirming that Pharos Lighthouse was built in three distinct sections, the base alone being over 100 feet and resting on massive blocks of red granite that were joined not by mortar but by molten lead so as to reinforce the structure against the heavy pounding of the sea. In this first section were government offices and military barracks, together with stables for at least three hundred horses. Above this area was a wide eight-sided enclosure with a spacious balcony. Here refreshments were sold to the tourists: morsels of roast lamb on sticks, fruits, and refreshing drinks. Exquisite sculptures decorated the balcony, and at the top of this section, about 350 feet above the sea, another balcony jutted out, giving the visitors a panoramic view of Alexandria and the Mediterranean Sea.

The third and by far the highest section was the cylindrical tower that led to the beacon chamber, where a fire burned day and night. Mariners knew the fire and directed their course accordingly, for it was visible even a hundred miles out to sea. By night, it looked like a brilliant star. A mirror was used to amplify the beam, most likely made from a curved sheet of polished metal.

Within the confines of the Lighthouse, a spiral ramp enabled donkey-driven wagons to haul fuel to the beacon chamber. Visitors also used this ramp to climb to the top. For those who could not manage the long hard climb, donkeys were available for a moderate price. Hundreds of windows lined each wall of the Pharos, providing ample light along the ramp and stairs. Braced on the very crest of the Lighthouse, a colossal statue of the sea-god Poseidon, trident in hand, stared down at the city.

Several theories have been advanced regarding Pharos's fate. One claims the Lighthouse remained in active service for more than a thousand years but was destroyed by an earthquake in A.D. 796. Another maintains that it was partially demolished in the year A.D. 850 as a result of a ruse. It seemed the emperor Michael III (A.D. 842–867) was envious of Alexandria, and he devised a plot to deceive the Arabs into destroying the Lighthouse, the city's greatest attraction, so he sent an emissary to the court of the caliph at Cairo with specific orders to spread a rumor that a trove of gold was buried underneath the foundation of the Pharos.

The caliph ordered the building to be torn down, and as the Arab workers began dismantling the cylindrical tower, the huge mirror of polished metal slipped away from its base and crashed into the sea. The beacon chamber was then stripped down as well as the eight-sided middle section and its two balconies. With only the base of the Lighthouse remaining, the caliph, realizing that he had been tricked, halted further destruction and ordered his workmen to start rebuilding the tower. But since the damage was now too extensive, the project had to be abandoned and instead of a tower a crude mosque was constructed.

These theories disintegrate with further historical analysis: When the Moor Idrisi visited Alexandria in A.D. 1115, the Pharos still stood. Yusuf Ibn al-Shaikh also found the Lighthouse in sound condition in 1165, although at that time a small mosque had taken the place of the beacon.

Pharos Lighthouse most likely met its fate in the earthquake of A.D. 1365. The magnificent blocks of granite and marble toppled into the harbor and interfered with shipping for almost a hundred years before a channel was cleared of the biggest pieces. As late as A.D. 1480, the stump of the tower still jutted from the Heptastadion. Shortly after that, the sultan of Egypt, Kait Bey, built a fortress and castle there, using the marble base of the fallen Pharos for walls.

As late as 1962, a young diver, searching for fish at a depth of 24 feet, spotted fragments of an immense statue, one piece alone measuring more than 20 feet long. Egyptian naval divers, together with experts from Alexandria's Greco-Roman Museum, were summoned to the area and after careful examination verified the young man's report, concluding that the huge section of the sculpture was a fragment of the colossal statue of Poseidon that rested for centuries on the top of Pharos Lighthouse. Returning to the site once again, the Egyptian divers and scholars discovered a smaller statue, several columns, and a sizable sphinx. However, the rough seas prevented them from recovering more of the fallen antiquities, and because of the mud and silt at the sea's bottom, they were unable to take any photographs.

Somewhere on the floor of the Mediterranean, this massive structure still rests, piece by shattered piece, buried under the muddy waters of the onrushing Nile. Skin divers from many nations routinely scour the murky depths of the harbor but up to now have discovered only a few artifacts of any archeological significance: Roman and Greek coins, marble coffins, columns of red granite, sculptures.

Nevertheless, the search goes on.

High in the old Egyptian quarter, on a hill overlooking the city, rose the Temple of Serapis. Here Greeks and Egyptians worshiped at common altars under a rigid priesthood whose spiritual succession dated back to the priests of Zeus and to the ancient hierarchies of Osiris.

"No description can do it justice," wrote the Roman author Ammianus Marcellinus in the fourth century A.D., "yet it is so adorned with extensive columned halls, with almost breathing statues, and a great number of other works of art, that next to the Capitol, with which revered Rome elevates herself to eternity, the whole world beholds nothing more magnificent."

The temple housed the "daughter library" of Alexandria, appropriately called Serapeiana, and is not to be confused with the Great, or Mother, Library of the Mouseion, whose praise the iambist Herodes sang in rapturous tones: "Think of it, everything that is or can be anywhere, is here: riches, power, comfort, glory, philosophers, gold, shows, young men, gymnasiums, wine, all good things the heart can possibly desire; women too, more in number than the stars, and as beautiful as the goddesses!"

"There it towered up, the marvel of the world, its white roof bright against the rainless blue; and beyond it, among the ridges and pediments of noble buildings, a broad glimpse of the bright blue sea!"

For many centuries, the Mouseion was unparalleled among institutions of learning. It was founded in Alexandria during the rule of Ptolemy Soter, who, after the death of Alexander the Great, chose Alexandria as the capital of his kingdom. After he ascended to the throne of Egypt, Ptolemy Soter began the erection of a great Mouseion on land adjacent to his palace and not far from the Mausoleum of Alexander. The modern word "museum" does not apply here. Properly speaking, a Mouseion was a shrine of the Muses, the goddesses of literature and the arts, and its head was a priest of the Muses, nominated first by the kings of Egypt and later by the Roman emperors. The entire complex was richly endowed, containing lecture rooms, libraries, laboratories, and botanical gardens. The official dedication of the Mouseion took place around 300 B.C., and Soter's successor, Ptolemy Philadelphus, called the most learned men in all fields to come to Alexandria and lecture. Most, if not all, came from Athens, and the largest numbers were scientists and philosophers.

Year after year, illustrious scholars lived in Alexandria under the patronage of the Ptolemies, and though most of them had already gained their fame, either in Athens or Rome, they sought to be an integral part of Alexandria's rich culture. Free from want and from taxes, they studied, wrote, collated manuscripts, researched, lectured, and theorized in their respective disciplines. "This unique establishment," wrote the German historian Ferdinand Gregorovius, "diffused a splendor over the civilized world which lasted longer than any other university, whether of Paris, Bologna or Padua. Long after the creative power of Greek genius was exhausted, encyclopedic knowledge and Greek sophistry were to be found in the Mouseion of Alexandria."

In a much broader sense, this was a university, consisting of sleeping quarters, refectory, walks along cloisters or colonnaded shelters with seats for rest and contemplation, theaters for lectures on philosophy and science, readings of the classic poets and historians, botanical gardens and animal parks for the study of flora and fauna. But more importantly, it offered to its privileged fellows, and subsequently to all the scholars of the world, the resources of the first real, and the most comprehensive and innovative, collection of intellectual materials ever assembled in antiquity.

❦

Other than scant knowledge furnished by late compilers, little information is available on the existence of libraries in the ancient world. Among those who were known to have collected books are Peisistratus, Polycrates of Samos, Euclid, Nicocrates of Cyprus, Euripides, and Aristotle. Plato was also a collector; and Xenophon refers to "the library of Euthydemus."

Peisistratus, the feared yet respected tyrant of Athens, was an aristo-crat and a man of culture who built temples and inaugurated the great Panathenaic Festival, admirably depicted by the sculptor Pheidias on the running frieze of the Parthenon. With his fondness for music and poetry, he appointed a committee of scholars to assemble and edit Homer's *Iliad* and *Odyssey*, the first critical attempt to arrange the two great epics. Over the years, Peisistratus accumulated a vast personal library, to which all free, male Athenians had access, justifying the statement of the Roman writer Aulus Gellius that "Peisistratus established the first Public Library at Athens."

Polycrates of Samos, another reputed tyrant, also honored the arts and letters, but as a descendant of the Carian pirates, he was a ruthless and unscrupulous ruler. Herodotus described him as being "ostentatious in his love for beauty, patronizing and petting his poets, dining and wining with them in continuous orgies." One day, his friend Amasis, king of Egypt, advised him to give up something he held most dear, to prove that the riches of this world had no real attraction for him. Without hesitation, Polycrates took his rare emerald signet ring cut by the famous Samian artist Theodore and cast it into the sea. Though Polycrates grieved for the sacrifice, soon a young fisherman made a catch of an unusually rare fish, presented it to the tyrant, and when the fish was opened, its belly revealed the signet ring. While Polycrates immediately took this as a good omen, Amasis suspected that the goddess Nemesis had turned down the tyrant's offering, and though Polycrates continued to prosper, Nemesis eventually caught up to him. He was lured to Asia by the satrap Orestes, where he was cruelly put to death.

Despite his ill repute, throughout his reign on Samos, with easy access to Asia, Greece, and Egypt to the south, and with his large fleet navigating a large territory, Polycrates was in the ideal position to invite the best scholars of his day to Samos and gather all their manuscripts and papyrus rolls for his own library.

Euripides, the great tragic poet, was also an ardent collector of books. Born in Salamis during the naval battle, he met his tragic end in Macedo-nia, torn to pieces by the hounds of his friend King Archelaus. Of his ninety-five plays, only eighteen have survived, and though he was a man of very limited means, he had the good fortune of having his intelligent and faithful servant Cephisophon, who was also an accomplished scribe and collaborator.

Plato, who created a world of ideas, and whose views on God and man exerted a profound influence on philosophy, religion, and politics, was an ardent collector of books. After the death of Socrates, he traveled extensively throughout Greece and made three journeys to Syracuse. In these long visits to the cultured cities of Greece and Sicily, he gathered manuscripts and records of the fifth century B.C. He paid the huge sum of one hundred minas to purchase three books on the Pythagorean doctrine by Philolaus of Croton. His main collections, not including those he had acquired in Greece, came from purchases at Tarentum and Syracuse.

Demosthenes, the famous orator and political leader, also possessed a very select library, most of which (according to Lucian of Samosata) included manuscripts he had copied with his own hand. Of these, he re-copied many beautiful manuscripts of Thucydides, either as gifts to his friends or for the purpose of sale. He is one of four Greek writers whose manuscripts have survived in the best condition.

Aristotle, pupil of Plato and author of works on logic, philosophy, natural sciences, ethics, politics, and poetics, was the first to collect, preserve, and use the culture of the past. He laid the very foundation of literary history. A man of universal knowledge and interests, he founded his own philosophical school, the Lyceum, on the outskirts of Athens, where he walked as he lectured and hence became known as the "Peripatetic philosopher." He was personally selected by Philip of Macedon to be the tutor of Alexander the Great, a position he held for three years. Alexander so deeply respected his teacher that with every conquest of Egypt, the kingdoms of Asia and the East, he arranged to acquire rare books and send them to Aristotle. These included precious Greek manuscripts from the sophisticated cities of Asia Minor, Egyptian papyrus rolls, and many oriental manuscripts, all of which Aristotle gathered together and classified in his vast personal library. Among these works were political records and materials from more than 150 communities throughout the Greek world, collected by his own students and reference scholars for his series on constitutions. One of these manuscripts was to be discovered in a tomb at Akhmin, Egypt, in the twentieth century. It was written on four papyrus rolls under the title *The Constitution of Athens*. His library also contained numerous literary scrolls, works of natural history written and sent to him by his many students and admirers, and, of course, his own voluminous writings, totaling over four hundred books, or as the writer Diogenes Laertius noted, "445,270 lines."

In his final years, with his health failing, Aristotle was pressed to name a successor, which placed him in a difficult position because he had two disciples who excelled the rest in learning and scholarship: Theophrastus of Lesbos and Eudemus of Rhodes.

> During an evening symposium at his home, Aristotle leaned back and said, *This wine I am drinking does not sit well with my health. Could you not fetch me some foreign vintage, say some wine of Rhodes and Lesbos?*
> His students, grasping his intent, brought the desired wines and gathered around their master as he first tested the wine from Rhodes. *This is truly sound and pleasant wine,* he said. He then tried the wine from Lesbos, and remarked, *Indeed, both are very good, but the Lesbian is the sweeter.*

Through this little anecdote (passed down from Aulus Gellius), Aristotle made his choice and thus selected Theophrastus of Lesbos to be his successor. At his death, Theophrastus left the library and works of Aristotle, plus his own library and writings, which amounted to 232,808 lines, to his relative and pupil Neleus of Scepsis. The will of Theophrastus was preserved by Diogenes Laertius. His property in Stagira he left to Callinus; all his books to Neleus.

According to the geographer Strabo, these books remained in the family of Neleus's heirs for many years, but because his descendants were subjects of Pergamum, they feared that the avaricious kings of Pergamum would take the books away from them. Consequently, they hid the entire library in a cave, and as the years passed, the manuscripts were forgotten until Apellicon of Teos, a Peripatetic philosopher and omnivorous collector of books, learned about this hidden library and somehow managed to acquire it. The books were in deplorable condition, molded and partly rotted from the cold and dampness of the cave; nevertheless Apellicon arranged to have them published, editing and even filling in the missing sections with additions of his own, which were later corrected by scholars.

The library of Apellicon was confiscated by the Roman general and dictator Sulla and taken to Rome after he conquered Athens in 84 B.C. Copies of the "Aristotle books" eventually reached the hands of Andronicus of Rhodes, the first of the great Aristotelian scholars, who subsequently devoted most of his years to the task of elucidating the complete works of this last genius of the Greek classical age.

Athenaeus, the Greek rhetorician and grammarian, however, has a different and more valid story: Neleus sold the complete libraries of Aristotle and Theophrastus to Ptolemy II (Philadelphus) for the newly created university in Alexandria, whose library would become the greatest the world has ever known.

⟨❦⟩

The Alexandrian Library became the central attraction for writers, teachers, and scientists from every part of the world. Its first curator and director was Demetrius Phalereus, a distinguished Athenian scholar. Under his aegis, the Library acquired more than 600,000 manuscripts, all neatly rolled in long-enduring papyrus. In addition to being its first curator and director, Phalereus was also instrumental in creating the Mouseion itself. Prior to coming to Alexandria, he had governed Athens from 317 to 307 B.C. as the agent of the Macedonian dynast Cassander, before being expelled by another Macedonian dynast. Phalereus had previously been an associate of Aristotle, who in his philosophical school at Athens had assembled a huge number of books with which he carried out researches in every branch of learning. Phalereus was thus well qualified to advise the king in the creation of a community of scholars and writers who would be associated with this extensive library. After the death of Ptolemy Soter, his son and successor, Ptolemy Philadelphus shared his father's lifelong enthusiasm for the project and the work was carried on to its completion.

The Library lay within the quarter of Alexandria that was originally called the Palaces, and later the Brucheion. Strabo, writing in the first century B.C., described this quarter as forming one-third of the main enclosure of the city. The Library had a covered walk, a portico, and a central block, to which the refectory of the scholars was attached. It has never been revealed how the Library functioned, or if its scholars and scientists lived on the premises. Direct evidence is also lacking as to whether or not these scholars actually taught or lectured there. However, one fact is certain: they indeed engaged in scholarly work of immense value, which was intimately connected with the Great Library that stood on their premises. Books and papyrus rolls were collected from every corner of the civilized world, with the aim of gathering together the writings of all men so far as they were worthy of attention. This massive collection of books and scrolls was not limited to Greek and Roman works. Oriental writings were translated into Greek and placed in the Library; as were ancient Egyptian texts, the Hebrew Scriptures, and writings ascribed to the Persian prophet Zoroaster.

The Ptolemies spared no expense in gathering works for the Library. The legendary physician Galen inferred that Ptolemy borrowed the original copy of the works of the great Athenian tragic poets in order to have them copied. Ptolemy was required to lay down as a deposit the sum of fifteen gold talents, but when the work was completed, he chose to forfeit his money and instead sent the copies back to Athens, retaining the originals.

It is difficult to ascertain the actual number of books that were contained in Alexandria's Library. The Byzantine monk John Tzetzes, living in the thirteenth century A.D., derived his figures from much earlier authority, and estimated that the external library (a much smaller library which was attached to the temple of the god Serapis) contained 42,800 rolls, while the royal library (belonging to the Mouseion) possessed 490,000 rolls. Of these, 400,000 were *mixed rolls* and 90,000 *unmixed*. A mixed roll contained several works, whereas an unmixed roll was confined to one work alone. Generally, a papyrus roll consisted on an average of twenty sheets, each sheet varying between 10 centimeters and 4.5 centimeters in width. The works of the ancient authors were divided into books that were more or less as large as the average roll, so that 490,000 rolls amounted to little more than 70,000 works.

Using these collections, the scholars affiliated with the Library were able to produce standard editions of the main Greek classics. With such brilliant minds gathered together under its roof, the Library became the cultural center of the eastern and western worlds, holding this position from 300 B.C. to A.D. 642.

There is no reason to doubt that geometry originated in Egypt. The Egyptians were led to its study by the necessity of restoring the boundaries of the fields after the yearly destructions wrought by the inundation of the Nile. The very word "geometry" means "land-measuring." The earliest Greek on record to have visited Egypt was Thales. He was engaged in trade there for many years, and on his return to Miletus in his old age, he brought with him the Egyptian science of geometry and astronomy.

Herodotus, "the Father of History," made an extensive visit to Egypt around 450 B.C., traveling widely throughout the country and ascending the Nile as far as the island of Elephantine at the foot of the Great Cataract. He devoted the entire second volume of his *History* to Egypt, and although his chief concern was the historical development of the people, he also dealt extensively with the geography of the country. Many of his ideas proved to be fundamentally sound, for he correctly conjectured that the lower part of the Nile Valley was once a gulf of the sea, which in the course of ages had become filled with sediments deposited from the swirling river.

In his observations of the dimensions of structures and the distances between places, Herodotus made use of various methods, including the foot, cubit, fathom, plethron, stade, and parasang. He also indicated the distances from one place to another by disclosing that it was so many days' sail by river, or so many days' journey by land. Along with the geographers of his time, he believed that the known land portion of the earth's surface consisted of three continents: Europe, Asia, and Libya (modern Africa). However, he did not agree with those who considered the Nile to mark the boundary between Asia and Libya, since that would involve the division of Egypt into two parts, one belonging to Asia, the other to Libya. Therefore, he regarded Egypt and the eastern desert as belonging to the continent of Asia, for after defining Egypt as the entire tract of which the soil had been deposited by the Nile, the only proper boundary between the two continents was the frontier of Egypt.

Herodotus theorized that Libya was known to be washed on all sides by the sea, except where it was joined to Asia. This observation was solidified by the fact that ships manned by Phoenician sailors under the service of Necho, a seventh-century B.C. Egyptian king, sailed from Egypt, by way of the Red Sea, into the Indian Ocean and returned by way of the Pillars of Hercules (Gibraltar) and the Mediterranean, after a voyage of more than two years.

This same King Necho was the first to attempt the excavation of a canal from the Nile to the Red Sea. It began at the Pelusiac branch of the Nile, a little above the city of Bubastis, and passed near Patumus to reach the Erythraean (Red) Sea. However, when 120,000 Egyptians lost their lives in the undertaking, and after an oracle informed him that only foreigners would profit from his labors, Necho abandoned the project. Even though he did not complete the canal, Necho constructed shipyards and built a fleet of ships on the shore of the Red Sea in the vicinity of the modern Suez, and it was from this location that his ships departed on their long voyage of circumnavigation around the continent of Africa.

Before leaving Egypt, Herodotus visited the pyramids of Giza and described them in detail, recording the history of their construction as it was related to him by the priests. He also measured the two largest pyramids and found that they were both 800 feet square but differed from each other in height, that of Cheops (Great Pyramid) being 800 feet high, while that of Chephren (Second Pyramid) was lower by 40 feet.

Ancient authorities on mathematics agree that the first person to compose a book of elements was Hippocrates of Chios, who lived and worked during the middle of the fifth century B.C. He is not to be confused with the Father of Medicine, who came from Cos. These authorities also maintain that a whole hegemony of mathematicians existed between the time of Hippocrates of Chios and that of Euclid himself, whose own *Elements* dated to 300 B.C. The object of any book on elements is to systematize all geometrical knowledge, which Euclid accomplished in a remarkable way. Even to this day, his work serves as the most systematic and comprehensive on the subject.

Before this, Plato complained that mathematicians gave no account of their hypotheses but instead assumed that they were evident to everyone; and in his *Posterior Analytics,* Aristotle held firmly to the argument that the starting points, which he specified as definitions, axioms, and hypotheses, must themselves "be indemonstrable yet also true."

More than anyone else, Euclid realized that once the starting points are set out, a body of theorems is demonstrated in a systematic way. Little is known of his life, except that he was of Greek descent, was born in Athens about 330 B.C., and lived most of his life in Alexandria. One thing, however, is certain: he wasn't the Euclid of Megara, with whom he has been erroneously confounded over the centuries, a disciple of Socrates, who, after Socrates' death in 399 B.C., left Athens and founded a school in Megara, which puts him a whole century before Euclid the mathematician.

The cloud encircling Euclid's identity in many respects is similar to that of Homer, but while seven cities vied for the honor of having given birth to the father of poetry; there was not one city, town, or hamlet that claimed or even desired to claim the father of geometry. His name is most appropriate, *eu* means "good," and *kleis* means "key": the good key.

Two hundred years before Herodotus measured the pyramids, there was a narrative about how the Greek philosopher and geometrician Thales determined the actual height of a pyramid. With Amasis the king standing beside him, he chose the time when his own shadow was equal in length to his height, which of course happens once a day when the sun's altitude is 45 degrees. Then, assuming that the shadow of the pyramid must also be equal to its height, he measured the former, and so deduced the latter. If Euclid had been around at that time, he would have found Thales' experiment quite elementary, since if two right-angled triangles have one of the acute angles in each equal, and the one triangle is isosceles, the other will also be isosceles. Nevertheless, Amasis the king was astonished at the ingenuity displayed by Thales.

The modern texts of Euclid's *Elements* are founded on an edition prepared by Theon, who was the father of Hypatia. His treatise contained a systematic exposition of the leading propositions of metrical geometry and of the theory of numbers. It was quickly adopted as the standard textbook on the elements of pure mathematics by the Alexandrians who, unlike the Athenians, treated the science as a subject wholly distinct from philosophy.

Euclid also published a collection of problems known as the *Data*. It contained ninety-five examples of the various deductions that are generally made in analysis, and was intended for those who wished to acquire the power of solving problems. His *On Divisions* is a collection of thirty-six problems on the division of areas into parts that bear a given ratio to one another. Another book on optics, treated geometrically, contained sixty-one propositions founded on twelve assumptions. It began with the assumption that objects are seen by rays emitted from the eye in straight lines, "for if light proceeded from the object itself we would not fail to perceive a needle on the floor."

His other treatises included studies on geometrical astronomy, spherical geometry, and the elements of music.

When King Ptolemy Soter asked Euclid if he (the king) could not learn geometry more easily than by studying the *Elements*, Euclid replied, "There is no royal road to geometry." For someone who carved his name so indelibly in science and in history, it is regrettable that very little is known about him, other than that he was a man of mild and inoffensive temperament, unpretending, and kind to all sincere students of mathematics.

As with mathematics, much work was accomplished in astronomy by Alexandrian scholars. In the beginning, the focus was on significant phenomena regarding events on earth, chiefly the fortunes of the king and the people of Egypt, whereas astronomers (particularly the Babylonians) followed the more scientific method of constructing tables that determined definite astronomical events. Their studies proved so accurate the Greeks used them in their own observations. As early as the fifth century B.C., the Pythagoreans had already made rapid advances in this field, assigning each of the planets as well as the sun and moon to separate circles, and working out a detailed theory of planetary motion. However, Aristotle, in his book *On the Heavens*, criticized the Pythagoreans for asserting that the earth itself moves, circling a postulated central fire like one of the planets.

The first detailed and coherent solution to the problems regarding the movements of the planets was given by Plato's younger contemporary, Eudoxus of Cnidus. A scholar and scientist of great renown, he contributed immensely to the development of astronomy, mathematics, geography, and philosophy, as well as providing his native city with laws. As a youth, he studied geometry with Archytas of Tarentum, from whom he acquired a deep interest in number theory and music, and in Athens he attended the lectures of Plato. His circle of friends in Cnidus raised enough money to send him on a journey to Egypt for a series of diplomatic discussions with King Nekhtanibef II on behalf of King Agesilaus II of Sparta, and also for the purpose of acquainting him with the various astronomical and mathematical methods practiced in Alexandria.

Eudoxus spent considerable time in Egypt, often in the company of the priests at Heliopolis, where he composed his *Octaeteris*, an eight-year calendric cycle. He next traveled to Cyzicus in northwestern Asia Minor and founded a school of astronomy, after which he paid a second visit to Athens and developed a closer association with Plato, the result of which was Plato's *Philebus*, written with the Eudoxian view of *hedone* (that pleasure, correctly understood, is the highest good) in mind.

After returning to Cnidus, Eudoxus lectured on theology, cosmology, meteorology, and astronomy. In addition, he wrote textbooks and enjoyed the respect of his fellow citizens. From his long sojourn in Egypt, and particularly Alexandria, he investigated mathematical proportion, the theory of exhaustion, and axiomatic methods. The pyramids at Giza encouraged him to make prolonged observations, as a result of which he concluded that the volume of a pyramid is one-third the volume of the prism having the same base and equal height, and that the volume of the cone is one-third the volume of the cylinder having the same base and height.

The most important achievement of Eudoxos was his application of spherical geometry to astronomy. In his book *On Speeds,* he expounded a system of geocentric, homocentric rotating spheres designed to explain the irregularities in the motion of planets as seen from the earth. Aristotle erroneously assumed the system to be a description of the physical world and complicated it by the addition of more spheres, but Eudoxus meant the system to be simply an abstract geometrical model.

Eudoxus was an astute observer of the fixed stars, and his knowledge of spherical astronomy led to the publication of the geographical treatise *Tour of the Earth.* Beginning with Asia, he systematically (while making use of Greek mythology) recorded each part of the known world, along with political, historical, and ethnographic details. Unquestionably, he learned much from his lengthy stay in Egypt, and it helped him become a dominant figure in the intellectual life of Greece during the age of Plato and Aristotle. Sadly, not a single work of his has survived. Equally as sad, the only thing the world remembers about him is Aristotle's remark: "The upright and controlled character of Eudoxus, made people believe him when he said: *pleasure was the highest good.*"

Although Archimedes was on intimate terms with, and probably related to, Hiero, king of Syracuse, and to Gelo, his son, he spent considerable time in Alexandria, attending the lectures of Conon of Samos, whom he admired as a mathematician, cherished as a friend, and to whom he communicated his discoveries before publication. After completing his long stay in Alexandria, he returned to his native city and devoted himself entirely to mathematical research. He was humble in nature and set no real value on the ingenious mechanical contrivances that made him famous, regarding them as beneath the dignity of pure science and even refusing to leave any written record of them, except for *On Sphere-Making,* where he explained the construction of a sphere, which was made to imitate the motions of the sun, the moon, and the five planets in the heavens.

His inventions impressed the popular imagination and figured largely in the traditions about him. He devised for King Hiero machines of war that terrified the Romans and prolonged their siege of Syracuse for more than three years. One such machine was a burning mirror that set the Roman ships on fire when they were within a bow shot of the walls of the city. Archimedes also invented the catapults that rained down on the Romans as they tried to seize Syracuse. They were constructed in such a way that their range could be made adjustable and thus discharged through a small loophole without exposing the artillery men to the fire of the enemy.

The principle in hydrostatics that bears his name resulted from the story of Hiero's question whether a crown made specifically for him, and purporting to be of gold, did not in fact contain a proportion of silver. This problem worried Archimedes for a long time until, one day as he stepped into a bath and observed the water running over, it occurred to him that the excess of bulk occasioned by the introduction of alloy could be measured by putting the crown and an equal weight of gold separately into a vessel filled with water and observing the difference of overflow. He was so thrilled with this wondrous discovery, he ran home naked, shouting: "Eureka! Eureka!" (I have found it! I have found it!)

At another time, he made this statement: "Give me a place to stand and I will move the earth." When Hiero asked him to submit proof that a very great weight could be moved by a very small force, Archimedes constructed a small mechanical device and fixed it upon a large and fully laden ship. Using this device. Hiero was able to move the ship by himself, and with little effort.

During the general massacre that followed the capture of Syracuse by Marcellus in 212 B.C., Archimedes was engaged in drawing a mathematical figure on the sand when a Roman soldier ran a sword through his body. No blame could be attached to General Marcellus for this deed, since he had given strict orders to his men to spare the house and life of the great Archimedes. In the midst of his triumph, Marcellus truly lamented the death of so illustrious a person, and after befriending Archimedes' surviving relatives, he directed that an honorable burial be given him. In accordance with the expressed desire of Archimedes, his tomb was marked by the figure of a sphere inscribed in a cylinder that stood for the discovery of the relation between the volumes of a sphere and its circumscribing cylinder, which Archimedes regarded as his most valued achievement. Fortunately, many of his works still survive.

Archimedes is foremost among the mathematicians, and his accomplishments have been acknowledged by the most distinguished men of succeeding generations. Cicero, who was born in Arpinum, visited Sicily in 75 B.C. and for a long time searched for the tomb of Archimedes. Near the Agrigentine Gate, he spotted a marble column jutting out between the rocks. It was overgrown with thorns and briers, and after brushing everything away, he noticed the figures of a sphere and a cylinder carved on the marble slab. "And so," he later wrote, "one of the noblest cities of Greece [Agrigento], once indeed a very great seat of learning, would have been ignorant of the monument of its most brilliant citizen, except that it was revealed by a man of Arpinum."

More astronomer than mathematician, Aristarchus of Samos, who lived and taught in Alexandria, is celebrated as the first man to have propounded the heliocentric theory of the universe (eighteen centuries before Copernicus). He was born on the island of Samos, just across from Miletus in Asia Minor, the cradle of Ionian science and philosophy. He was a pupil of Strato of Lampsacus, who was the third head of the Lyceum founded by Aristotle.

Aristarchus's heliocentric theory can be traced to the early Pythagoreans, a religiophilosophical school that flourished in southern Italy in the fifth century B.C. Concerning Aristarchus's greatest work, *On the Sizes and Distances of the Sun and Moon*, Archimedes had this to say: "His hypotheses are that the fixed stars and the sun are stationary, that the earth is borne in a circular orbit about the sun, which lies in the middle of the orbit, and that the sphere of the fixed stars, having the same center as the sun, is so great in extent that the circle on which he supposes the earth to be borne has such a proportion to the distance of the fixed stars as the center of the sphere bears to its surface."

Yet after reporting Aristarchus's views, Archimedes proceeded to criticize him for setting up a mathematically impossible proportion, pointing out that the center of the sphere has no magnitude and therefore cannot bear any ratio to the surface of the sphere.

Basically, Aristarchus believed that the moon received its light from the sun, that the earth had the relation of a point and center to the sphere of the moon, and that when the moon appeared to us to be exactly at the half, the great circle dividing the light and dark portions of the moon was in line with the observer's eye. Furthermore, the breadth of the earth's shadow (during eclipses) was that of two moons.

He followed these assumptions with eighteen propositions containing demonstrations of proof. Throughout his work, he rigidly asserted that the sun was the center of the universe, and that the earth revolved around the sun, a view rejected by his contemporaries. As Galileo was to be attacked and condemned many centuries later by the theologians, Aristarchus too had to answer many heated charges, particularly those of the Stoics. Nevertheless, his propositions on the measurement of the sizes and distances of the sun and moon were accurate in principle and accepted as correct.

More than a thousand years later, it was revealed that Copernicus was sorely distressed to know that Aristarchus, and not he, discovered the heliocentric theory. In fact, Copernicus deliberately suppressed a statement in which he had acknowledged his awareness of Aristarchus's theory. The statement, deleted from the autograph copy of *De Revolutionibus Orbium Coelestium*, appears in a footnote in the 1873 edition of that work. Elsewhere, Copernicus speaks of his "search for classical precedents for his new ideas about the heavens, and of finding in Plutarch the views of Philolaus, Heraclides, and Ecphantus," but the name of Aristarchus is never mentioned.

The theory of heliocentricity was considered for a time but was ultimately rejected by other Alexandrian astronomers, including the great Ptolemy (Claudius Ptolemaeus), who frequently discussed the question of whether any movement can be attributed to the earth. However, he rejected any such notion for astronomical and physical reasons, since if the earth actually rotated, "we would expect visible effects on the objects around us. Clouds and missiles in the air would never move eastward because the movement of the earth would always anticipate them."

In ancient times, other factors weighed against the acceptance of heliocentricity, primarily the appeal to the "common sense" doctrine of

Aristotle, which stated flatly that all heavy objects must be subject to the same laws and move in the same direction toward the center of the earth.

In the third century B.C., the Stoic philosopher Cleanthes suggested that the Greeks ought to indict Aristarchus of Samos on a charge of impiety, for putting in motion the Hearth (earth) of the Universe. Fortunately, his advice was never taken seriously.

Another Aristarchus (of Samothrace), the better known of the two, settled in Alexandria after leaving his island home in early youth. He studied under Aristophanes of Byzantium, and later succeeded him as librarian of Alexandria's Mouseion. A respected grammarian and critic, he founded a school of philologists, named after him Aristarcheans, which flourished for a long time in Alexandria, and after that at Rome. He wrote more than eight hundred commentaries, and also edited the works of Hesiod, Pindar, Aeschylus, Sophocles, and other authors. However, his chief fame rests on his critical and exegetical edition of Homer's *Iliad* and *Odyssey*. To obtain a thoroughly correct text, he marked with an obelus the lines he considered spurious, while various other signs were used to indicate notes, varieties of reading, repetitions, and interpolations. His principle as a critic strongly maintained that the author should explain himself without recourse to allegorical interpretation; and in grammar, he laid chief stress on analogy and uniformity of usage and construction.

On the ascension of the tyrant Ptolemy Physcon (who was his former pupil), Aristarchus realized that his life was in danger and he withdrew to Cyprus, where he died from dropsy, hastened by voluntary starvation.

Among the most notable Homeric critics of antiquity was Zenodotus of Ephesus. He was installed as the first head of the Alexandrian Library by Ptolemy Philadelphus, and although he was sometimes reproached for having an insufficient knowledge of Greek, he nevertheless achieved universal fame as the first editor of Homer. After collating the Homeric manuscripts in the Library, he expunged or obelized doubtful verses, transposed or altered lines, and introduced new readings. He also divided the Homeric poems into twenty-four books, using capitals for the *Iliad*, and small letters for the *Odyssey*. It is not known if he ever wrote any commentaries on Homer, but his Homeric lists of unusual words formed the source of all explanations in Homer. While his colleagues at the Library (Alexander of Aetolia and Lycophron of Chalcis) were allotted the tragic and comic writers, Zenodotus worked mostly on Homer and the epic poets. He also lectured on Hesiod, Anacreon, and Pindar. Suidas flattered

Zenodotus when he called him an epic poet; a further and more deserving honor came when three epigrams in *The Greek Anthology* were assigned to him.

Whereas the ancient Greeks wrote in continuous sentences, using only capital letters, Zenodotus was responsible for inventing the use of accents on words for pronunciation. During his long reign as head of the Library, most of the literary scholarship of Alexandria sprang up, including that curious by-product, the scholarly joke. One man wrote a poem that had, when transcribed, the shape of a bird; another poet created his words in the shape of a double-headed ax; and a third rewrote the entire *Odyssey* without using the letter *s*.

The donnish wit of the Mouseion even infected the Royal Palaces and was practiced by the Ptolemies themselves. When a scholar named Sosibius complained to Ptolemy Philadelphus that he had not received his salary, the king replied: "The first syllable of your name occurs in *Soter*, the second in Sosigenes, the third in Bion, and the fourth in Apollonius. I have paid these four gentlemen, and therefore I have paid you."

Twenty-five years after the death of Archimedes, Apollonius of Perga settled in Alexandria and lectured there until his death in 200 B.C. His brilliant treatise *Conics* gained him the title of "the Great Geometer." He was not as well loved as Archimedes. His contemporaries saw him as vain, jealous of the reputation of others, and ready to seize every opportunity to depreciate them. He and the geographer Eratosthenes, his fellow lecturer at the University, bore the nicknames of Epsilon and Beta by their students because they always used the rooms numbered (in the Greek capital letters) 5 and 2 respectively.

Apollonius spent a number of years at Pergamum, where a university had been recently established in imitation of the one in Alexandria, but he felt more at home with the cultural challenge of Alexandria, and he returned there to spend the rest of his life.

In his great work *Conics*, he so thoroughly investigated the properties of curves that he left very little for his successors to add. However, his proofs were long and involved, and most students, assured that his demonstrations at least were valid, were content to accept a brief analysis of his work. To satisfy them, Apollonius later brought out a second edition, considerably revised and improved, but before submitting it to his students and contemporaries, he sent it to his friend Eudemus in Pergamum for criticism and suggestions. One of his envious colleagues asserted that much of the material in *Conics* had been stolen from an unpublished work of Archimedes, but critical examinations of both books proved this accusation to be false.

Apollonius first defined a cone on a circular basis. He then investigated the different plane sections and showed that they were divisible into three kinds of curves, which he called ellipses, parabolas, and hyperbolas. His work contained most of the propositions found in modern textbooks, developing the theory of lines cut harmonically, and treating the points of intersection in all systems of conics. Beyond his work in geometry, Apollonius was credited by Claudius Ptolemaeus (Ptolemy) with an explanation of the motion of the planets by a system of epicycles, and he also made researches in lunar theory. But it is on *Conics* that his fame rests.

Although Apollonius and Archimedes were the most able geometricians of that era, their works were distinguished by a marked contrast: in attacking the problem of the quadrature of curvilinear areas, Archimedes established the principles of geometry that are devoted entirely to measurements, a system which did not differ from the method later to be used by Newton. As for Apollonius, by investigating the properties of conic sections, he established the foundations of the geometry of form and position. These two giants of geometry, together with Euclid, made up the triumvirate of scientists at the Alexandrian school. Those who followed them, although lesser known, were equally as great.

෴

Eratosthenes, a native of the Greek city of Cyrene in North Africa, studied for a time in Athens before being invited by Ptolemy III (Euergetes) to Alexandria, where he was placed in charge of the Mother Library, a position of the highest distinction. He occupied this post until 194 B.C., when, after losing his sight by ophthalmia (a curse of the Nile Valley), and refusing to live when he could no longer read, he committed suicide by voluntary starvation.

As a youth in Cyrene, Eratosthenes was surrounded by the highest culture. The city was widely acclaimed among the ancients for its intellectual life. It had a famous medical school, as well as a sound university. It produced Aristippus, a pupil of Socrates, and the founder of the Cyrenaic school of philosophy, which (like Eudoxus) held that pleasure was the highest form of existence. Cyrene continued for many years to sustain its intellectual life. It was the birthplace of Carneades, founder of the New Academy at Athens and one of the first skeptics. It also was the home of Synesius, a disciple of the Neoplatonist Hypatia.

Eratosthenes arrived in Alexandria at the same time as Archimedes and was a personal friend of the mathematician. Distinguished for his athletic and literary, as well as his scientific, achievements, Eratosthenes acquired a reputation known throughout the world. He was one of the most learned men of antiquity and wrote on a great number of subjects. Although he laid the foundation of mathematical geography in his book *Geographica*, his greatest accomplishment, and the one that earned him enduring fame, was his attempt to determine the magnitude of the earth. He did this by employing a method that was perfectly sound in principle: first ascertaining by astronomical observations the difference between the latitudes of two stations situated on the same meridian, also by terrestrially measuring the distance between the same two stations, and finally, on the assumption that the earth was spherical in shape, by computing its circumference.

The two stations selected by Eratosthenes were Syene (modern Aswan) in the south of Egypt, and Alexandria in the north. He assumed the general belief at the time that Syene was situated exactly under the tropic of Cancer, which meant that on the day of the summer solstice the sun would pass exactly through the zenith there, while at Alexandria on the same day, the sun would pass to the south of the zenith at an angular distance; and since the rays from the sun's center were considered to be parallel at the two places, they would obviously be equal also to the difference of latitude between them.

Applying this method, Eratosthenes determined that the only quantities of which he had to obtain a knowledge in order to be able to calculate the circumference of the earth were: the zenith distance of the sun at Alexandria on the day of the summer solstice, which he could find by observation, and the direct distance from Alexandria to Syene, which he assumed to be 5,000 stades. (According to Herodotus, one stade was equivalent to 600 Greek feet, or 185.3 meters, which was the ordinary Olympic stade used to measure a footrace course.)

For his observation of the zenith distance of the sun, Eratosthenes made use of a *scaphe,* or bowl, having the form of a concave hemisphere, from the floor of which projected a verticle gnomon whose upper extremity coincided with the center of the sphere itself. When the sun came to the meridian at Alexandria on the day of the summer solstice, the shadow of the gnomon was found to cover an arc of the scaphe equal to one-fiftieth of the circumference; and since the gnomon would cast no shadow in Syene at this distance, this arc was the measure of the difference between the latitudes of Syene and Alexandria. By this simple proportion, Eratosthenes concluded that the circumference of the entire earth was fifty times the distance between Syene and Alexandria, i.e., 50 × 5,000 (or 250,000 stades), which he subsequently amended to 252,000 stades, since it was more conveniently divisible by 60.

Contrary to the accepted belief of the time, Eratosthenes proved that the world was round, and that the complete circumference of the earth was 25,000 miles, the diameter 7,850 miles. He was correct on his first figure but missed the diameter by 50 miles; but this slight error is understandable, since it resulted from a common belief of the time that the distance between Alexandria and Syene was 5,000 stades, or 926 kilometers, when in fact the true distance is 842 kilometers, or 4,544 stades.

His *Geographica* was furnished with a map which, for the first time, used a system of parallels of latitude. Regrettably, his great mathematical and scientific treatises are lost. Of the few fragments that have come down to us, one of the most interesting is a passage (preserved by the geographer Strabo) relating to the Nile River and its tributaries, from which it appears that Eratosthenes had much better information about the upper reaches of the great river than Herodotus, or any subsequent writer down to Claudius Ptolemaeus. In this passage, Eratosthenes asserted that the Nile resembled in its course the letter *N* reversed, for after flowing for about 2,700 stades from Meroe toward the north, it turned again to the south and to the winter sunset, continuing its course for about 3,700 stades, when it was almost in the latitude of Meroe. It then entered far into Africa, and after making another bend, it flowed to the north for a distance of 5,300 stades, up to the Great Cataract (Wadi Halfa). From here, it inclined a little to the east, traversed a distance of 1,200 stades to the smaller cataract at Syene, then 5,300 stades more to the sea. Two rivers, which issued out of some lakes to the east and encircled the city of Meroe, emptied themselves into the Nile. One of these rivers, the Astaboras (now called the Atbara), flowed along the eastern side of Meroe; and the other (now called the Blue Nile) was the Astapus.

Eratosthenes also founded the science of chronology. One of his treatises fixed the dates of the chief literary and political events, beginning with the conquest of Troy. In addition, he was a capable cartographer and wrote extensively on moral philosophy, history, the theater, and poetry. He was a man of universal learning and broad scholarship, deserving the appropriate title of Beta given him by his peers (Alpha being reserved for the divine Plato). Another version submitted by later historians stated that he was given the title of Beta because he was the second head of the Library, having succeeded Callimachus, who was the first.

After having attained a reasonably accurate estimate of the circumference and diameter of the earth, Eratosthenes then proceeded to lay out the foundations for a scientific theory of geography. This required a prime meridian, which he naturally established through Alexandria. It passed through Syene and along the course of the Nile, through the land of the Nubians, to the country of the Sembritae, who were supposed to reside on the edge of the known world. Northward from Alexandria, it passed through Rhodes, thence through the Euxine (Black) Sea, to the mouth of the Borysthenes (Dnieper) River.

For his primary parallel, he took a line through Rhodes and ran it through the Malea Promontory of the Grecian Peloponnesus, touching westward the toe of Italy, passing through the Strait of the Columns (Gibraltar), and from there to the Sacred Promontory (Cape St. Vincent), which at that time was believed to be the most westerly point of Europe. Eastward from Rhodes, the line passed through the Gulf of Issus and along the southern base of the Taurus Mountains, which were regarded as a vast barrier across Asia.

The most northerly point of his meridian was the island of Thule, which lay on the edge of the frozen sea. This mysterious island has never been fully identified, but Pliny (quoting Pytheas, a native of Massilia) said,

"Thule was six days' sail from the north of Britain, and had a day six months in length and a night of equal duration."

Eratosthenes' other works are mostly extinct, and we know of them only through the reference of contemporary writers. In his treatise *Arithmetic*, he invented a method called the "sieve" (*koskinon*) for finding prime numbers. To employ the system, one writes down consecutively the odd numbers starting with 3 and continuing as long as desired; then, counting from 3, one passes over two numbers and strikes out the third (a multiple of 3, and hence not prime) and continues to do this until the end. The same process is gone through with 5, but this time passing over four numbers and striking out the fifth.

On the subject of chronography, Eratosthenes wrote two books, both of which entailed considerable original research. He was the first writer to have made a scientific study of the dating of events, such as the Fall of Troy (1184 B.C.), the Dorian migration (1104 B.C.), the First Olympiad (777 B.C.), the invasion of Xerxes (480 B.C.), and the outbreak of the Peloponnesian War (432 B.C.).

He also wrote extensively on literary criticism, his chief work being *On the Old Comedy*, which comprised twelve volumes, its contents ranging over textual criticism, discussion of the authorship of plays, the dates of performances, and the meanings and usages of words. These books were highly regarded by ancient scholars for decades, as was a separate work, *Grammar*. In addition to this, he had a wide reputation as a poet, his chief poetical works (all extant) bearing the titles *Hermes*, *Erigone*, and *Hesiod*.

Surpassing most of the other great scholars of the Alexandrian Library, Eratosthenes saw the clear significance of the works of Homer. "All wisdom is not to be found in them," he said. "They are esteemed for what they are—beautiful poems, written to charm the imagination of men, not to instruct them."

He was eighty-one when he took his own life. His body was not brought back to Cyrene but was buried in Alexandria, and the brief eulogy was delivered by Dionysius of Cyzicus:

> A mild old age, no darkening disease, has put out your light, Eratosthenes, son of Aglaus; and now that your high studies are finished, you sleep the appointed sleep. Cyrene, your mother, did not receive you into the tombs of your fathers, and now you are buried on this fringe of Proteus' [mythological king of Egypt] shore, beloved even in a strange land.

The Greek historian Diodorus came to Alexandria from Sicily and remained there for most of his life, spending endless months in the Mouseion, where he compiled a voluminous work called *Library of History*. It was written in Greek and completed about 30 B.C. The first volume is devoted chiefly to an account of the myths, kings, and customs of Egypt, with added remarks concerning the geography of the country. One of these myths (as given to Diodorus by the Egyptian priests) was an account of the first appearance of human life on earth, maintaining that when the universe was created, men first came into existence in Egypt because of the favorable climate of the land and specifically for the nature of the Nile. This stream, which produced much life and provided a spontaneous supply of food, amply supported all living things in the land.

As proof that animal life appeared first in their country, the Egyptians offered the fact that the soil of the Thebaid at certain times of the year generated mice in such numbers and of such size as to astonish all who witnessed the phenomenon. Some of these creatures were fully formed as far as the breast and front feet were concerned, and they were able to move while the rest of the body was unformed. They also claimed that if in the flood, which occurred in the time of Deucalion, most living things were destroyed, it was probable that the inhabitants of Egypt survived, since their country is rainless for most of the year. Subsequently, when the moisture from the abundant rains, which fell on other nations, was mingled with the intense heat that prevailed in Egypt, it was reasonable to assume that the air became very well tempered for another creation of living things. Even to this day during the inundations of Egypt, new generations of animal life can clearly be seen developing in the pools that remain the longest. When the river begins to recede and the sun has thoroughly dried the surface of the slime, living animals seem to take shape—some of them fully formed, and others only half so, yet still actually united with the very earth.

The myth of half-formed mice being found still attached to the earth may sound absurd, but the idea was quite credible to the Greeks, since Anaximander in the sixth century B.C. taught that fish, or animals closely resembling fish, sprang from heated water and earth, and that human fetuses grew in the animals to a state of puberty, so that when at length the animals burst, men and women capable of nourishing themselves proceeded from them.

Diodorus particularly described the geography of Egypt in his *Library of History*. He saw the country as oblong in shape, and extending in a general way from north to south, excelling all other kingdoms of the world in natural strength and beauty of landscape. Moreover, the country was afforded natural protection by deserts on the east and west, and, in case of a threatened invasion by sea, by the absence of any safe harbor other than that of Alexandria along the northern coast. But it was the Nile that fascinated him most. He traced its source to the extremity of Ethiopia, in a region that had been unapproachable because of the excessive heat. He deduced that the river's course from the mountains of Ethiopia to the Mediterranean Sea, including its many windings, was some 12,000 stades (2,220 kilometers). Except at the cataracts, where it was greatly agitated owing to the abundance of rocky obstructions, the river flowed without violence. He enumerated more than seven hundred islands in the Nile, the largest being the splendid city of Meroe. Here he found mines of gold, silver, iron, and copper, as well as ebony and every kind of precious stone.

The Nile finally divided into several streams to form the Delta and entered the Mediterranean by seven mouths called (in order from east to west): the Pelusiac, Tanitic, Mendesian, Phatnitic, Sebennytic, Bolbitine, and Canopic. At each mouth there was a walled city, divided into two parts by the river, with pontoon bridges and guard houses. From the Pelusiac branch there was also an artificial canal, the construction of which was started by Necho, continued by Darius (who left it unfinished because he was told that the Red Sea was at a higher level than Egypt), and completed by Ptolemy II "Philadelphus," who provided it with a lock, and after whom it was called the Ptolemy River.

Of the many cities in Egypt, Diodorus spoke at length about Alexandria, which was the capital of Egypt at that time. He specifically remarked on its advantageous situation close to the harbor of Pharos; and as one of the greatest cities of the world, it far surpassed all others in beauty, in the grandeur of its buildings, and in riches. Ideally situated between the sea and Lake Mareotis, with streets aligned to give access to the cool Etesian winds, Alexandria possessed not only an agreeable climate, but more importantly, it could be approached by only two narrow land passages and was easy to defend.

The official records at the time of Diodorus (59 B.C.) reveal that the city had a population of more than 300,000 citizens and yielded an annual revenue to the king of more than six thousand talents (weight of gold). These historical appraisals were followed by more accurate geographical findings.

*

The oldest systematic account of Alexandria and the geography of Egypt was written by the celebrated Greek geographer and historian Strabo. Born at Amasia in Pontus, Asia Minor, he nevertheless resided for a considerable time in Alexandria, "drawn there," he wrote, "by its marvelous treasures and institutions of learning." He traveled the full length of Egypt in 25–24 B.C., and ascended the Nile as far as the island of Philae, in company with his friend Aelius Gallus, who was governor of Egypt under the rule of Augustus.

His treatise on geography, the most complete descriptive work on the subject that survived antiquity, was not finished until A.D. 19, when he was about eighty years of age. In the first two of the total seventeen books, he gave a detailed review of geography's progress from the earliest times to his own day, providing valuable information from earlier writings now lost, especially those of Eratosthenes. In the remaining fifteen books, his aim was to bring together all that was important for men of liberal education to know about the various countries of the world and their inhabitants.

Strabo mainly accepted the views of Eratosthenes regarding the shape and size of the earth and its relationship to the universe. However, he was the first to adduce the convexity of the sea as an additional proof of the earth's sphericity, stating that "sailors cannot perceive lights at a distance when placed at the same height as their eyes, but if raised on high, they become at once perceptible to vision."

Philo (like Eratosthenes) had observed the sun to cast no shadow in Syene at noon forty-five days before the summer solstice, and he had also observed the relative lengths of the gnomon and its shadow during the two solstices at that place. The exact date of Philo's observations is unknown, but it is believed to have been prior to 246 B.C., and the observations may therefore be presumed to have been known to Eratos-thenes.

According to Strabo, the ancients gave the name of Egypt only to that part of the country inhabited and watered by the Nile. Later writers up to his time included on the eastern border the entire tract between the Arabian Gulf (the Red Sea) and the Nile, and on the western side the tract extending to the Oases and the parts of the Mediterranean coast from the Canopic mouth of the Nile to the Catabathmus and the kingdom of Cyrenaica. The kings who succeeded the Ptolemies even joined Cyprus to Egypt.

Strabo regarded the Nile as the true boundary between Asia and Africa, adding that it flowed through Egypt in a straight line from Syene to the vertex of the Delta, where it divided into two main branches: the Pelusiac and the Canopic. There were others between these, but they were mostly false mouths. The whole Delta was cut up into islands by minor branches of the river and by canals, so that every part of it was accessible by boats. Farther to the south, Lake Mareotis, which contained eight islands, was more than 150 stades (28 kilometers) in width, and 300 stades (56 kilometers) in length.

Strabo compared the inhabited section of Egypt to a rolled-out bandage, a tract of land on each side of the Nile, 740 kilometers long and seldom exceeding 35 kilometers in breadth. As for the annual rise of the Nile, he concurred with Diodorus that it was caused by the abundant summer rainfall in the mountains of Upper Ethiopia. He journeyed at length up the Nile, visiting the pyramids and other famous sites of ancient Egypt, but unlike his predecessor Herodotus (who was reputedly awestruck by the monuments), Strabo considered them devoid of artistic beauty and overall wasted work.

Nevertheless, he loved Alexandria and spent most of his Egyptian days there, going almost daily to the Mother Library, comparing notes with its students and teachers, conversing with shopkeepers, merchants, and travelers, absorbing the rich aura of the city. At night, he was engrossed with the Alexandrian sky, studying the stars, planets, and each constellation of the universe. Since it was only by astronomical observations that the latitudes and longitudes of places on the earth's surface could be determined, he held that no one could become truly proficient in geography without a knowledge of astronomy.

Alexandria's most illustrious astronomer and geographer was Claudius Ptolemaeus (Ptolemy), of no relation to the royal families of the same name. Earlier historians identified his birthplace as Pelusium, but later writers revealed that a mistake had arisen from a misreading of the Arabic form of his name, and that the most probable place of his birth was Ptolemais in Upper Egypt. Whatever may have been his birthplace, it is certain that he passed most of his life in Alexandria, where he studied and made astronomical observations, and where he wrote his famous treatises on astronomy and geography, *Almagest* and *Geography*. His work has always been associated with Alexandria and, as he himself said, he never wished to live anywhere else.

Even during his lifetime, Ptolemy was viewed as a man elevated far above other men by his singular focus and tranquility of mind. In his *Almagest*, he wrote, "I know that I am mortal and ephemeral, but when I scan the multitudinous circling spirals of the stars, no longer do I touch earth with my feet, but sit with Zeus himself, and take my fill of the ambrosial food of the gods."

His first recorded observation, an eclipse of the moon, was made in A.D. 127, during the reign of Marcus Aurelius. He had the good fortune to live under the reign of Rome's best emperors—Trajan, Hadrian, Antoninus Pius, and Marcus Aurelius—while Alexandria still basked in scholarly tradition, because of its celebrated Library. Ptolemy most likely took advantage of this opportunity, spending much of his time sifting through the Mouseion's books and reference material. Along with Euclid, he composed primers that were to remain standard works in their chosen fields for more than a thousand years.

Ptolemy's fame reached the attention of the known world with the publication of the two books *Almagest* and *Geography*. The former (whose title was derived from the Arab use of the Greek superlative *Al Megistes*—The Greatest) consisted of thirteen books, the first two devoted entirely to an introduction in which Ptolemy explained his astronomical assumptions and mathematical methods. His *Star Catalogue*, Books Seven and Eight of *Almagest*, was the earliest catalogue of stars to have survived. It listed over one thousand, arranged according to forty-eight constellations, and gave each star's longitude, latitude, and magnitude.

The last five books of the *Almagest,* which dealt with planetary motions, were Ptolemy's most famous works. While previous astronomers imagined the planets to be attached to a complicated system of moving spheres, Ptolemy maintained that a planet revolved uniformly in a circle (epicycle), the center of which revolved uniformly on another circle (deferent), around a point not agreeing in position with the earth (eccentric). He refused to listen to the counterargument of Aristarchus of Samos, who rejected the moving sphere theory because it did not agree sufficiently with observations of the period. Although Ptolemy's system was marked by error, his earth-centered view of the universe earned him the most prestigious title ever given by the Alexandrian school: the Great Astronomer. His ideas proved extremely attractive to medieval theologians, who regarded man and the earth as the main purpose of creation. Furthermore, his theory that the solar system was centered upon the earth influenced mankind for almost two thousand years.

His *Geography* consisted of eight books and was a remarkably factual and scientific achievement, in that it attempted to map the world as it was known at the time. The main body of the work contained (for the very first time) the longitudes and latitudes of principle cities, rivers, and mountain ranges. It also included accurately drawn maps.

The greatest improvement adopted by Ptolemy in his *Geography* was the introduction of a scheme of projection by which he could represent scientifically upon a plane map the positions of places actually located upon the spherical surface of the earth, and although the imperfect observations and instruments of his day marred the importance of this scientific endeavor, Ptolemy so thoroughly set the standard for modern maps that his methods continue to be employed by cartographers.

Undeniably, the intellectual creche of the Alexandrian Mouseion fostered progressive ideas unmatched for centuries. The great sphere of the earth was clearly perceived by them, and all that was known of place and distance had now been mapped upon its surface. Yet mankind was hesitant about accepting their visions. When Christopher Columbus embarked in his three small vessels and dared to sail westward to the wonders of Cathay, he little appreciated the measurements of Eratosthenes,

Ptolemy, and the astronomers of the Alexandrian Mouseion. This was attested by his letter to the treasurer of Aragon in 1493:

> As I know you will be rejoiced at the glorious success that our Lord has given me in my voyage, I write this to tell you how in thirty-three days I sailed to the Indies with the fleet that the illustrious King and Queen, our Sovereigns, gave me, where I discovered many islands, inhabited by numberless people. And when I came to Juana, I followed the coast of that isle toward the west, and found it so extensive, I reasoned it to be the mainland, the province of Cathay.

Perhaps Columbus never would have fallen into the error of believing he had reached India after a voyage of thirty-three days had the cartographers of his time been as advanced as the Alexandrians.

Shortly after the establishment of the Mouseion in Alexandria, medicine was included in the program of learning, and within a very short time, it achieved remarkable success. One of its greatest physicians was Herophilus. Born in Chalcedon in the latter part of the fourth century B.C., he was summoned by Ptolemy Soter to Alexandria at a time when Euclid was still flourishing there. In the "Golden City," Herophilus eventually became the founder of anatomy and, after Hippocrates and Galen, was regarded as the greatest physician of antiquity.

He believed in the empirical method in his study of anatomy, making direct observations rather than by conjecture. His work was detailed and masterful, and his descriptions (according to such valid authorities as Galen and Celsus) were of the highest order. He gave accurate descriptions of the brain, examined the difference between tendons and nerves, and studied the eye extensively. The vascular system too was examined by observing and distinguishing the arteries, veins, and chyliferous vessels. He also introduced the water clock, by which the pulse could be measured accurately.

Through his studies, Herophilus concluded that the body is governed by four forces: heat in the heart, perception in the nerves, nourishment in the liver, and thought in the brain. The liver and pancreas were studied with accurate detail, as were the functions of the salivary glands. In addition, he introduced many new drugs in treatment and believed in the efficacy of bloodletting in the healing of disease. His pioneer work in obstetrics set a model for future generations, and his textbook on the subject remained in wide use for centuries.

Like most physicians of the time, he was influenced by Hippocrates, whose *Corpus* was a fundamental text for understanding ancient medicine. In one of his famous "case histories" found in the extant *Epidemics*, Hippocrates related how a certain soldier named Tychon was wounded during a battle while leading an assault on the main gate of Datos. Tychon received an arrow in his back, but the wound seemed quite minor, since the missile entered at a sharp angle and was easily pulled out by a fellow soldier as the mercenaries retreated from another unsuccessful attempt to gain entrance into the city. Much controversy followed this last failure, and Tychon kept reaching over his right shoulder with his left hand to touch his wound, which had now stopped bleeding. Meanwhile, the company commander went among the dejected troops, encouraging them with plans for a new assault on the stubborn city and adding that, with their newly acquired seize machinery, victory would soon be theirs. Tychon meanwhile sipped from his cup of Chian wine and exchanged tales with a veteran soldier sitting beside him, who boasted about having fought with the great Spartan general Brasidas at the seige of Potidaea.

As dusk settled, the soldiers posted their guards and the camp began to hear soft moans from where Tychon lay beside his cooking fire. When the moans became louder and wrenched with agony, the commander presumed that they were the customary squabbles over spoils seized the day before when the troops had sacked a neighboring village. However, Tychon was alone, moaning and groaning in a most unusual posture, his back arched, his jaws locked tightly together. Shortly after this, he stumbled backward and fell to the ground, writhing in pain. A soldier friend forced some wine between his teeth, but Tychon was unable to swallow and the wine was expelled in spurts from his nostrils. Alarmed, his friend ran off to summon a physician, who had been seen in the neighboring village about five miles away. While he was gone, the rest of the army settled back into sleep. Tychon's loud moans continued through the night, and late in the afternoon of the following day, the physician named Demosthenes arrived and found Tychon still in his arched posture. His saliva had become frothy, and Demosthenes observed that the wound not only felt hot but there was a formation of pus on the surface of the gash. Whispering softly to the commander, Demosthenes indicated that there was very little he could do except to soothe the wound with cooling plasters and reduce the amount of yellow bile around the gash. The next morning, as a cock crowed in the distance, Tychon died.

This case reveals that even a country doctor like Demosthenes was well schooled in the various theories on opisthotonos that were current as early as the fourth century B.C. Tychon died after being wounded by an arrow in his upper right back, and although the death occurred within twenty-four hours, it unquestionably resulted from tetanus. Demosthenes knew that opisthotonos described exactly what happened when the tendons in the back of the neck are diseased. Its treatment was generally the injection of warm liquids through the nose, or cold water if one was able to withstand it. Underlying these practical actions were the physician's assumptions about humors, and about the functions of medical care in restoring the balance of those basic liquids in the living human body. From his command of the theory of humors and related notions, Demosthenes was thus able to make a sound prognosis.

The Alexandrian physicians most assuredly knew that the first requirement for health and life was air, and that too much or too little of it, could be a major cause of disease. Along with this were the humors, which were known to all ancient physicians and easily identified through examination and experience. After all, blood was everywhere in the human body: phlegm dribbled out of the nose and appeared to keep the inner lining of the mouth moist; bile caused the bitter taste often mentioned by the ill; and physicians constantly saw escaping fluids in the urine and the feces. There was, however, uncertainty about the number of humors, even though there was general agreement that an ideal balancing or blending of them produced perfect health. Ill health resulted if one humor increased too much because the patient had eaten something that promoted the overproduction of that humor, or if some action or ill-advised portion of the diet caused too much of a humor to escape from the body. Also, food that remained in a state of indigestion could produce a humor that rose to the head and thereby caused a discharge that could affect any part of the body.

The medical scholars of the Alexandrian school reasoned that an accumulation of humors was the major cause of disease, and along with the theories of Hippocrates in *Nature of Man* (written by his son-in-law Polybius), a new and fourth humor was added: black bile. All Alexandrian physicians were familiar with the black feces of stomach ulcers, the black vomit of intestinal cancer, and the fever that produced a blackish urine from malaria. They also knew that humors alone were not entirely responsible for health or disease. Something else had to be present, some other power that made humors from food, kept them moving, mixed them, cast out excesses, and maintained the necessary balance. Along with the studies of Aristotle, these physicians extended the concept of innate heat, which (according to Hippocrates) had its seat in the left ventricle of the heart. This was why the heart was hot, and why it was cooled through respiration. They correctly reasoned that babies have the most innate heat because they continually grow, whereas the elderly (whose growth is on a decline) have the least. Pepper is hot, and a rose is cold, not because they are unmixed or simple, but because the characteristics of heat and cold are dominant within them.

For the Alexandrian physician, innate heat was a basic part of man's nature, and diseases could be cured only by examining and understanding their specific characteristics. An overpreponderance of cold, resulting in a depletion of innate heat in the human body, might cause illness which, through a natural course, could be recorded in the list of fevers and other symptoms—as in pneumonia, where changes occur in coughing, the consistency of the sputum, and finally the *krisis*, which stops the coughing. Thus all the natural causes of disease produce an excess of a particular humor that has to be expelled in order to restore a proper balance.

It was in the academic setting of Alexandria that the work of Herophilus reached its highest recognition. He made significant contributions to the study of human anatomy, and much is quoted from his major work, *On Dissections*, which reveals astonishing results of his examinations of the brain, eye, and nervous system. He was the first to use the word "neuron" in reference to ligaments. In his observation of the confluences of the blood sinuses in the brain, he named them the *lenos* (winepress), a structure that is still called the torcular Herophili. He observed a netlike membrane in the eye—the retina—and his most famous anatomical coinage is the "duodenum," the length of part of the small intestine in the human body.

He also discovered the ovaries, which he compared to the male testes.

Moreover, he devised a method of classifying pulses according to their rates and rhythms, each depending upon the age and constitution of the patient. Quite amazingly, he employed various theories of music in his work with the pulses, using the musician's upward and downward beats, arsis and thesis, to describe the dilation and contraction of an artery.

More than two thousand years before Sigmund Freud "discovered" the theory of psychoanalysis, an Alexandrian physician had already detected a strong link between sexual problems and nervous afflictions. A case in point was Antiochus, son of King Seleucus. Upon the death of his wife, Seleucus married the beautiful young Stratonice and immediately proclaimed her queen of Upper Asia. When young Antiochus laid eyes on the new queen, he fell passionately in love with her. These feelings persisted even after Stratonice made Seleucus the father of a son. Antiochus struggled with this problem, and when he resolved that his strong desire for Stratonice was wholly unlawful, his malady past all cure, and his powers of reason too feeble to act, he decided to starve himself to death under the pretense of being ill. Seleucus, alarmed at seeing his son wasting away, summoned the distinguished Alexandrian physician Erasistratus to the palace. His wife accompanied him on the journey.

One look at the ailing Antiochus and Erasistratus quickly perceived that the problem was love, but since the young man wasn't talking, the physician decided to undertake a long vigil and wait in the patient's bedchamber, particularly observing any change of emotion and countenance whenever the young women of the court made their visit to the sick prince. Erasistratus soon noticed that the presence of these beauties produced utterly no effect on Antiochus, but when Stratonice entered the bedchamber, the physician readily detected Sappho's symptoms: the faltering voice, the face flushed up, the stealthily staring eyes, the sudden sweat, the irregular and violent beatings of the heart, and finally the faintness, prostration, and pallor.

Erasistratus reasoned further upon these symptoms, and also upon the difficulty of making a diagnosis of this nature to Seleucus. Aware that the situation was now life-threatening, the physician at last found the courage to speak to the king and tell him the malady was love, a love that was impossible to gratify and relieve. Plutarch recounted the event:

> The king, extremely surprised, asked him, *But why impossible to relieve?* *The fact is,* lied Erasistratus, *your son is in love with my wife.*
>
> *Really?* said Seleucus, *and will our friend Erasistratus refuse to bestow his wife upon my son and only successor, when there is no other way to save his life?*
>
> *You,* replied Eristratus, *who are his father, would not do so if he were in love with Stratonice.*
>
> *Ah, my friend,* answered Seleucus, *if any means, human or divine, could cure my son's illness, I would gladly part not only with Stratonice, but with my whole empire.*
>
> Seleucus uttered these words with such sincerity, shedding tears, that Erasistratus took him by the hand, and softly said, *In that case, you have no need for Erasistratus; for you, who are the husband, the father, and the king, are the proper physician for your family.*
>
> Accordingly, Seleucus summoned a general assembly of his people and declared to them that he had resolved to make Antiochus king and Stratonice queen of all the provinces of Upper Asia, and then without further delay, proceeded to unite them in marriage.

Erasistratus succeeded Herophilus as head of the Alexandrian School of Medicine and flourished as "the Father of Physiology" in the Mouseion during the middle of the third century B.C. His achievements in anatomy were second only to those of Herophilus, and he excelled as the founder of comparative and pathological anatomy. Were it not for his belief that the arteries were filled with air, he might very easily have anticipated William Harvey's discovery of the circulation of the blood, which was not published until twenty centuries later, since he suspected that the final ramifications of the arteries and the veins were connected; and he had already reached the conclusion that every organ was connected by the threefold system comprised of arteries, veins, and nerves.

Erasistratus, like Herophilus before him, firmly rejected the theory that occult causes were inherent in the behavior of bodily functions, but he displayed a marked difference from Herophilus in his methods of explaining the various functions in the living human body. One observation recorded blood vessels dividing again and again to the point that they decreased their size far beyond the limits of human vision. It was generally believed in his time that organs were nourished and sustained through a specific power, but Erasistratus argued that nature's tendency to fill a vacuum was far more important to human physiology. The main part of this power was the pneuma, which transmuted food into a form appropriate to replace the matter that was taken away. Thus this quasi-air, or pneuma, was the most important part of human living functions, so much so that it formed the basic force that sustained life.

Subsequently, Erasistratus proved that the arteries contained only pneuma, whereas the veins had blood. He strengthened this theory with the important observation that bodily parts have a vein, an artery, and a neuron, and that each of these parts is nourished by the vein. However, it was the pneuma that was central to all bodily functions. During digestion, the pneuma (coming into the stomach through the arteries) gave the stomach the appropriate grinding motion. In respiration, outside air passed from the bronchi to the lungs, then to the left ventricle of the heart by way of the aorta and ascending arteries, then to the body and to the head.

Erasistratus was the first physician to discount the outdated humoral theory of Hippocrates, distinguishing between therapeutics and hygiene, and laying particular emphasis on bodily cleanliness and exercise in relation to health. Unlike Herophilus, he opposed the use of too many drugs and too much bloodletting in the treatment of disease.

Aulus Cornelius Celsus (c. first century A.D.) in his treatise *Of Medicine* revealed that both Herophilus and Erasistratus practiced vivisection on human beings. As pains and various other disorders attacked the internal parts, they believed that no person could apply proper remedies to those parts of which he is ignorant, and that therefore it was necessary to dissect dead bodies and examine their viscera and intestines. Herophilus and Erasistratus took this method further: they procured criminals from prison, by royal permission, and dissected them alive, contemplating (while they were still breathing) all the concealed parts of the body, after which they studied their position, color, figure, size, order, hardness, softness, smoothness, and roughness. They were fully aware that when any inward pain occurred, a physician could not discover the seat of that pain if he had not learned where every viscus or intestine was situated; nor could the part that suffered be cured by one who did not know what part it was. When the viscera happened to be exposed by a wound, if the physician was ignorant of the natural color of each part, he could not know what was sound and what was corrupted. In the mind of Erasistratus, this practice was by no means cruel, for "by the tortures of a few guilty persons, the whole innocent race of mankind could be saved."

As can very well be imagined, the sometimes violent reaction to this inhumane method of searching for remedies to heal the sick reverberated even down to the time of St. Augustine. Especially strong in his denunciations was Tertullian, one of the important writers of the Roman Church.

Next to Hippocrates, Claudius Galen was considered to be the most famous physician of the ancient world. He followed the Father of Medicine by almost six centuries, and considerable progress in medicine was made during that long period of time. Galen came originally from Pergamum, the prosperous Roman province in western Asia Minor. His father, Nikon, from whom he received his early education, was a wealthy architect in the city and played a leading role in the design and construction of the imposing buildings that became famous in Roman Pergamum. Nikon made certain that his son was well trained in Greek literature, art, and language. Furthermore, he insisted that Galen also study with the best-known teachers of philosophy. As a young student, Galen boasted of his expertise in Plato and Aristotle, employing Stoic categories in his discussions, and detesting Epicureanism in all its forms. He spoke glowingly of his father, but was quite adamant about his feelings toward his mother. He had the good fortune to have as a father a highly amiable, just, good, and benevolent man. His mother, on the other hand, possessed a very bad temper; she often bit her serving maids, and she was perpetually shouting at Galen's father and quarreling with him. After comparing the excellence of his father's disposition with the disgraceful passions of his mother, Galen resolved "to embrace and love the former, and to avoid and hate the latter."

Nikon named his son Galenós,* and although Galen eventually turned out to be a man of elevated character, his propensity for controversy most likely came from his maternal inheritance.

At the age of sixteen, he began to study medicine, and on the death of his father, five years later, he left Pergamum and went to Smyrna for a

*Galenós—Greek for "peaceful, tranquil."

69

short period of time. After several brief journeys, he at last arrived in Alexandria and remained there for a considerable length of time, studying, experimenting, and writing. Unlike Herophilus and Erasistratus, he chose not to work on human dissection but preferred instead to conduct all his experiments and observations on apes, dogs, and swine.

He lived in Alexandria during the most turbulent times, when internal strife and disturbances plagued the city. Nevertheless, he carried on his work unmolested. In the year A.D. 130, the emperor Hadrian visited the city and took the occasion to establish new professorships at the Mouseion. Scholarship at this time was veering more toward the direction of metaphysics and the occult, and the political situation was in such turmoil that the people of Alexandria were devoting most of their efforts toward the stars, seeking to find answers for their deplorable situation rather than speculating on the arts and sciences.

When he completed his studies in Alexandria, Galen returned to his native city of Pergamum and assumed the office of medical advisor to the athletes of the gymnasium whose buildings lay adjacent to the Temple of Aesculapius, but after a few years a revolt compelled him to leave his position and travel to Rome.

In the capital city, he achieved swift success, especially after having cured Eudemus (a famous Peripatetic philosopher) and many other prominent citizens of the empire. Their praises brought him a large and lucrative practice among the best families of Rome, and his skill became so greatly admired that he was invested with the titles "Paradoxologus" (Wonder-Speaker) and "Paradoxopoeus" (Wonder-Worker).

However, the main body of Roman physicians harbored jealousy and bitter resentment against him, primarily because he had acquired his medical knowledge in the rival city of Alexandria rather than in Rome, and worse still, he was not even a native citizen but an alien Greek. Medical practice in Rome at this time was at a low ebb, and Galen (revealing once again traces of his mother's impetuosity) took no pains to conceal his contempt for the ignorance, charlatanism, and venality of the Roman practitioners.

Despite his social popularity, he raised such antogonism in medical circles he was forced to flee the city hurriedly and secretly in A.D. 168, and returned to his home in Pergamum, where he planned to spend the rest of his life in the quiet enjoyment of scholarship and experimentation. But he was in Pergamum only a short while when the emperor Marcus Aurelius summoned him back to Rome, preparatory to an expedition against the Germans, for which Galen was to serve as his personal physician.

Galen declined the appointment. He had no desire to subject himself once again to the hostility of the Roman physicians, but upon the emperor's insistence, he agreed to at least return to Rome. As physician to Marcus Aurelius, he prepared one of his famous theriacs, an antidote to poison and the bites of venomous animals. Needless to say, theriacs occupied a very important place in the pharmaceutical cabinet of all emperors during these turbulent times. Long before this, King Mithridates the Great of Pontus devoted considerable attention to the preparation of antidotes. The most powerful monarch of his time, he was generally thought to have been a more zealous promoter of discoveries for the benefit of mankind than any of his predecessors, a fact evinced not only by many positive proofs, but by universal report as well. It was he who first thought (the proper precautions being duly taken) of drinking poison every day for the purpose of becoming habituated to it, and thus to neutralize its dangerous effects. He was also the first to discover the various kinds of antidotes, one of which indeed still retains his name (the mithridates); and it is generally supposed that he was the first to employ the blood of the ducks of Pontus as an ingredient in antidotes, because they derived their nutriment from poisons.

Since Galen still refused to accompany Marcus Aurelius on his expedition into Germany, the emperor persuaded him to remain in Rome as the personal physician of the young prince Commodus, after which he finally returned to Pergamum, where he devoted the rest of his life solely to writing. His influence upon future generations of physicians and researchers was enormous. He was one of the most prolific writers of antiquity. Many of his works became landmarks in the history of medicine. In one of his earliest surviving treatises, *On Anatomical Procedures*, he meticulously demonstrated dissecting techniques gained from numerous investigations of the Barbary ape. His *Hygiene* was a useful handbook on how to stay healthy; and his *Antidotes* contained a vast number of collected recipes, medical botany, toxicology, and pharmaceutics. Yet these books represented only a fraction of Galen's total output. He wrote extensively, the titles including *On Medical Experience, On Anatomical Procedures, On the Parts of Medicine, On Cohesive Causes, On Regimen in Acute Diseases in Accordance with the Theories of Hippocrates,* and *On the Variety of Similar Parts of the Body.* All in all, he produced more than five hundred treatises on subjects as varied as logic, ethics, grammar, and medicine. Although he differed greatly with Hippocrates on his theories on humors, Galen, like most of his contemporaries, staunchly upheld the sacred oath of the Father of Medicine.

ᏸᎢᏆᏆᎯᎩ

The literature that developed in the Alexandrian school, unlike that of the Golden Age of Greece, was not concerned with the basic problems of life and death, nor even ethics and morals. It was enough for the Alexandrian poets to have a graceful and amusing style, sarcasm and wit; and whereas the poets of classical Greece wrote of heroic deeds and accomplishments, the Alexandrians sang of love, creating their epigrams and idylls in a way no other civilization had ever experienced. Darts and hearts, sighs and eyes, breasts and chests, all originated in Alexandria because of the intimate relationship between Palace and Mouseion. "Indeed, love flitted through the literature of Alexandria as through the thousands of terra cotta statuettes that have been exhumed from her soil."

The poet most responsible for setting this tone was Callimachus, who was called by Ptolemy Euergetes from Eleusis to serve as director at the Library. Callimachus was a man of great learning, and he knew how to use it with wit and charm. He was a stickler for neatness and detested the ponderously heavy volumes published by his contemporaries. "A big book," he'd say, "is a big evil."

He is best known for his marvelous epigrams, the most famous of which is:

> Someone told me, Heracleitus,
> Someone told me you were dead.
> They brought me bitter news to hear
> And bitter tears to shed.
> I wept as I remembered
> How often you and I,
> Had sunk the sun with talking;
> And now here you lie,
> A handful of grey ashes,

My dearest Carian friend.
But your nightingales, your songs, are still awake,
For Death who taketh all, these he cannot take.

Sadly, the prophetic reference to the immortality of the "nightingales" never came to pass, and not one of Heracleitus's poems exists today.

During this time, a young aspiring poet with exceptionally thin legs came to Alexandria from the island of Rhodes to study under the great Callimachus. His name was Apollonius and his one ambition was to write a long epic, something Callimachus vehemently frowned upon. Nevertheless, Apollonius persisted, and although he was only eighteen at the time, he was permitted to give a reading at the Mouseion. Callimachus attacked him and his epic poem "Argonautica" in front of the audience and a violent argument ensued. Apollonius was expelled from the University for his arrogance, and Callimachus, still sizzling from the incident, wrote a satire in which his young rival's legs were mocked and ridiculed. Apollonius and his friends quickly struck back. It was a bitter battle and the peaceful atmosphere of the University was shattered for many years to come. After the death of Callimachus, Apollonius was summoned back to Alexandria from Rhodes and, within a short time, assumed the post of librarian.

Unfortunately for Callimachus, the long epic poem of Apollonius survives to this day. Presumably written in the style of Homer, it recounts the voyage of the *Argo* in search of the Golden Fleece, but here any similarity to Homer ceases. Homer's Troy was Troy in all its details—as was Aulis, the isles of the Aegean, Scylla, Charibdis, and Ithaka—but Apollonius's epic, even though it speaks of foreign lands and barbaric people, never quite makes it out of Alexandria, and consequently Jason's heroic quest is almost entirely buried under the excessive baggage of Apollonius's style. What saves it is an infiltrating yet graphic description of Alexandria, her idiosyncracies and charm.

The greatest of the Alexandrian poets was Theocritus, who came to Alexandria at a later age, via the islands of Cos (his birthplace) and Sicily. His initial aim was to stay briefly at the University, but he was so impressed with the cultural challenges of the city, he remained there the rest of his life. Like Callimachus and Apollonius, he cast his poetry through a decorative treatment of love and fantasy, but unlike his two predecessors, Theocritus wrote with an ardor and experience they were never able to muster; and whereas their poems soon became required reading in the Alexandrian schools, his were sparklingly refreshing and appealed chiefly to the liberal spirit of Alexandria. Each of these works he prefaced in the same manner: "I, Theocritus, who wrote these Idylls, am of Syracuse, a man of the people, the son of Praxagoras and famed Philina."

His poems paint an elegant portrait of both the pastoral and sophisticated life of Alexandria, detailing the air and sun, the fragrant smell of a meadow in early spring, the song of birds, the bleating of goats and sheep, and the intimate affairs of women and men who lived in the Greek quarter near the Temple of Serapis. His "Idylls" gave Alexandria a new voice.

The poems that sprang from the sophisticated city of Alexandria at the time ring so pertinent and true, they could be heard today in the salons of Paris, London, or Rome. With each masterly word, Theocritus resurrects an entire city from its buried ashes and fills every corner, every street, with steaming vibrant life.

PART THREE

THE POWER
OF THE CITY

I T WAS A CITY of nicknames. When a statesman assumed office or a king succeeded to the throne of Egypt, he was immediately given a moniker to tag him for the rest of his life. Thus, Ptolemy X was called "Bloated," Ptolemy XI "Vetch," Seleucus "Pickled-Fish Peddler," and Vespasian "Scullion." Ptolemy XII, called "the Piper," evidently earned his name by drinking copious amounts of wine and playing the flute during most of his reign. When the Roman governor of Syria, Agrippa, a staunch friend of the Hebrews, passed through the city on his way to a contested throne, Alexandrian Jews dressed up an unfortunate creature whom they had found in the streets, put a paper crown upon his head and a reed in his hand, then led him through the city, hailing him as king of the Jews. When Vespasian demanded repayment for a small, six-obol loan from one of his friends, another crowd marched through the streets chanting and ridiculing the emperor. The sport Alexandrians made of mocking their emperors extended into the reign of Caracalla, whom they ridiculed for his small stature and attempt to style himself after Alexander the Great. This time, though, they dealt with the wrong man. Caracalla retaliated by ordering his Roman legions to seize every young man and woman of the city and herd them to the crest of Rhakotis Hill, where they were butchered like animals, then burned in one massive pyre.

Despite Caracalla's brutality, the impish Alexandrian wit continued to find its target in the countenance and character of its emperors. Their rebellious political songs spread through the empire and reverberated on the lips of citizens in other towns. Comedians entertaining large audiences in the city found that jokes about the emperor or another government official were especially popular.

"The people of Alexandria," observed the emperor Hadrian, "are wholly light, wavering, and flying after every breath of a report. They are seditious, vain, and spiteful—though as a body wealthy and prosperous."

Aside from entertaining themselves at the expense of their rulers, the Alexandrians thrived on ancient traditions and love of the theater. The whole city lived for excitement, and when the festival of Apis (the sacred bull) took place, all the inhabitants of the city celebrated with music and horse races. In their daily work, they were quite serious, even sober, but the instant they entered the theater or the Race Course, they immediately became possessed, as if by some intoxicating drug, so that they no longer knew nor cared what they said or did. This hedonism and sense of abandon overtook even the women and children, and even after the first madness had passed, all the streets and byways continued to seethe with activity.

Stereotypes at the time described typical Alexandrians as preoccupied by their appearance and so well-to-do that the luxury of their homes exceeded that of the Romans. Aside from displays of wealth, they were obsessed with the culinary arts and thought of little else but food. Being fickle and easily influenced by the moment's emotion, they were most prone to treachery. As for patriotism, they shunned all forms of political interest, except to revolt constantly against the government over petty issues and to disturb the peace with noisy street rioting.

Yet despite this reputation for frivolity, Alexandria fueled itself through business, and many of her citizens engaged in lively commercial enterprises. Although it was distinguished by the most important corn market in the world, the city was also engaged in many other forms of commerce, and throughout the reign of the Ptolemies was recognized as the greatest trading center in the world. Here East and West met in the busy Emporium, and the city had already begun to cast its eye toward a new trade route to India. The University was now at the height of its glory, and the eyes of the world were focused on Alexandria's great philosophers, scientists, teachers, and scholars.

At this stage, the city was ready to accept one of its most famous and capable rulers.

Born of Macedonian blood in 69 B.C., Cleopatra was the daughter of Ptolemy XII (the Piper), who had become king of Egypt in 80 B.C. Unlike her father, who in all respects was a weak and inefficient ruler, Cleopatra was to be the last of a long series of ruthless yet patriotic women of the Ptolemaic dynasty obsessed with power. "She was a brilliant linguist, who easily turned her tongue to any language she wished. It was rare that she had need of an interpreter, for she dealt with most matters herself, talking with Ethiopians, Troglodytes, Jews, Arabs, Syrians, Medes and Parthians."

Although her predecessors had not bothered to learn Coptic, the language of most Alexandrians, Cleopatra mastered it, along with Greek, at an early age. She would also converse freely in Latin with Julius Caesar and Mark Antony. It was said that while in her company one was touched by an irresistible charm. Her form, along with the persuasiveness of her conversation and her charisma, combined to beguile even the stoniest of foreign statesmen.

Her image engraved on coins, wrote Plutarch, suggests a woman of the eastern Mediterranean—dark-haired, fine-boned, and well proportioned. As a queen, privileged by rank, she was schooled in etiquette, hospitality, and seduction. Despite this training, there were only two men in her life: Julius Caesar, by whom she had one son, and Mark Antony, the father of her other two children. She was a dedicated and devoted mother, and fought to have her children inherit her throne and her vast empire. Her charm was the important weapon in achieving this goal. It made her Caesar's wife and mistress of the Roman Empire and also Antony's wife and queen of the Eastern Empire. Though Jewish historian Josephus inferred that she was "a slave to her lusts," his own friendship with the infamous Nero calls into question his own morality instead of hers.

In addition to her linguistic talents, she had a fondness for the arts and sciences. Working through her lover, Antony, she acquired the famous library of Pergamum, which contained almost a quarter of a million manuscripts, for Alexandria. She also befriended and funded great artists and scientists of the Mouseion; and she introduced Caesar to the famous astronomer Sosigenes, who subsequently reformed the Roman calendar and liberated it from its state of utter confusion.

Like Caesar and Antony, Cleopatra was a military genius, the last person to seriously challenge the authority of Rome in the East. She did this not as an Egyptian, but as a civilized Greek (all of the Ptolemies were Greek, not Egyptian), for deep in her heart she regarded the Romans as barbarian invaders. If she had succeeded in her challenge, she would have established a Greco-Roman kingdom and extended the Hellenic influence upon the entire Roman world, making Alexandria, not Rome, the capital of this immense empire.

She was ten years old when her father, Ptolemy XII, granted his people an amnesty in 59 B.C. Diodorus Siculus, the Greek historian, visited Egypt at this time and recorded an incident that illustrates the antipathy between Alexandrians and Romans. It stemmed from the Alexandrian superstition that killing a cat would bring disaster to their city. Standing in the street one day, Diodorus saw a Roman citizen riding in a carriage run over a cat and kill it. The incensed crowd converged upon him, but he managed to escape to his house, bolting the door and windows. But the mob stationed itself outside and clamored for his life, even though the act had been an accident. Diodorus witnessed messengers "arriving from Ptolemy himself, begging the crowd to spare the Roman's life. All to no avail. The next morning, the Roman citizen's unrecognizable corpse lay battered and broken in the empty street in front of his house."

At a time when Cleopatra was most impressionable, this cat incident seemed to ignite the long-standing antipathy of her people for the Romans. Most likely, she also listened to her father speak of Caesar and of Pompey many times. During this period, they both toyed mercilessly with Ptolemy and Egypt, rendering the country economically destitute and impoverished. The coinage under her father was so debased, each coin had less than one-third silver in its composition; and because Rome refused to officially recognize "the Piper" on his accession to the Egyptian throne, the Egyptian burden of tolls and taxes steadily increased.

Growing up in the disordered environment of her father's court while he attempted to preserve the rich ceremonials and pretenses of a once-great past, Cleopatra came to know that a stronger hand was needed to save her people from shame and ruin. Aside from this, the Piper had only a weak claim to the throne and was constantly at odds with his half brothers and sisters, who kept putting in their own claims, threatening his dynasty. Ptolemy decided that bribery was the only way to secure his right to the throne. So in 63 B.C., as the powerful Pompey was taking Judaea after a string of successive victories in the East, the Piper, in a rare display of intelligence, sent him an enormous gold crown, and even offered to provide him with a cavalry force of 8,000 men in his campaign against the Judaeans. Ptolemy then extended an invitation for Pompey to visit him in Egypt, which would be a great show of strength for the Egyptians and a solidification of the Piper's claim to the throne. Pompey accepted the bribe, but did not make the visit. Nevertheless, the Piper felt safe in the knowledge that Pompey had now become his patron and, as a Roman, would probably not abandon him in a time of need.

Meanwhile, Caesar, always short of funds, had been hoping to blackmail Ptolemy in return for Rome's official recognition of the monarchy. This was not unusual during these turbulent times. Indeed, Rome had forgotten what honesty was. "A person who refused a bribe was seen not as dishonorable, but as a personal enemy."

Neglected by Pompey, Ptolemy, left with no other choice but to seek official Roman sanction of his title, embarked for Rome, his royal barge laden with a bribe of six thousand talents (about four million dollars). Julius Caesar, nearly bankrupt, readily accepted the money, then moved a resolution in the Senate, after which Ptolemy was confirmed on his throne and acknowledged as a friend and ally of the Roman people.

Naïve, assuming that the Romans could be trusted, the Piper returned to Alexandria, exhilarated. Egypt was now under his full control. But a disastrous event in Cyprus would destroy his euphoria.

His younger brother was king of Cyprus, the last foreign possession of what had once been the rich Ptolemaic empire. Since the Romans had just concluded an arrangement with the Piper, they felt no obligation to keep his brother on the throne of Cyprus. They prepared to launch an invasion of the island, so the king, fearing permanent banishment and imprisonment, took poison and died. He had accumulated a considerable treasure during his brief reign, more than seven thousand talents, which the Romans seized and paraded through the Forum. For the Egyptian people, it was a sad day when Cyprus, which had long been a center of Greek culture and the financial treasury of the Ptolemies, fell without bloodshed into Roman hands. Dreading that the Romans' next step would be the complete annexation of Egypt, the populace rose up in revolt against the Piper and blamed him not only for having failed to protect his brother, but, far worse, for paying such an exorbitant bribe to claim his throne while his people struggled with poverty and starvation. A general rebellion ensued, and the Piper had to flee Egypt and seek asylum in Rome, the city that had betrayed him.

On his journey across the Mediterranean, he learned that Cato, the general who had conquered Cyprus, was visiting Rhodes. The Piper seized this opportunity to make one final plea to secure his patronage through Cato, despite his involvement in the death of his brother and in wresting control of Cyprus from the Ptolemies. And so, he dispatched an invitation to Cato to visit. Cato's reply was curt: "If Ptolemy wants to see me, he had better come here."

Cato didn't bother to rise when the Piper made his appearance. He pointed to a chair, asked him to sit, then advised the Piper not to go to Rome because he'd be cheated as he had been before. Furthermore, Cato told him to return to his country and make peace with his people. After carefully considering the suggestion, the Piper still decided to continue to Rome.

During his absence, his daughter Berenice IV declared herself queen of Egypt. Cleopatra was only eleven at the time, and the economic condition of the country was steadily getting worse. The once-efficient agricultural methods that had enriched Egypt had been abandoned, and rather than pay exorbitant taxes, farmers forsook their lands and fled farther up the Nile. Under Berenice, gold coins were replaced by silver and, in time, silver was replaced by copper. Goods coming into Alexandria from foreign lands were too expensive for the populace and were left unsold at the Emporium. What little food products arrived, perished. The country, on the verge of total collapse, was ripe for anarchy.

In Rome, meanwhile, the Piper stepped up his efforts, frantically trying to persuade important senators and government officials to carry out Rome's guarantee of his reinstatement to the throne. Here again, he relied on large sums of bribe money, but since he had depleted his funds on the previous bribe to Caesar, he was now forced to go to the wealthy moneylenders of Rome and issue them promissory notes on the guarantee of repayment on his ascension to the throne. Pompey was one of the many recipients of his bribes. The Piper stayed at Pompey's Roman villa near the Alban district and was assured by Pompey that he would be his patron through the unpleasant situation.

Soon enough, the Alexandrians heard what was going on in Rome and, determined to prevent the detested Piper's restoration to the throne, they dispatched a delegation to Rome, led by the philosopher Dion. After landing at the port of Puteoli on the Bay of Naples, they managed to get lodgings in the Alexandrian embassy. But before they embarked for Rome, they were attacked by the Piper's assassins, who killed the majority of them. Those who survived were bribed into silence. Dion alone managed to escape to Rome, but shortly after arrival he was poisoned on the Piper's orders.

Largely through Pompey's efforts, the Roman Senate eventually concluded that the interests of Rome would be best served by the Piper's restoration to the throne, but stipulated that Egypt would be maintained under Roman jurisdiction and arms. In addition, the Piper would have to pay heavily for this favor: the corn and grain so desperately needed by the citizens of Rome was soon to be theirs, and all the rich commerce on the docks of Alexandria would fall under complete Roman control. Ptolemy would gain the throne by climbing on the backs of the Egyptian people.

The Piper did not return directly to Alexandria. Instead, he stopped briefly in Ephesus, while at the same time a shattering event rocked Rome. The colossal statue of Jupiter on the Alban Mount was struck by lightning, and in panic the Romans consulted the Sibylline Books* for a prophetic answer to the calamity. It was revealed to them strong and clear: "If an Egyptian king should come asking for help, do not refuse his friendship, but do not go to his aid with force, for if you do, you will meet dangers and difficulties."

Could the Piper have bribed the Sibyl prophetess too?

At any rate, the message to the Romans was quite plain: no Roman military involvement in Egypt.

In the days that followed, debates erupted in the Senate, and finally it was decided to send a delegation to Egypt to demand the abdication of Berenice. But who should lead it? The names of Pompey and Crassus quickly came up. Crassus succeeded in moving the issue out of the Senate, into the public Forum, where, despite resistance, he convinced everyone that Pompey was not the man for the job. But Cicero took charge and managed to find a way to circumvent the Sibylline prophecy against using force to restore the throne for the Piper. He determined that neither Pompey, Caesar, nor Crassus would lead the delegation into Egypt.

Meanwhile, the Alexandrians had arranged a marriage between

*A collection of prophetic writings, also called "Sibylline Oracles."

Berenice and Archelaus of Cappadocia (according to custom, she could not marry her brother because he was still only a child). Such a marriage was contrary to the Roman plans. Seeking an excuse to invade Egypt, they operated under the pretext that the Egyptians were encouraging pirates on their coastlines, thus interfering with Roman ships of trade. War was declared on Archelaus and Berenice, and the Romans, under General Aulus Gabinius, set out with their legions across the desert from Gaza, into the fortress town of Pelusium, which lay sprawled along the coast at the eastern edge of the desert. Commanding the Roman cavalry was a brilliant twenty-seven-year-old officer named Mark Antony.

Pelusium fell quickly, and with the road to Egypt open, Aulus Gabinius personally escorted the Piper into Alexandria. Archelaus was killed during a minor skirmish outside the city, and the Piper immediately had Berenice executed. The palace soldiers, realizing that all was lost, deserted and joined forces with the Romans.

With the death of her sister Berenice, Cleopatra became the rightful heir to the throne. Mark Antony remained only a short time in Alexandria, yet Cleopatra's beauty and intelligence most likely made a strong impression on him. He was also taken by the superb sights of the city: the exquisite harbor, the wide avenues, the porticoes, Library, Mouseion, and the Pharos Light throwing its powerful beam across the sea.

The Piper's time to enjoy his newly recovered throne was finally at hand, and although constant rebellions plagued the city, he indulged himself as the "New Dionysus," entertaining his guests with wine, music, and revelry. Determined to launch his rule in appropriate style, he staged a grand procession in honor of Dionysus one winter's day. Mechanical statues were paraded on huge floats; wine ran freely from vast urns; sweet refreshments were handed out to all the spectators. Actors and throngs of women joined public officials who had dressed as satyrs in a performance that included scenes of Dionysus's drunken return from India, the figure of Alexander the Great, and an enormous gold phallus 180 feet long, covered with ribbons and tipped with a large gold crown. The Morning Star led the way, while the Evening Star brought up the rear. In between marched 2,000 oxen adorned with gold, 2,400 dogs, giraffes, Indian parrots, elephants, a gnu, ostriches pulling carts, and an enormous white bear. The figure of "Corinth" led a parade of women named after the cities of Ionia and the islands. This procession was a clear allusion to the League of Corinth and the Ptolemies' concern for Greek freedom. Thousands of slaves dragged the carts and floats through the streets of Alexandria. The procession lasted from dawn to sundown, and the festivities that followed continued into the early hours of morning.

In the spring of 50 B.C., the Piper made out a will, placing one copy in his palace vault in Alexandria and another with his patron Pompey in Rome. In it, he requested that the throne of Egypt should be held jointly by his eldest daughter, Cleopatra VII, and her younger brother, Ptolemy XIII, who was to be her husband upon the death of their father.

When the Piper died the following year, he was succeeded by an eighteen-year-old Cleopatra and her brother, only ten. Upholding Egyptian tradition, they were formally married, and because the young Ptolemy was a minor, three guardians were appointed to look after him. One was Achillas, a commander of the army; another, a Greek teacher named Theodotus, who was to supervise the young king's education; and a third, the eunuch Pothinus, Egypt's minister of finance and a man of devious character. All three realized that if they were to succeed in their positions they would have to keep close to the boy-king and eventually dispose of Cleopatra.

⌒ⱳⱳⱳ◡

In 55 B.C., the Roman governor of Syria sent his two sons to Alexandria, seeking permission from the authorities to release all the legions stationed in the city so they could assist the Syrian governor's army in a war with the Parthians. The Roman soldiers rebelled against the idea. Most of them had settled down quite well in Alexandria, taking wives and mistresses, enjoying all the comforts of a cultured city, and they had no desire to march north over endless hills of sand in oppressive heat to wage battle against the most feared and despised enemies of Rome. In the heated exchanges, a mutiny broke out, ending in the murder of the Syrian governor's sons.

Cleopatra, aiming to solidify her position with the Romans, ordered the immediate arrest of all the mutineers, then sent the ringleaders to Syria to stand trial and eventual execution. The strong position taken by Cleopatra did not sit well with the triumvirate protecting her brother. Foreseeing the development of still another court intrigue, Cleopatra was advised to flee the country and seek refuge in Syria, where she knew she would find a favorable reception, after having sent back the mutineers and murderers of the governor's two sons. In only a few years, she had developed into a capable leader. Furthermore, the lessons of intrigue, political corruption, bribery, and murder had now endowed her with an even greater sense of diplomacy and sharpness of character.

And she was more beautiful than ever.

Across the sea, in Rome, the three powerful figures Caesar, Pompey, and Crassus broke up and went their separate ways. Crassus, envious of both Caesar's and Pompey's military fame, hoping to gain a fortune from the wealth of the East, put together a large Roman force and set out for Parthia. The results were disastrous. His army was destroyed at the Battle of Carrhae, and Crassus himself was killed, leaving Caesar and Pompey to combat each other in the struggle to control Rome.

Before fleeing to Syria, Cleopatra had officially received Pompey's elder son Gaius in response to an appeal from Pompey, whose troops needed food in the raging civil war between him and Caesar. While in Alexandria, Gaius was accorded hospitality fit for a king, and before leaving he had Cleopatra's full assurance that several merchant ships laden with wheat would immediately be dispatched to Pompey's hungry legions. As her father before her, Cleopatra too had deep trust in Pompey and considered him a patron to Egypt. But to her misfortune, Pompey was defeated in the fields of Pharsalia in Thessaly and fled from the scene, both his dreams and his army shattered.

Cleopatra was in Syria when she learned about the catastrophe. She was also told that Pompey was on his way to Egypt with his wife Cornelia to claim proper acknowledgment for his help and patronage, and that his large galley would be stopping at Cyprus on its pleasant favorable-wind crossing of the Mediterranean. In preparation for the visit, Cleopatra raised an army in Syria and was ready to invade Egypt and overthrow her brother. The Egyptian forces, encamped at Pelusium on the border of Syria and Egypt, were under the command of Achillas. Not too far away, Cleopatra and her forces stood arrayed in full battle attire.

The fortress of Pelusium stood on low desert ground overlooking the sea. It was the most easterly port of the Nile Delta and it lay on the main caravan route between Egypt and Syria, forming the Asiatic gateway to the Ptolemaic kingdom. Pompey's galley dropped anchor near the barren headland to the west of the little harbor, and while he waited for the young Ptolemy's emissaries to greet him officially, a heated argument developed among the three protectors of Ptolemy—Achillas, Theodotus, and the eunuch Pothinus—about what type of reception they should accord this defeated Roman general, who only a short time ago seemed destined to become master of the whole Roman Empire. "It was a tragic situation, that the fate of Pompey the Great should have been determined by three such men; and that he, riding at anchor off the shore, should have been forced to wait on the decision of such a tribunal."

After a long debate, Theodotus came up with the ultimate solution: they would lure Pompey ashore, seize him, and thus prevent Cleopatra from seeking his assistance in her battle to recapture the throne of Egypt. More importantly, their act against Pompey would place the victorious Caesar under an obligation, and give the young Ptolemy's reign the sanction and protection of Rome.

As commander of the Egyptian army, it was appropriate that Achillas be selected to greet Pompey, and to provide further authenticity, he was accompanied by Septimius, a Roman officer who had at one time served under Pompey. A Roman centurian named Salvius rowed them in a small boat to escort Pompey ashore, and as they pulled up alongside the large Seleucian galley, Septimius stood up and saluted Pompey by his military title. Achillas then invited him to step aboard, explaining that the galley had too deep a draught to enter the small harbor. A short distance away, a large number of Egyptian warships cruised off the shore, and the sandy beaches were alive with troops. Pompey's wife Cornelia immediately became suspicious and cautioned her husband not to leave the Seleucian galley, but he paid no heed. Together with a freed slave named Philip and a slave called Scythes, he calmly stepped into the smaller boat, looked back at Cornelia, raised his hand in fond farewell, and quoted these lines from Sophocles:

> *He that enters at a tyrant's door*
> *Becomes a slave, even if free before.*

As the boat slid through the water, which at this time of year (the end of September) was discolored by the Nile mud gushing down from the first swell of the annual floods, Pompey glanced over his shoulder and said to Septimius, "Surely, I may be mistaken, but were you formerly my fellow soldier?" Septimius's answer was a silent nod of the head. Pompey did not press the matter. His eyes once again flitted toward the troop movement on the beaches, then, opening a little book, he began reading. After the boat reached the shore, he closed the book, stood up, and was about to take hold of freed slave Philip's hand, when Septimius drew his sword and stabbed him in the back. Both Achillas and Salvius quickly brought out their swords and continued the attack. Pompey never uttered a word. Groaning softly, he drew his robe over his head, fell back into the bottom of the boat, and within a few minutes was dead. Cornelia, witnessing the murder from the deck of the Seleucian galley, gave out a piercing cry and, before fainting on the deck, saw the murderers stoop over the body and stand up again with the severed head of her husband held aloft. Fearing for Cornelia's life and for the safety of his crew, the captain issued orders to weigh anchor at once, and the Seleucian galley sped off into the open sea before the Egyptian warships could prepare themselves for pursuit.

The assassins had severed Pompey's head so as to have tangible proof for Caesar when he arrived in Alexandria, but the body was left in the sand, stripped of all clothing and battered by the breaking surf. After Achillas and his accomplices carried the head to the royal camp of the young Ptolemy, the freed slave Philip, who was unmolested by the murderers, made his way back to the beach, waited along the desolate shore until he was certain everyone had retired to the town, then knelt over Pompey's body, washed it with seawater, and wrapped it in his own robe. An aged Roman soldier, who had served under Pompey, suddenly appeared on the beach and helped the freed slave gather up driftwood for a funeral pyre, and as soon as they collected enough wood, they placed the body on the pile and set fire to it.

The brief but illustrious reign of Pompey the Great was over. The whole Roman Empire now belonged to Caesar.

While the forces of Cleopatra and the young Ptolemy remained near Pelusium, confronting each other, waiting for the appropriate time to attack, Caesar arrived in Alexandria and learned about the brutal murder of Pompey. A few days later, the instigator of the plot, Theodotus, returned to Alexandria from Pelusium, and as he proudly displayed the head and signet ring of Pompey, Caesar burst into tears. Theodotus, who no doubt had expected a reward from Caesar, was dismissed abruptly and forced to flee from Egypt, wandering as a refugee for years through Syria and Asia Minor. His travels brought him eventually to Rome, where he was recognized one day by Marcus Brutus and, as a punishment for having orchestrated the murder of the great Pompey, was dragged through the streets of the capital city in shame, then crucified.

Pompey's ashes were recovered from the beach at Pelusium and Caesar arranged to have them sent to Pompey's widow, who then buried them in the grounds of his Alban villa, the same villa where Pompey had given sanctuary to Cleopatra's father, the Piper. After this, Caesar ordered the severed head to be buried near the sea, in the grove of Nemesis at the eastern walls of Alexandria where, under the cool shade of cedars, a bronze bust was erected.

At first, the Alexandrians were affronted when Caesar offered his protection and friendship to all the imprisoned partisans of Pompey, but the eunuch Pothinus and Achillas, endeavoring to escape the same fate as Theodotus, advised the populace to accept Caesar's decree, knowing full well that Caesar would eventually leave Alexandria, and if not, they could always find a way to dispose of him, as they did with Pompey.

With the armies of Cleopatra and the young Ptolemy still encamped against each other near Pelusium, Caesar landed at Alexandria and quickly moved into the vacant Royal Palaces, one of the finest structures in Alexandria: marble steps, columns, and porticoes, elegant furniture, spacious gardens, flowers and spouting fountains. He was exhausted after the endless campaigns of a civil war and a victory against Pompey at Pharsalia in central Greece. Now, with the death of Pompey, he was the chief representative of Rome, making him responsible for the execution of the Piper's will. Conqueror of half the world and the greatest soldier since Alexander the Great, Caesar was in his early fifties when he took up his residence in one of the Royal Palaces at Alexandria. He was an extremely active soldier, "a clever, graceful swordsman, powerful swimmer and excellent athlete." In battle, he had proved himself brave and coolheaded; even in his earlier years, he had been regarded as a dashing young officer. By the age of twenty-one, he had already won the Civic Crown, one of Rome's most prestigious awards, for saving a soldier's life at the storming of Mytilene. At the height of the action, he exposed himself bareheaded among his men, cheering them and encouraging them by his own good spirits; and on another occasion, in the same battle, when a distraught standard-bearer was fleeing for cover, Caesar turned him around and compassionately suggested that he had mistaken the direction of the enemy.

There was still another side to his character. It was openly asserted, not only by his enemies, but by his soldiers who loved and respected him, that he took male lovers, among them Nicomedes, king of Bithynia, which laid him open to insults from all quarters: "Whatever Bithynia had, and Caesar's paramour!" Nevertheless, Caesar persisted with the relationship, and when he celebrated his Gallic Triumph, the soldiers who followed behind his chariot, mockingly sang:

> *All the Gauls did Caesar vanquish, Nicomedes vanquished him;*
> *Lo, now Caesar rides in triumph, but where is Nicomedes?*

However, Caesar's reputation as a womanizer was also well known in Rome. He was the inevitable corespondent in every fashionable divorce, and despite the long list of women linked with him, Roman society and a veritable legion of cuckolds permitted him to survive unscathed to middle age. The marvel is that he did not end in some dark street, a dagger between his ribs. He seduced the wives of most of his friends, including Crassus, Gabinius, and Pompey's Cornelia, but his greatest passion was reserved for Servilia, the mother of Marcus Brutus (who was to be one of his assassins). In fact, it was rumored that he was even Brutus's father. During the long Gallic Triumph, Caesar's legionaries shouted verses that attested to his sexual activities even beyond Rome:

> *Home we bring the bald adulterer,*
> *Romans, lock your wives away!*

He was a robust man, tall of stature, with a fair complexion, shapely limbs, a full face, and keen black eyes. He enjoyed good health, though during his later years he was subject to fainting fits and nightmares. He was twice attacked by the falling sickness (epilepsy) during several campaigns. He was assiduous about his appearance, kept himself well trimmed and shaved, even plucking out superfluous hair from his nose and around his eyes. His baldness greatly bothered him, and because of it, he used to comb his thin locks forward over the crown of his head. Out of all the honors voted him by the Senate, there was none that he enjoyed more than the privilege of wearing the laurel crown at all times. He was extremely fastidious about his dress, and always wore a senator's tunic, with fringed sleeves to the wrist.

Although his soldiers often mocked and derided him openly, they nevertheless had the deepest admiration for him. Unlike other generals, he would be the first to swim across a river, and was indefatigable on the battlefield, challenging and surpassing even the youngest and strongest of his soldiers. A superb horseman, he cared very little for food and ate moderately. What spare time he had, he devoted almost entirely to the collection of precious gems he used to entice and seduce his women. He was on his fourth marriage when he arrived in Alexandria. His current wife was Calpurnia, the daughter of Calpurnius Piso, who served as consul in 58 B.C.

Above all other virtues, Caesar was a man with a restless passion for honor. His drive and ambition (often seen as extreme cockiness and self-confidence) are unmatched in history. These characteristics were evident even in his early life, when he was captured by pirates and taken to the island of Pharmacusa off the Asia Minor coast city of Miletus. The pirates demanded that he send for a ransom of twenty talents (several thousand dollars) as payment for his release. Caesar laughed and said he was worth far more than that, at least fifty talents, a sum he ultimately paid them, but not before assuring them he would return to their island one day and have them all executed. Meanwhile, as he waited for the ransom to be sent, he willingly joined in their orgies, never for a moment letting them forget that although he was their prisoner, he was still their superior. He castigated them for their coarse and uncivilized manners, and when it came time for him to sleep, he demanded they keep silent. Soon after he was freed, he collected a small force and, true to his word, came back to the island, rounded up all the pirates, and ordered their crucifixion; but in a moment of weakness, he changed his mind and commanded their throats to be cut rather than have them suffer a long and painful death on the cross.

Once he was settled in the Royal Palaces at Alexandria, Caesar summoned the young Ptolemy to meet with him for the purpose of settling his long and bitter dispute with Cleopatra. Overriding his counselor's objections, Ptolemy accepted the invitation and left immediately for Alexandria, accompanied by the eunuch Pothinus. They found the Royal Palaces guarded by Roman soldiers and the city entirely under Roman rule. During their audience with Caesar, he demanded a huge sum of money, claiming he had lent that amount to Ptolemy's father, the Piper, in order to restore him to the throne of Egypt. Before dismissing his two visitors, Caesar counseled them to cease their campaign for the throne and arrive at a peace with Cleopatra. Finally, he urged the young Ptolemy to disband his army and withdraw at once from the frontier near Pelusium.

The eunuch Pothinus, refusing to be intimidated by Caesar's advice, sent a hasty message to Achillas at Pelusium, ordering him to bring his entire army into Alexandria. Caesar, in the meantime, positive that he was on the threshold of a final conclusion to the dispute, sent word to Cleopatra and invited her to come to Alexandria also. Here again, Cleopatra revealed her daring courage by deciding to undergo the perilous journey through enemy lines. Thus early in the morning, she secretly embarked in a ship at a remote cove near the harbor of Pelusium and set sail for Alexandria. She anchored off Pharos Island and waited until nightfall, when her faithful servant Apollodorus pulled up beside her galley in a small boat and quietly rowed her to a familiar dock directly below the great walls of the Royal Palaces. He then wrapped Cleopatra in a carpet, tied it securely with cords, and slung her over his shoulder. He was stopped several times by guards, but he managed to proceed by telling them he was one of the palace servants on an important errand. Once he got inside, two guards accompanied him through the great halls of the palace to Caesar's suite of rooms. Apollodorus waited until Caesar himself made his appearance, then carefully laid the carpet on the floor, untied the cords, and to Caesar's great astonishment, the little queen of Egypt rolled out and leaped to her feet, her hair disheveled, her face scarlet. This ruse of Cleopatra instantly opened the way to Caesar's heart. He had known scores of women throughout the world, but he had never encountered one like this.

Knowing Caesar's reputation, it is conceivable they became lovers that same night—she perhaps for the first time in her life, even though she was no virgin when it came to political intrigue. As a Ptolemy, she would stop at nothing to achieve her ultimate goal: the throne of Egypt.

After Caesar had arranged a reconciliation between Cleopatra and the young Ptolemy, he learned from his barber that the eunuch Pothinus and Achillas were devising a plot to assassinate him. Acting quickly, he hosted an elaborate banquet to celebrate the union between brother and sister, and during the festivities, Pothinus was seized by soldiers, dragged outside, and executed. Somehow, Achillas managed to escape and return to his army. Caesar, realizing that war was imminent, and that his few thousand Roman soldiers were hardly enough to withstand an assault from Achillas's army, sent his friend Mithradates after additional forces in Syria and Asia Minor, hoping, by a rear attack, to defeat the Egyptian army stationed at Pelusium. To ensure the success of his plan, Caesar held not only the young Ptolemy, but also his sister and her tutor Ganamydes as security in the palace. However, his scheme was foiled when Achillas left Pelusium without warning and headed for Alexandria. When his army reached the outskirts of the city, they were greeted enthusiastically by the inhabitants. This news was discouraging for Caesar, who now had to deal with the fanatical mobs of Alexandria as well as Achillas's army of 20,000 foot soldiers and 2,000 cavalry.

Suddenly, Ptolemy's sister loomed as a heroine to the Alexandrians, something Achillas viewed with displeasure, since his allegiance was with the young Ptolemy. Knowing that Achillas would never bend from this position, Ptolemy's sister had him executed, then proclaimed Ganamydes general of the Egyptian army and leader of the revolt against Caesar.

The Roman galleys carrying the Thirty-Seventh Legion from Asia Minor had now reached the Egyptian coast, but because of contrary winds, they were unable to proceed toward Alexandria. At anchor in the harbor off Lochias, the Egyptian fleet posed an additional problem for the Roman ships. However, in a surprise attack, Caesar's soldiers set fire to the Egyptian ships, and the flames, spreading rapidly in the driving wind, consumed most of the dockyard, many structures near the palace, and also several thousand books that were housed in one of the buildings. From this incident, historians mistakingly assumed that the Great Library of Alexandria had been destroyed, but the Library was nowhere near the docks. The Roman historian Lucan reported that Caesar, besieged in the palace, ordered torches to be soaked with pitch and thrown on the Egyptian ships. The fire immediately spread to the rigging and to the decks, which were coated with resin. Devoured by flames, the first of the Egyptian ships began to sink, while the fire spread rapidly toward the rest of the ships. The houses nearest the docks caught fire too; and the flames, driven by gusts of wind, streaked the sky like meteors over the rooftops.

The most immediate damage occurred in the area around the docks, in shipyards, arsenals, and warehouses in which grain and books were stored. Some forty thousand book scrolls were destroyed in the fire. Not at all connected with the Great Library, they were account books and ledgers containing records of Alexandria's export goods bound for Rome and other cities throughout the world.

When the sea finally calmed, the Roman galleys appeared off Pharos Island. Caesar was transported there and personally escorted them into the harbor, after which a select force of legionaries under his command set out to capture Pharos. They planned to make one assault from the sea, the other from the eastern harbor, then swing around and take the great promontory Heptastadion. The landing on Pharos was successful and the northern part of the Heptastadion was quickly secured. Caesar himself led the attack to gain the southern section of the promontory that faced the city, but he met with unexpected resistance and soon found himself trapped on the Heptastadion between two attacking Egyptian forces. Several galleys and boats were summoned to his assistance and Caesar got into one of the small boats, but it was so heavy with survivors and wounded it overturned and sank, forcing him to swim two hundred yards to another vessel.

That night, in the company of Cleopatra and several officers, he remained silent during dinner, then withdrew to his bedchamber. Not only had he underestimated the strength of the Egyptian forces, but in the struggle to take the Heptastadion, he had lost a great number of sailors, 400 of his best legionaries, and his favorite purple general's cloak.

Farther east, Mithridates and his army had already taken the fortress at Pelusium and were advancing down the Nile. The Egyptian force at Memphis was no match for them, and after an easy victory, Mithridates crossed the western bank of the Nile and headed for Alexandria. When the young Ptolemy learned that Mithridates and his army were converging on the city, he took immediate charge of his troops and marched south to battle. Caesar, waiting until the Egyptian army had withdrawn from the city, left a small guard in the palace and sailed eastward, presumably toward Pelusium, but under the cover of darkness, his galleys reversed their direction and sailed quietly back to the western harbor of Alexandria, where he joined forces with Mithridates' army, and together they headed north to attack the Egyptians, who were still under the assumption that Caesar had sailed away from Alexandria.

The ruse succeeded. In the two-day battle that raged on a fortified hill rising between a marsh on one side and the Nile on the other, the Egyptian army was annihilated. Some survivors tried to escape in small boats across the Nile, the young Ptolemy among them, but as he jumped into one of the crowded boats, it overturned and sank, and he drowned with all the others. His body, later recovered and identified by the golden corselet he wore, was brought to Alexandria and buried with full honors. The following evening, Caesar entered the city in triumph. After five weary months, the Alexandrian War had finally come to an end, and he now was ready to install on the throne of Egypt a queen who would soon bear his child.

A few months later, in early spring, he and Cleopatra boarded a magnificent barge and embarked on a voyage up the Nile. This Ptolemaic state barge was 300 feet long, 45 feet on the beam, and rose 60 feet above the water. It was propelled by many banks of oars, and contained bedchambers, banquet rooms, shrines, grottoes, gardens, and courtyards with porticoes and colonnades. A fleet of galleys and supply ships followed close behind; also several thousand Roman troops as a precaution against any attempt to assassinate the new queen. In all, four hundred ships accompanied the barge as it moved slowly up the Nile. News of this voyage rapidly circulated through the country and crowds of people "came flocking along both sides of the river to view the spectacle, for in their minds, they beheld a gigantic vessel transporting their god Ammon and the goddess Isis through the very heart of Egypt."

The display of wealth and echo of Egyptian gods and goddesses set the stage for Cleopatra's reign as queen. Because she presented herself to the Egyptian people as royalty, they would thereafter accord her with near-mystical powers that would protect them and their kingdom.

⌘

Typical of the Alexandrians, they slyly called Cleopatra's son Caesarion (Little Caesar), but the actual name was Ptolemy Caesar. Soon after the child's birth, Caesar's most pressing problem was to terminate once and for all the constant uprisings in the turbulent East. Since the Jews of Alexandria had displayed a peaceful temperament and had not joined the Egyptians in their fight against the Romans, Caesar rewarded their brethren in Judaea by exempting them from both military service and the payment of tribute. After appointing Antipater (who was well liked by the Jews) procurator of Judaea, Caesar left Judaea and joined his legions at Zela, four hundred miles north of Ephesus, where he crushed the armies of Pharnaces. After the battle, he wrote these famous words to his friend Amantius in Rome: "Veni, vidi, vici!"

He had one more battle to fight before his triumphant return to Rome. The following April, he crushed the Pompeian forces at Thapsus in North Africa. Three of the enemy generals were subsequently executed, and the other two, Scipio and Cato, committed suicide. The old guard of the Roman Republic had met its end; the road was now open for the new empire.

In preparation for the grand celebration of his victories, Caesar summoned Cleopatra and her son Caesarion to Rome and, in a gesture of politeness, her surviving brother also, the eleven-year-old Ptolemy XIV, who posed no real threat to her throne.

Cleopatra arrived in Rome with her son, and with her full retinue of slaves, eunuchs, bodyguards, and courtiers. Caesar promptly transported her to his country house on the right bank of the Tiber, an elegant estate with courtyards, gardens, porticoes, and sculptures, while his legitimate wife Calpurnia remained in his town house within the city. Caesar made no attempt to hide his relationship with Cleopatra. Everyone in Rome knew that, as the father of Caesarion, he was thinking seriously about entering into a legal union with Cleopatra to establish a royal line.

The Triumph was a four-day celebration, the largest and most expensive Rome had ever seen. On the opening day, as Caesar ascended the Capitol steps, he was proclaimed conqueror of Gaul by the same legions that had spewed their bawdy songs about "the bald-headed adulterer." The long ceremony culminated with the spectacle of Vercingetorix (the leader of the Gauls) walking in chains through the streets of Rome toward his execution.

During the celebration, Caesar seized the opportunity to dedicate a temple he had built at his own expense to Venus the Mother of All (Venus Genetrix). Alongside the statue of the goddess, he had installed a gold statue of Cleopatra, the implied message of which did not sit well with the Romans: *Cleopatra is the incarnation of Isis, who is the Egyptian equivalent of Venus. We are both of divine origin!*

The link to Isis was no accident. From her early adolescence, Cleopatra loved to dress as the goddess Isis, and to be called the New Isis. Apuleius, a Platonic philosopher and author of *The Golden Ass*, described one such occasion, when her long thick hair fell on her neck, and she wore an intricate chaplet woven of exotic flowers. Just above her brow shone a round disc, like a mirror, or like the bright face of the moon. Vipers rising from the left-hand and right-hand parting of her hair supported this disc, with ears of corn bristling beside them. Her many-colored robe was of finest linen—part glistening white, part crocus yellow, part glowing red. Along the entire hem a woven border of flowers and fruit clung and swayed in the breeze. But what caught and held Apuleius's eye more than anything else "was the deep black lustre of her mantle. She wore it slung across her body from the right hip to the left shoulder, where it was caught in a knot resembling the boss of a shield, some of it hanging in innumerable folds as the tasselled fringe quivered." This mantle was embroidered with glittering stars—not only on the hem, but everywhere else—and in the middle beamed a full and fiery moon.

On the second day, after the Gallic Triumph was completed, the Egyptian Triumph began, with lavish ceremony and splendor. A statue of the Nile god was paraded around the city, together with a model of the Pharos Light to remind the Romans of Egypt's importance in the world; also portraits of the defeated Achillas and the eunuch Pothinus. These were followed by a procession of African animals unknown to Rome, particularly the giraffe. Arsinoe (Cleopatra's spiteful sister) was also led through the streets in chains but was later granted her freedom.

On the third day, Caesar's victory over Pharnaces at Pontus in Asia Minor was highlighted by the procession of a huge tablet bearing the words "Veni, vidi, vici!" After the Triumphs, Caesar rewarded his soldiers with large gifts and entertained the people with banquets, feasting them all at one time on twenty thousand dining couches, and furnishing spectacles of gladiatorial and naval combats.

While Caesar went about the business of governing the empire and, more importantly, constructing new roads and buildings for Rome, Cleopatra was comfortably lodged with her son in the country house overlooking the Tiber, surrounded by her chambermaids, eunuchs, and courtiers. The Romans did not take to this kindly; nor were they much impressed with the Egyptian costumes and manners of her ménage. A letter written by Cicero to his friend Atticus tells of a gift Cleopatra had promised to grant him in return for a service he had rendered her: "I detest the queen, and the voucher for her promises. Her insolence too, while she resides in Caesar's trans-Tiberian villa, I cannot endure without a pang. So I will have nothing to do with that woman!"

Paying no heed to the gossip, Cleopatra tactfully avoided all contact with the society life of Rome just across the river. As a result, throughout her seclusion in Caesar's villa, she missed some of the most endearing aspects of that magnificent city: "The drip of water from the aqueduct that passed over the gate from which stretched the dusty and squalid Appian Way, the garrets under the tiles where the pigeons sleeked themselves as the rain drummed on the roof, the narrow streets choking with shoppers and carts, the pavements ringing with the echo of military boots, the tavern waiters moving about with trays of hot dishes on their heads, the flower pots hanging from high window ledges, the shuttered shops, a sudden street brawl, the city's darkness quivering under a flare of torches as elegantly-dressed gentlemen and ladies passed along from a dinner party with their accompaniment of servants and slaves."

Compared to Alexandria, Rome was still a provincial city. More than anyone else, Caesar knew that the real wealth of the world lay in the East, as did the greatest unconquered enemies of Rome, the Parthians. The disaster at Carrhae in Mesopotamia, in 53 B.C., could never be forgotten by the Romans, as the great general Crassus was slain there, and most of his legions were annihilated by quick Parthian horsemen and their showers of arrows. It was Caesar's ambition to punish these Parthians and destroy them once and for all. His vast empire, containing Gaul, Spain, and most other regions in Europe, already surpassed that of Alexander the Great. And Alexander had been proclaimed a god, the son of Jupiter Ammon.

At about this time, all records of Cleopatra's younger brother, Ptolemy XIV, faded from the scene. He had entered into these world-shattering events like a shadow, and like a shadow he abruptly disappeared. The Jewish historian Josephus inferred that he was murdered by Cleopatra and Caesar, but this accusation was never substantiated. In all probability, the boy died of a sudden illness.

Despite the young Ptolemy's death, the drama of Caesar's return continued to unfold. It was now February 15, a day of great celebration for the Romans, the annual festival of the Lupercalia. Lupercus was identified in Roman legend with the god of nature, Pan. He represented the return of spring, the growth of plants, the mating of animals, the reproduction of human beings. A goat and a dog were sacrificed, then two young nobles of the Order of Lupercus cut the skins of these animals into strips called *februa* (hence February). Running through the streets, they used the skins as whips and lashed out at every woman they passed, in the belief that these women would become pregnant during that year. Women who wanted to bear a child competed fiercely to be struck by the *februa*.

On this festive date in 44 B.C., Caesar was seated on a golden throne in the Forum and Mark Antony happened to be one of the young noblemen brandishing the *februa*. Bounding into the Forum, Antony hailed Caesar as Lupercus in the flesh, then dashed forward, mounted the rostrum, and tried to place a crown upon Caesar's head. Caesar's many supporters stationed at key areas in the Forum began shouting and begging him to accept it, knowing full well that had he done so, this would have made him king of Rome as well as emperor. Unquestionably, this whole incident was conceived by Caesar and Cleopatra, with Antony's help, so as to test the reaction of the Roman people to the idea of having King Caesar and Queen Cleopatra rule over them.

But the Romans detested the word "king." It reminded them of the long bitter struggle their ancestors endured to rid themselves of the Etruscan kings. Despite the cheers of some supporters, Caesar sensed the overall mood in the Forum and quickly handed the crown back to Antony. His action was roundly applauded, but Antony, under the assumption that Caesar was merely making an outward gesture of refusal, persisted, and again handed him the crown. When the crowd once more voiced its disapproval, Caesar bowed to their wishes and emphatically rejected the crown and the throng burst into cheers. Curbing his disappointment, Caesar ordered the crown to be taken and placed upon the head of Jupiter's statue in the Capitol, then decreed that the whole incident be duly recorded in the public records: "On this day, acting on the wishes of the people, Mark Antony offered Caesar the royal crown, but the Emperor refused to accept it."

In the weeks that followed, Caesar launched preparations for his campaign in the East, planning first to create the empire's frontiers in Dacia (modern Hungary and Romania), then head south through Armenia and launch an assault against the Parthians. During this hectic period of mobilization, he consulted a passage of the Sibylline Books, in which a prophecy was interpreted unequivocally that "no war could be successful against the Parthians unless the Roman armies were led by a king."

It is not certain whether or not Caesar had a hand in this prediction, but if it were a ruse, it made the following event even more disastrous. On March 15, the Ides of March, the Sibylline prophecy was to be debated in the Senate, and the proposal to crown Caesar king was to be laid before all the members. Meanwhile, a plot to assassinate Caesar had been brewing for weeks and, under pressure of the Sibylline prophecy and Caesar's planned invasion of Parthia, the conspirators had to move fast. Otherwise, if Caesar came back from the Parthian war victorious, there could be no denying him the crown.

A group of senators, all of whom had personal and political grievances against Caesar, collaborated in the plot to kill him. The leader in the conspiracy was Gaius Cassius, who had served under Pompey as an admiral. A fervent Republican, he had no use for dictators and autocrats. Brutus, a coconspirator, was of a different nature. His scholarly intellect provided the moral justification for the act, and in all probability he had another reason to do away with the dictator: it was whispered on every street corner in Rome that Caesar had had an affair with Brutus's mother Servilia, both before and after Brutus's birth. The rumors persisted that Brutus was Caesar's son, though he claimed himself to be the legitimate son of Junius Brutus, a hero of the Romans in their war against the Etruscans. Still, Caesar treated Brutus like a son, which made all the difference. He gave special orders that Brutus not be harmed in the Battle of Pharsalia and repeated them during the escape of the surviving Pompeian army. In the Senate, Brutus was a moralistic prig obsessed with principles of ethics and behavior, who assailed his fellow senators on these points during and outside of their debates. At one time, his remarks became so unbearable, Caesar was prompted to say, "I don't understand what the young man means, but whatever it is, he means it vehemently."

The other leading conspirators were the two Casca brothers, Trebonius (to whom Caesar had just offered the post of proconsul of Asia), Tillius Cimber, and Servus Galba. All of these men had been for a long time supporters and confidants of Caesar, yet each had his own reason to join the conspiracy: idealization of the old Republic, a personal hatred of Caesar, or a self-serving desire for fame and recognition. It is difficult to comprehend why they would resolve to commit such an act. They saw Caesar daily, pretended to share his views, his ideas, his plans for the empire, and even feigned friendship.

Because Caesar's last day in Rome before embarking with his army for Parthia would be on March 15, and because this would be the appropriate occasion for him to ask the Senate that he be crowned king "to ensure victory," as the Sibylline passage had prophesied, the conspirators decided that the Ides of March would be the date of the assassination. The place would be the Hall of Pompey, where the Senate would be meeting. The plan was ideal. Caesar, trusting that all the senators had sworn they would never see him harmed, would enter the hall unarmed and without a bodyguard.

Plutarch writes that on the day before the assassination, Brutus was tormented with anguish. He couldn't eat and wouldn't speak to anyone. He tossed so fitfully in his sleep his wife Portia finally asked him what was troubling him, and, on the point of tears, he revealed all the details of the plot, knowing that he not only was risking the lives of the conspirators but, far worse, was involving his own wife in the crime.

A few days before the Ides, an old soothsayer named Spurinna came to Caesar and warned him to beware of the Ides of March. On March 14, it was reported that a small bird carrying a sprig of laurel in its beak had been observed flying into the Hall of Pompey, pursued by other birds, which attacked it and finally killed it. That same night, as Caesar was lying next to Calpurnia in his town house, all the doors and windows suddenly burst open as if struck by a violent gale. At the height of the turbulence, the ceremonial armor of Mars, which was given to Caesar, fell from the wall with a loud crash. Calpurnia moaned in her sleep, and when Caesar awakened her, she told him that she had dreamed he was being murdered and begged him not to leave the house.

In the morning, his doctors concurred with Calpurnia and strongly advised Caesar to remain at home. At the same time, Caesar received a report from the priests and augurs, stating that the sacrifices of that day had proved ominous. All signs indeed pointed toward an evil day and should have convinced Caesar to stay away from the Senate. Meanwhile, as time dragged on and Caesar had yet to make his appearance, the conspirators began to feel edgy. Brutus must have wondered if his wife Portia had leaked the plot to a friend, who might have informed a government official, bringing Caesar with his legionaries to surround the Hall of Pompey and take his revenge. In this terrified state, the conspirators decided to send an emissary, Decimus Brutus Albinus, who had been a close and trusted friend to Caesar and was to receive the consulship the following year. He arrived at Caesar's town house and found him greatly distraught. Caesar apparently had now paid full credence to all the portents and prophecies and had already sent for Antony with the intention of postponing his visit to the Senate.

Decimus nevertheless insisted and urged him to go to the Senate in haste, reminding him of the many business details that needed his attention before he left Rome for Parthia, but more importantly, if Caesar was to be proclaimed king, it would be imperative for him to be there to receive the honor. This persuaded Caesar, and he agreed to come.

Satisfied, Decimus returned to the Hall of Pompey and informed his fellow conspirators that Caesar was on his way. As with Decimus, their daggers were hidden under their cloaks.

As Caesar was being borne through the streets of the city, he received still another warning from the old soothsayer Spurinna, but he cast it aside and laughingly said, "You see, the Ides of March have arrived!" To which Spurinna replied, "Yes, but they are not over yet." Farther down the same street, a man darted out from the crowd and thrust into Caesar's hand a small scroll revealing all the details of the assassination plot. Apparently, Caesar did not bother to open it.

Inside the Hall of Pompey, the priests again offered sacrifices and once more the signs proved unfavorable. Suddenly, news was circulated around the senators that Brutus's wife Portia was either dead or dying. (In fact, she had fainted in her house from the strain.) At this point, a senator, Popilius Laenus, whispered to Brutus and one of the Casca brothers: "I wish you luck with your scheme, but I advise you to be quick, for people are talking."

When Caesar at last entered the building, every senator stood on his feet and applauded. The Senate was about to proceed with the business of Caesar's kingship and the forthcoming Parthian campaign when the conspirators, led by Tillius Cimber, formed a circle around Caesar so as to cut him off from the main body of the Senate. Cimber then asked a favor of Caesar, requesting that his brother be recalled from exile. Caesar refused. However, Cimber persisted and in the Roman gesture of supplication, placed his hand on Caesar's robe. Before Caesar could draw back, Cimber had pulled the purple robe off the emperor's shoulders: a signal to the other conspirators. Immediately, they crowded around Caesar, who now stood there in his simple Roman toga. Casca, standing directly behind him, struck the first blow at Caesar's neck, but missed and pierced only his shoulder. Caesar spun around, grabbed Casca's arm, and ran it through with his stylus. In the next instant, Casca's brother stabbed Caesar in the side, and Cassius thrust a dagger into his face. They were now upon him like a pack of wild dogs, stabbing at his chest, his thighs, his back. They were so driven by frenzy and blood lust, several of their own number were wounded. Caesar, striking out left and right with his stylus, fought desperately for his life and once again grabbed Casca by the arm, but there was no strength left in his body. Leaning against the statue of his old enemy Pompey, he looked up and for the first time noticed Brutus coming toward him with a dagger in his hand. Caesar's last words, spoken in Greek, were addressed to Brutus: "And you too, my child!" With this, he covered his head with his toga, slid to the floor, and died. Twenty-three dagger wounds were later counted on his body, but it was so bloodied and lacerated there may well have been many more.

⟨๛⟩

The conspirators never anticipated that the Roman people would decry Caesar's murder. "Who now," the populace moaned, "will lead our legions against the Parthians? Who will administer our huge empire that extends from far-off Gaul to distant Asia?"

While the anger in the city raged, Caesar's body lay in state in the Forum for five days. The date of the funeral was finally fixed for March 20. Toward evening, Antony went to the Forum and found throngs of people wailing and lamenting around the corpse, soldiers pounding their shields on the floor, women beating their breasts and pulling their hair. Seizing a spear from one of the soldiers, Antony jabbed it into the blood-spattered purple robe that lay beside the dead body and held it aloft

for everyone to see, and after calmly waiting for the vengeful cries to subside, he pulled out Caesar's will from under his toga, unrolled it, and
began reading:

> I bequeath to every Roman citizen 300 *sesterces;* I also give to the
> Roman people my vast estates and gardens on the other side of the
> Tiber [where Cleopatra was staying]. Three-quarters of the remainder
> of my estate is bequeathed to Octavian, my adopted son, and the other
> quarter is to be divided between my two nephews, Lucius Pinarius and
> Quintus Pedius. I further decree that Octavian be my official heir.

Not one word of reference to Cleopatra, or to her son. Yet she had
been one of the first to learn of Caesar's death. An unknown senator dispatched a messenger to the villa with the grim news, and it was as though
the twenty-three dagger thrusts had mortally wounded all her plans. The
grand scheme for a Julian-Ptolemaic dynasty would never come to pass.
Far worse, she now feared for her life, and for the life of Caesarion.

Antony's funeral oration and the reading of Caesar's will drove the
crowd into such a frenzy that they began shouting for revenge upon all the
conspirators. Someone in the throng recalled a derogatory speech made
against Caesar by a man named Cinna shortly after the assassination, and
when a minor poet, also called Cinna, was addressed by one of his friends,
the mob attacked him, thinking he was one of the conspirators. His body
was torn limb from limb, then trampled.

The enraged throng then grabbed benches, tables, all available wood-
work, and built a great pyre in the center of the Forum. On top of it, they
placed Caesar's body, laid out on sheets of purple and gold. Torches were
applied to the pyre, and in the warm spring night the flames rose quickly,
illuminating the fierce faces of the crowd and the walls and pillars of the
surrounding buildings. In time, the charred body of Caesar collapsed into
the core of the fire, and before the flames died down, the crowd took flam-
ing brands from the blaze and hurried off to burn the houses of the conspirators.

Caesar's will proved shocking to Cleopatra. In her dilemma, she vac-
illated between proclaiming her son the rightful heir to Caesar's throne or
fleeing the country in fear. And who was this Octavian? Caesar hardly
spoke of him in her company. It was only later revealed to her that Caesar
had taken a fancy to this obscure nephew of his during the Spanish War.

Although the young man had been weak after a severe illness, he was determined to join Caesar in Spain. His devotion gained Caesar's admiration. Octavian had endured shipwreck and roads infested with the enemy to reach the Roman army, and when he finally got there, he fought valiantly by his uncle's side. When he received news of Caesar's death and his appointment as inheritor to the throne of Rome, he was still pursuing his studies in Apollonia.

Cleopatra, however, was not to give up that easily, reasoning that if, with Antony's support, her son were to be recognized officially as Caesar's child, Octavian would then be cast aside forever, since by law a son held preference over a nephew. Antony also knew that if Octavian established himself on Caesar's throne his own power in Rome would vanish. Furthermore, if he were to support Cleopatra, he would retain his regency for many years and might even take Caesar's place as Cleopatra's husband, thus ascending to the throne by way of his stepson.

For these reasons, Antony persuaded Cleopatra to remain in Rome a while longer. Soon after, he stood up in the Senate and declared that little Caesarion had been acknowledged by Caesar to be his rightful son. It was denied at once by Oppius, who favored the claims of Octavian. While the Senate argued the matter, Octavian, now nineteen, had already left Apollonia and was on his way to Rome to claim his rights. The city immediately cast aside the issue of the conspirators and positioned itself into two factions: one supporting Octavian, the other upholding Antony's claim. The situation became so grave that Antony advised Cleopatra to return to Alexandria with her son and wait there until the strife was over. Antony also urged her to raise troops and ships to support him against the impending threat from Octavian.

The Roman statesman and author Cicero, in a letter to Atticus from Sinuesa, commented on the news that "Cleopatra left Rome a few days before April 15th." As the Seleucian galley carried her across the Mediterranean, her mind was tormented by the events of the past and the precarious fate of the future. Two things were certain, however: she was determined that the great personality of Caesar would resurrect itself in his little son and that Antony would be true to his word and champion her cause to the death.

In early October of 43 B.C., a plot by Octavian to kill Antony failed. In retaliation, Antony began spreading the story that Octavian had been adopted by Caesar only because of their homosexual relationship, to which Octavian responded accusing Antony not only of having immoral relations with Curio, the young son of the wealthy Caius Scribonius Curio, but that the affair had become so notorious the father forbade Antony from even entering his house. Largely through Cicero's efforts, the two combatants briefly reconciled. Nevertheless, Antony advised Octavian that he should make no attempt to claim his inheritance because he was far too young to assume the responsibility of leadership.

During the uneasy peace, the two agreed to become allies in the pursuit of Cassius and Brutus. Shortly thereafter, Octavian fell ill, and it was decided that Antony alone was to assume the task of tracking down the two conspirators. Such odd behavior was typical of Octavian. Many times, even in public, he was derided for his cowardice. Even after the Spanish War when he had fought beside his uncle, as the prisoners were led before the conquering generals, they saluted Antony respectfully but cursed Octavian in the foulest language.

With his powerful army, Antony passed swiftly through Greece and into Asia Minor. In late summer of 41 B.C., he established temporary headquarters at Tarsus, from where he sent an officer named Dellius to Alexandria, inviting Cleopatra to meet with him and discuss the situation.

Cleopatra already knew what kind of man Antony was. She had observed his faults and virtues firsthand in Rome, and his reputation was known throughout the world. "The people of Alexandria regarded him as a colossal child, capable of conquering the world, but incapable of resisting any form of pleasure." To many, he seemed good-natured, a personification of Bacchus; but to the thousands of people he conquered, he was the Devourer, someone to be greatly feared.

Undeniably, he was a man of remarkable appearance: tall, well built, heavily muscled like a gladiator, thick hair curling about his head, the perfect image of Hercules, from whom he claimed lineal descent. His forehead was broad, his nose aquiline, his mouth and chin strong. His great physical strength evoked admiration among men; and to women he was irresistible. Cicero despised him and likened him to "a prize fighter, with that heavy jaw, powerful neck, and mighty flanks." Nevertheless, Antony had a lovable nature and was revered by his soldiers. This devotion was due to the nobility of his family, his eloquence, his frank and open manners, his ease in talking with everybody, and his kindness visiting the poor and unfortunate. After a battle, he went from tent to tent to comfort the wounded, often breaking into tears, upon which they, with radiant faces, would seize his hands and call him their emperor and their general.

He was a notorious drinker and womanizer. In his early military career, he traveled throughout Italy with his mistress, the actress Cytheris, accompanied by a whole train of musicians, actors, actresses, concubines, and brothel-keepers. He loved every aspect of the theater—its actors, musicians, writers, and directors. With this lifestyle of extravagance, it was inevitable that he should constantly be in debt, and when Pompey's splendid town house was put up for sale after his death, Antony simply stepped in and acquired it, confident that Caesar would never ask his most faithful supporter for money. But he was mistaken. Caesar at once demanded payment and Antony was forced to oblige. During his occupancy of the house, many choice works of art were either destroyed or given away in endless parties and orgies, during which even the slaves slept in Pompey's purple coverlets. The house depreciated so greatly in value, Antony thought seriously about selling it, but changed his mind at the last moment, fearing Caesar's reaction.

He loved to play tricks, especially on his wife Fulvia, a woman not born for spinning or housewifery, nor one who could be content with ruling a private husband, but a woman prepared to govern and even give orders to a commander-in-chief. To keep such a strong-minded woman content and happy, Antony indulged in boyish pranks, like bouncing out at her from behind dark corners of the house and taking childish delight in her surprise. Shortly before Caesar returned from the war in Spain, a false rumor circulated that he had been defeated and that the enemy was marching on Rome. Antony found this an opportunity for yet another practical joke on his wife. Disguising himself as a bedraggled soldier, he made his way back to his house and managed to enter by convincing the servants that he had an urgent letter from Antony to be delivered into Fulvia's hands. He was subsequently shown into the presence of the agitated Fulvia and stood before her as she took the letter in her trembling hand. In a choking voice, she asked this mysterious figure if something dreadful had happened to her husband, but he made no reply. As she nervously tore open the letter, he suddenly pulled the ragged cloak off his shoulders and swept her into his arms, laughing and kissing her on the neck.

At other times, he delighted in wandering around the city, disguised as a servant and tapping on the doors and windows of his friends' houses to alarm them. Often he was ill-treated and beaten even though they knew who he was.

As Caesar's successor, Antony set out to amass his own private fortune, and at the urging of Fulvia, who was perhaps the most unscrupulous woman of her day, he managed to inherit not only Caesar's entire wealth and property, but also Caesar's private accountant Faberius, with whose help he falsified documents and even created others supposedly found among Caesar's papers. The pillaging was so flagrant that it became public knowledge that everything belonging to the empire was for sale at Antony's house: titles, privileges, estates, even towns. Strangely, the Romans weren't offended by this. Whereas previous emperors and dictators had been grossly corrupt and sought in every way to hide their wickedness, Antony, with his remarkable warmth and openness (which explains why the common people and his own soldiers loved him), never bothered to conceal his wrongdoing. But unlike Caesar, who also had laid aside an immense fortune for himself, Antony was unable to manage the affairs of the empire and keep Rome on a sound basis. He allowed nothing to interfere with his pleasures; running the empire was of secondary importance.

One morning in Rome, while still suffering from the effects of an all-night drinking orgy at the wedding of his comedian friend Hippias, he was called upon to deliver an important public speech. Standing on unsteady feet in the Forum, he was about to begin his address when he was overcome with nausea and unashamedly vomited before the large throng.

Incidents of this nature made him repulsive to the refined classes of Rome. During the greater part of his life, he played the clown, drank heavily, brawled, enjoyed women, and was uncouth in his temperament and speech. In addition, the glamour of the stage had special appeal to him. He was particularly enamored of the actress Cytheris who accompanied him on many official visits to various parts of the country. During these journeys, huge pavilions were erected and sumptuous feasts prepared for the entire company. After this, all the people in the town were entertained by clowns, musicians, buffoons, and chariots drawn by lions. Because of his indulgences, Antony fell into heavy debt, but the big loser was the empire. Treasury funds fell to an all-time low, and to save the situation, Cicero decided this was the appropriate time to summon Caesar's rightful heir to Rome.

Alexander the Great, here represented in both marble bust and marble head, became an icon of Hellenic beauty. *Pella Museum, Greece.*

His image was replicated on money, here on a silver four-drachma coin, struck by the famous sculptor Lysippus (355–281 B.C.). Alexander was the first king in history to be represented on money, making him the most famous figure of his time.
Athens Numismatic Museum.

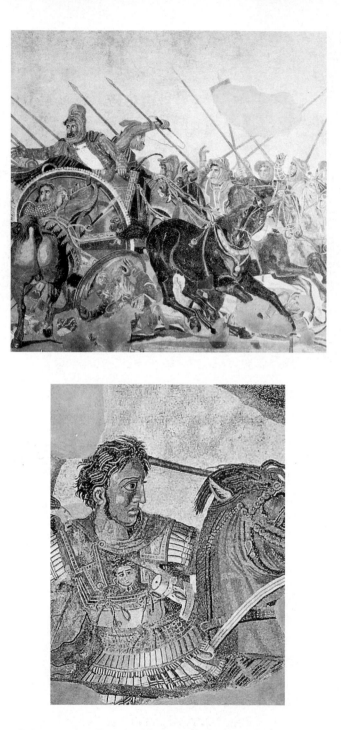

These mosaic images taken from the Alexander Sarcophagus (c. 320 B.C.) suggest the
momentum that built Alexander's empire, and the frantic retreat of the Persian king
Darius in the Battle of Issus (333 B.C.). Alexander is shown here on his legendary horse
Bucephalus (Head of an Ox). *National Archeological Museum, Naples.*

King Philip of Macedonia and his wife, Olympias, dwarf their young son Alexander in this ivory sculpture, but it was Alexander, through his later conquests and the founding of his great city, who made the family famous. *Thessalonika Museum, Greece.*

Pharos Lighthouse, regarded by ancient historians as one of the Seven Wonders of the Ancient World, guided and attracted merchants and travelers to Alexandria's Great Harbor. *From an early reproduction after Thiersch, Greco-Roman Museum, Alexandria.*

In a woodcut by André Thévet, from his book *Portraits and Lives of Illustrious Men* (Paris, 1584), Euclid, the Father of Geometry, who studied in Alexandria, is shown working on a series of figures. *Houghton Library, Harvard University.*

This woodcut, also by Thévet, shows the mathematician and inventor Archimedes contemplating a problem. Beside his hand is one of his models of war machines. *Houghton Library, Harvard University.*

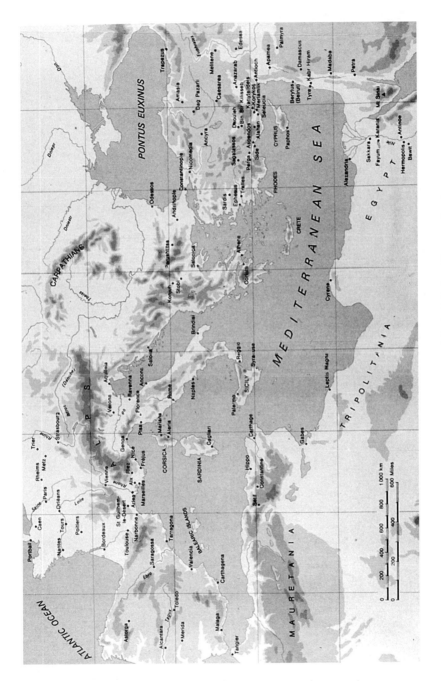

A map of the Mediterranean as it looked during Cleopatra's reign.
Courtesy of the Greco-Roman Museum, Alexandria.

In this limestone relief, Cleopatra and her son Caesarion make an offering at the Temple of Hathor in Dendara. *Photo: Vas Vrettos.*

Cleopatra's hopes for saving the Alexandrian empire were crushed when Julius Caesar (right) was assassinated by Brutus and other members of the Roman Senate. *Vatican Museums.*

The robust yet self-indulgent Mark Antony ultimately squandered both Cleopatra's fortune and her chances to defend her vast empire against Octavian's forces. Like Cleopatra, he committed suicide in Alexandria. *Vatican Museums.*

Emperor Constantine, here shown on his horse in a fourth-century sculpture, had a vision integral to the eventual spread of Christianity and to the flowering of cultural thought in Alexandria. *Vatican Museums.*

Napoleon, fascinated by Egypt and a fervent admirer of Alexander the Great, was perhaps the last western emperor to find his fate determined in the waters off the coast of Alexandria. *Painting by Antoine Gros (1799), Musée Légion d'Honneur, Paris.*

On a spring day in 44 B.C., Octavian arrived in the capital city under a good omen. As the crowds gathered around the Forum to greet him, a bright halo formed around the sun, its rays falling directly over Octavian's head. The populace took this as a divine message and their cheers filled the Roman air. Deep down they had another reason for applauding Octavian: Antony, with his excessive wastefulness and profligacy, had never paid the people the money Caesar had promised them in his will, and now (on Cicero's urging) Octavian had given them his solemn word that they would receive it.

During the reception that followed, Antony impetuously scorned Octavian and even went out of his way to shame him, insinuating he had been named Caesar's heir only because he was Caesar's lover. Octavian remained stoic during the accusation.

The relations between Antony and Octavian had been strained from the very beginning. As Plutarch remarked, "Antony on many occasions had publicly displayed his dislike for this presumptuous young man who had the audacity to claim not only Caesar's inheritance but the very mantle of the great emperor." Soon after Caesar's death, Octavian tried several times to occupy Caesar's golden chair. The first time, because he was forbidden to do so by a tribune of the people, he stepped down and was subsequently applauded by the crowd; on the second occasion, during the celebration of the funeral games for Caesar, although Antony had vehemently forbidden it, Octavian once more attempted and was again applauded for his effort.

Octavian learned from Cicero how to handle the public. "Give them games, bread, wine, spare them from war and improve their lives. This is all they ask." On the last day of the games, another sign appeared which, together with the halo around the sun, offered proof to the Romans that the gods were with Octavian. A comet revealed itself in the sky and, proclaimed the Julian Star, it was a sure sign that Julius Caesar had indeed joined his ancestress Venus among the immortal gods, and that he was now blessing his adopted son Octavian before the eyes of the Roman people.

This sudden turn of events did not bode well for Antony. Nevertheless, he agreed after prolonged arguments and a near civil war to a second reconciliation with Octavian in the autumn of 41 B.C. The two rivals, still mistrusting each other, were both searched for weapons before sitting down to talk. It was finally decided that a triumvirate should be formed, consisting of Antony, Octavian, and Lepidus, an old friend of Caesar who held the rank of master of the horse. He was to act as the mediator between Antony and Octavian and prevent them from warring against each other; the three men were to govern Italy jointly. Antony and Lepidus were assigned the greater portion of the empire, while Octavian was given only Africa, Numidia, and the Mediterranean islands. The first goal of the triumvirate was to avenge the murder of Caesar.

The reconciliation of Antony and Octavian was particularly distressing to Cleopatra. Her son Caesarion, whom she had groomed to inherit Caesar's throne, had been entirely dispossessed by Octavian, and now she could only hope that Octavian would lose his life in the war that was about to break out against the conspirators. Cassius and Brutus had already raised a large army in Greece, and to combat them the triumvirate, desperately needing finances, launched an orgy of killings, the most sordid and despicable of the century. One hundred senators and more than two thousand rich men of distinction were accused as conspirators and their properties and wealth were seized. Fathers betrayed sons, and sons betrayed fathers. Everywhere throughout Italy, spies sought out the condemned victims and handed them over for large rewards. Cicero was among these. He had infuriated Antony with his speeches, condemning him for his scandalous behavior and improper handling of Roman affairs. Octavian, who owed so much to Cicero, stood by and allowed this powerful and influential Roman to be killed, assuming that Cicero, an old man, could be of no further help to him.

Displaying remarkable courage, the philosopher, orator, and perhaps greatest Latin writer in history, met his death in flight. His friends had arranged his escape by ship from Italy, but as the wagon in which he was being borne passed through the main part of the city, Cicero lifted his head from under the covers and was detected by a centurion standing guard at one of the city gates. One quick thrust of the sword, and Cicero's head fell to the street. The centurion then seized the hand with which Cicero had written his philippics against Antony and cut that off also. The heads of all the proscribed enemies were taken to the triumvirs for identification, and when Antony's wife Fulvia caught sight of the detested head of Cicero in the pile, she leaned over and stuck a long pin through the tongue that had dared to revile her husband.

With their treasury stocked with ample finances, the triumvirs began raising an army to destroy the rest of the Republican conspirators. They didn't have to worry about Dolabella, the most treacherous among those who had plotted Caesar's assassination. Cassius had defeated him and his forces in Syria, propelling him to suicide. At first, Cleopatra had chosen to support Dolabella despite his having been one of Caesar's murderers. But the four Egyptian legions she dispatched did not reach him in time, sparing her any humiliation.

On October 1, 42 B.C., in two battles near Philippi in eastern Macedonia, Antony's forces annihilated the armies of Cassius and Brutus. Cassius was slain in the first battle, and the remaining troops under Brutus were thoroughly routed in the second attack. The Republican cause was now dead. Brutus was advised by his counselors to make his escape but he refused. "Fly?" he exclaimed. "Yes, we must fly, but with our hands—not our feet!" With this, he seized his sword and killed himself. And so "the noblest Roman of them all" came to a bitter end. Somehow, Shakespeare's words do not ring true. After all, Brutus was a traitor. He conspired to murder a man he had sworn to protect and defend, a man who respected and loved him, who had saved his life in Pharsalia and who in all probability was his own father.

With his glorious victory at Philippi, Antony was now destined to assume Caesar's place as the most powerful ruler of the western world and, as such, to once and for all bring about the ultimate destruction of the despised Parthians. Cleopatra, cognizant of these events, proceeded to carry out her own plans toward positioning herself and her son Caesarion as sovereigns of the Eastern Empire.

⚬⚬⚬

Before embarking for Asia Minor, Antony and his large army made a triumphal tour through Greece, where he was hailed as Caesar, the Conqueror, Hercules, Mars, and, the title that flattered him most of all, the New Dionysus. He basked in this atmosphere of adulation and enjoyed himself to the fullest, partaking of wine, food, and women. He was now forty-two, twice the age of Octavian who, in his own subtle way, was quietly gaining strength and popularity back home.

In Asia Minor, Antony stayed for a while in the rich city of Ephesus, which he had entered as the New Dionysus, accompanied by young women dressed as Bacchantes, and youths parading as satyrs and fauns. Unlike Caesar, who had always planned ahead and made certain he left everything in a stable condition, Antony lived only for the moment, surrounding himself with his daily company of fiddlers, dancers, actors and actresses, jugglers, tumblers, and of course prostitutes and courtesans.

In the summer of 41 B.C., he left Ephesus and arrived at the ancient city of Tarsus, the capital of Cilicia, which was situated about twelve miles above the delta of the Cydnus River. Here again, he was hailed as Conqueror and the New Dionysus. Pompey the Great had made Tarsus the capital of the eastern province, and since it was the administrative center, Tarsus was always subjected to heavy taxation. Antony, however, carried it to extremes, placing double taxes on the populace, and causing one of his tax-collectors to remark, "If you intend to raise two taxes a year, you must also see to it that each year contains two summers and two autumns for harvesting."

Egypt was under the protection of Antony and his legions, and since he had personally known Cleopatra, first in Alexandria where he had arrived as a young soldier, then in Rome before Caesar's assassination, he dispatched a message to Alexandria requesting Cleopatra to meet with him at Tarsus. She was well aware of Antony's excessive tastes and voracious sexual appetite, and although he liked to claim descent from Hercules, she knew that he, however powerful and famous, was but a commoner, whereas in the eyes of her Egyptian subjects, she was Isis incarnate. Consequently, she did not hurry to accept Antony's invitation but chose to make him wait until she decided to go to Tarsus. Meanwhile, the best minds of her court and of the Mouseion dedicated themselves to making sure that when she arrived in Tarsus it would be one grand event. Shakespeare, inspired by Plutarch, colorfully described the occasion:

> The barge she sat in like a burnish'd throne,
> Burn'd on the water: the poop was beaten gold;
> Purple the sails, and so perfumed that
> The winds were love-sick with them; the oars were silver,
> Which to the tune of flutes kept stroke, and made
> The water which they beat to follow faster,
> As amorous of their strokes. For her own person,
> It beggar'd all description: she did lie

In her pavilion—cloth-of-gold of tissue—
O'er-picturing that Venus where we see
The fancy outwork nature: on each side her
Stood pretty dimpled boys, like smiling Cupids,
With divers-color'd fans, whose wind did seem
To glow delicate cheeks which they did cool,
And what they undid, did.

Cleopatra's royal barge, accompanied by its escort and supply ships, sailed up the Cydnus River and weighed anchor in the busy harbor of Tarsus. Antony, who had been informed of the queen's arrival, seated himself on a throne at the public tribunal in the marketplace, assuming that she and her courtiers would come ashore and present themselves to him. But he was mistaken. Knowing that Antony loved to claim the title of the New Dionysus (which her father had also borne), Cleopatra made her appearance to the people of Asia Minor not as Isis incarnate, but as Venus risen from the waves. Everyone in the city rushed to the docks to view this amazing barge. The sight staggered them. The queen of Egypt reclined under a golden canopy in the guise of Venus, surrounded by Cupids and serving women dressed as Graces and Nereids. This was theater in the ultimate and the crowds burst into cheers as a voice proclaimed, "Aphrodite has come to revel with Dionysus for the good of Asia!" Indeed, the spectacle of a dazzling queen, with her remarkable ship and remarkable wealth, convinced the populace of this Asia Minor city that she was no mortal woman but a true goddess. While all this was going on, Antony sat silently on his throne in the marketplace, together with his guards and a few Roman citizens.

Later that day, Antony sent a messenger to Cleopatra, inviting her to dinner. She declined politely and instead extended an invitation for him to dine with her on the royal barge. At this time, Antony was most anxious to form an alliance with her. His relations with Octavian had reached the breaking point and he realized that a coalition with the queen of Egypt would give him the advantage needed to destroy his rival once and for all. In the extravagance of Alexandria, the robust and lusty Antony had immersed himself for the first time in his life with men and women of culture, and the new role instantly appealed to him. He had even cast aside his Roman dress and clothed himself in the square-cut Athenian costume, with white Attic sandals. Having a sound knowledge of Greek, he also spent considerable time in the Library and Mouseion, and visited with the most learned men of the time.

Here in Tarsus, he knew that Cleopatra needed him as much as he needed her. She was now twenty-nine years old and at the height of her physical beauty and intellectual powers. As a young "widow" whose first union had been so short-lived, she was eager for a satisfactory marriage that would grant her not only the comfort of a strong husband and ardent lover, but, more important, the firm establishment of an empire over which they would jointly rule.

The wit and charm, the sparkling conversation, the voice and manners that had fascinated Caesar, were now to overwhelm Antony as he proceeded toward the royal barge that was moored on the city side of the lake. He was followed by his staff officers and the chief dignitaries of Tarsus. After the formal meeting and reception, everyone moved below to the huge dining hall. Antony was no stranger to ships, but this was no mere ship. The walls of the barge were hung with purple tapestries and embroidered with woven gold. Scores of large mirrors reflected their brilliant light over the whole room as a fragrant scent of incense wafted delicately through the air. Twelve embroidered dining couches were placed around the area. Set in front of each couch were tables with goblets of gold and silver dishes inlaid with precious stones. Antony voiced his amazement over such a splendid banquet, but Cleopatra, with a flick of her Alexandrian wrist, expressed deep regret that there had not been sufficient time to do more, then added, "If you would return tomorrow evening, I will personally make certain that things are better prepared."

The company now moved out to the upper deck of the barge, where illuminated lanterns hung above their heads. On the shore, thousands of onlookers watched in awe, convinced that their Venus was feasting with Dionysus for the benefit of all Asia. When the festivities at last came to an end, Cleopatra presented Antony and the other guests with gifts of everything used for the occasion: couches, gold goblets and silver dishes, embroideries.

True to her promise, Cleopatra's grand feast for Antony and her other invited guests the next evening surpassed even the wildest expectations. It began with sea hedgehogs, oysters, mussels, spondyli, fieldfares with asparagus, fattened fowls, black-and-white sea acorns, roe ribs, boar's ribs, purple shellfish, sow's udder, fish pasties, ducks, boiled teals, and hares. After this followed a course of peacocks from Samos, grouse from Phrygia, cranes from Melos, young goats from Ambracia, tunnyfish from Chalcedon, sturgeons from Rhodes, nuts from Thasos, and acorns from Spain. During the long meal, the master of revels mixed the wine into large bowls and young maidens in gay costumes filled the goblets of the guests, who lay on couches that were arranged around three sides of a table. Prior to their seating, chaplets of flowers were placed on the heads of each guest. Cinnamon and sweet perfumes were then sprinkled over their hair and bodies. Throughout the dinner, they were entertained by dancing girls, musicians, actors, acrobats, clowns, dwarfs, and gladiators.

Antony obligingly responded to Cleopatra's hospitality and invited her to a banquet at one of the richest estates in Tarsus, but the attempt, exceedingly provincial compared to the Egyptian queen's extraordinary affair, was marked by a rustic awkwardness. Nevertheless, Antony, with his charming way of turning failure into a joke, made no pretense of hiding his shortcomings as a host, thus endearing him to Cleopatra. As Plutarch observed, "From that very moment, he became convinced that with this woman as his wife, and with the vast wealth of Egypt at his fingertips, he would at last crush Octavian and be the most powerful ruler in the world."

Antony and Cleopatra spent that winter in Alexandria, in endless banquets, parties, revelry, and lovemaking. "It would be tedious to chronicle Antony's many follies in Alexandria." Indeed, he became more Alexandrian than the Alexandrians, and in addition to adopting all the Greek customs of the city and dressing in the Greek tunic and white Attic sandals, he founded an exclusive club, called the Society of the Inimitable Livers, whose sole purpose was for the members to contrive the most extravagant banquets and entertainments for each other. Antony and Cleopatra took special pride in setting the tone for this hedonistic group. In the Royal Palaces at Lochias, the kitchens were ready for a feast at any hour of the day or night. On one occasion, when a visitor saw eight wild boars turning on spits, he asked what great banquet was being prepared, and the head cook laughingly replied, "We only have a small party tonight, but because we never know when a meal will be required, we always have several in preparation at different times so that everything can be ready in a few minutes."

Throughout these long winter days, Cleopatra worked diligently with Antony, instructing him in every aspect of court life, especially its politics and intrigues. An eager student, he was thrilled with the idea of being molded into a new person by this infinitely intelligent queen. She, of course, had her own reasons. She was willing to initiate this coarse Roman soldier into the elegant mysteries of Alexandrian life, to guide him and even flatter him, but in turn, she expected to receive something from him: to be his rightful queen and co-ruler of the vast Roman Empire. She also participated in his practical jokes. On one occasion, after he had been fishing for a long while in the harbor without making any catches, he paid a local diver to swim down under his line and affix several large fish to his hooks. Cleopatra was not easily deceived. The next day, she arranged for another diver to attach something to Antony's lines, and when he felt the sudden weight of a huge fish, he eagerly drew it up to the surface, only to find that his trophy was a salted fish from the Black Sea, a staple diet of Alexandria's poor during the harsh winter months. Cleopatra burst into laughter when Antony discovered it was a prank. "General," she taunted him, "leave the fishing rod to others. Your game lies in cities, in provinces and kingdoms."

Meanwhile, Antony's wife Fulvia and his brother Lucius were bungling their campaign against Octavian in Italy; and in the East, the surging armies of the Parthians had advanced into Syria and slain Antony's newly installed governor. The Parthians next pushed onward into Judaea and captured Jerusalem, forcing Herod to seek refuge in the mountain citadel of Masada. Antony was blamed for both these events. By neglecting Italy, he had allowed Octavian to gain a firm foothold for future operations, and with the loss of Syria and Judaea, the once-powerful eastern provinces of the empire now lay in shambles.

Like a man aroused from sleep after a drunken orgy, Antony came to his senses and realized he had to leave his mistress and Alexandria, but by this time his brother Lucius had already surrendered to Octavian, and Fulvia was fleeing to the East.

After bidding Cleopatra a sad farewell, Antony set out on his mission, stopping for brief visits in Tyre, Cyprus, and Rhodes before finally reaching Athens, where Fulvia impatiently awaited him. Under the sparkling Attic sun, they took turns chiding each other. She, because he deserted her for Cleopatra, and he, for the failure of the campaign in Italy. After a few days in Athens, Antony decided that he should proceed immediately to Italy for a final confrontation with Octavian, who now held the strong hand, having gained not only Italy but Gaul and Spain as well. But here fate intervened. Exhausted and weak from her long ordeal, Fulvia became gravely ill and died.

On his arrival in Rome, Antony, true to his weak nature, placed the full blame for the Italian campaign on Fulvia's shoulders and offered to come to terms with Octavian. Anxious to avoid still another civil war, and mindful that he had a recently widowed sister Octavia, Octavian proposed that Antony should marry her and thus seal the agreement between them, which called for Octavian to rule over the western half of the empire and Antony the eastern. And so, in late autumn of 40 B.C., Antony was formally married to the young Octavia, who, according to Roman historians, surpassed even Cleopatra in beauty and intellect. Needless to say, the Romans, eager to at last put away their weapons and live in peace once again after suffering through the long civil wars that ravaged their country, voiced immediate approval of the marriage.

For Cleopatra, who two weeks prior to this had given birth to Antony's twins, a boy and a girl—Alexander Helios and Cleopatra Selene (the Sun and the Moon)—the marriage was a terrible disaster. It was a bitter loss for Egypt as well, because the country had expected to be incorporated as an eastern province of the Roman Empire. The fact that Octavia was young and exceedingly beautiful was especially unsettling to Cleopatra. Her carefully devised plans and schemes, from the time of her arrival in Tarsus and throughout that long Alexandrian winter, now seemed utterly destroyed. Her only hope was that Antony's promiscuous way of life would bring about an estrangement with Octavia and thus cause a split between the two Roman generals. Octavian too was aware of this, and to strengthen his position he married Scribonia, who was much older than he and already had gone through two husbands. However, she also happened to be a close relative of Sextus Pompeius, and it was easy to see that Octavian had proposed the marriage only as a political move since Pompeius was the last of Pompey the Great's sons.

The following year, as the fleet of Sextus Pompeius lay at anchor and the armies of Antony and Octavian were assembled on the shore, the three men reached an agreement at Misenum near Naples. To celebrate the event, a great banquet was planned, and when Antony inquired where it should be held, Sextus Pompeius replied, pointing to his admiral's barge with its six banks of oars, "There, for this is the only ancestral home that is left to Pompey."

He said this to reproach Antony, who was occupying the house in Rome that had once belonged to his father, Pompey the Great. He then brought his ship in to anchor close to the shore and made a kind of bridge between it and the headland of Misenum so that the visitors could pass on board. After this, he gave all of his guests a hearty welcome, and when the festivities (accompanied by many coarse jokes about Antony and Cleopatra) were at their height, a pirate-chief named Menas, who was one of the guests, whispered to Pompeius: "Shall I cut the cables and make you master, not only of Sicily and Sardinia, but of the whole Roman Empire?" Pompeius, after a moment's thought, replied: "Menas, you could have done this without telling me beforehand; but now we must leave things as they are. I cannot break my word."

Pompeius's response displayed rare conduct for that tumultuous period, yet it was fitting for the son of so distinguished a father. And it saved Antony from assassination.

In September 39 B.C., Octavia presented Antony with a daughter named Antonia, who would become the grandmother of the emperor Nero. Shortly thereafter, Antony sailed to Greece, taking up his quarters once more in Athens and resuming the same lifestyle that he had enjoyed in Alexandria. Like Cleopatra, Octavia could not prevent his infidelities, especially since his endeavors to emulate Hercules often led him to boast of the scores of children he had fathered. The New Dionysus indulged in such wild sprees that he astounded even the most hedonistic Athenians. No doubt, good news from the East did much to encourage his frivolities. The rebel leader Bessus had defeated the Parthians in two important battles, and among the heavy losses were the king's son and the Parthians' most able general.

The alliance made at Misenum was already crumbling. The fleets of Pompeius continued to harass the supply routes by cutting off the grain ships that were so critical for the Roman economy, and to offset this, Octavian, now certain that he and Pompeius would eventually have to battle each other, launched a massive shipbuilding program of his own. Since his relations with Pompeius were at the breaking point, Octavian had no further use of Scribonia. The marriage was dissolved and he attached himself to Livia Drusilla, a direct descendant of the ancient house of the

Claudii. Only nineteen, she was already married and pregnant with her second child by her husband Tiberius Claudius Nero. This did not deter Octavian. Acting as a Roman triumvir, he declared that Livia's marriage to Tiberius be immediately dissolved, then annulled his own marriage with Scribonia on the very day she bore him a daughter. In January, 38 B.C., he married Livia and three months later she gave birth to her second son, whom Octavian sent to her former husband. Consequently, the cynical Romans began circulating songs and verses congratulating Octavian and Livia on their miraculous feat of having a three-month child.

There was no question that Antony, who exuded charm and vitality, was more admired than Octavian with his thin frame and sickly nature. Moreover, Octavian was a curious-tempered man, morose, quietly cruel, and secretly vicious. So many persons were tortured and crucified by him that he became known as the Executioner. His manner was stiff and always controlled in public, but in private life he indulged in wild orgies, gambled, and surrounded himself with rough companions. During his reign of terror, most of the Roman populace hated the very sight of him.

In further contrast to Antony, Octavian's appearance was unimposing. He was short in stature and careless in his deportment. His pock marked complexion was sallow and unhealthy, and his teeth were much decayed. He never looked well groomed or clean and was notably averse to taking a bath. In the summer, he always wore a broad-brimmed hat to protect his head from the sun's brilliance, and in the winter he dressed in a thick toga, at least four tunics, a shirt, and a flannel girdle, while his legs were swathed in yards of warm cloth. Despite these obsessive preventative measures, he constantly suffered from colds in his head and was always sneezing and coughing.

He was the exact opposite of the New Dionysus, who dissipated his robust body in endless bouts of drinking and sexual indulgence. Antony had willingly allowed Cleopatra to take full control over him and make him into one of her own creatures. Under her influence, he became as foreign as she, putting away his Roman clothes and dressing in a manner not in accordance with the customs of his native land. More than anyone else, Octavian was repulsed by his unpatriotic behavior. "Let nobody henceforth consider him to be a Roman citizen," he pronounced, "but rather an Egyptian; let us not call him Antony, but rather Serapis. He has discarded all the august titles of his native land and become a cymbal player from Canopus."

By circulating such criticism, Octavian hoped to reduce his Roman rival to a foreign woman's plaything. After all, it was impossible for anyone who indulged in a life of royal luxury and spent most of his time with a woman to have a manly thought or do a manly deed. But instead of hurting Antony, the ugly rumors and accusations somehow endeared him even more to the populace. This, plus his well-executed victory over the Parthians, the first in Roman history, catapulted him to the heights of popularity.

In the spring of 38 B.C., Octavian's inexperienced and badly trained fleet engaged Pompeius at sea and was soundly defeated. Octavian was not disheartened, and though he launched plans for a second attack on Pompeius, he knew that his real enemy was Antony. In preparation, Octavian gathered the brilliant military strategist, Agrippa, and the richest and most influential men of Rome, including the poets Virgil and Horace, to his side. Antony, on the other hand, had only his concubines, his jugglers, entertainers—and Cleopatra.

In January, the Triumvirate was renewed for another five years. Antony's wife Octavia was instrumental in gaining this alliance between the three rivals, for no matter how disturbed she was about her husband's notorious antics, she was prepared to prevent any conflict between Antony and her brother. Octavian, embarrassed by his first loss to Sextus Pompeius, quickly set out to build an even larger naval force, but to achieve this goal he had to enter into an uneasy agreement with Antony whereby he was to supply 20,000 legionaries for Antony's second and much-larger-scale Parthian campaign, in return for which he would receive 130 ships from Antony. Unlike the first disastrous operation against the "Son of Neptune" (as Pompeius boastfully called himself), Octavian was determined that this encounter would not fail through lack of preparation, and throughout that whole year, with Agrippa at his side, he worked diligently, constructing even more ships and training crews for the ultimate confrontation with Pompeius.

Agrippa's skills went far beyond the military. He was a brilliant administrator and planner. He knew that to defeat Pompeius, the first requirement was a really good harbor, protected from storm and foe alike. Near the shore east of Misenum, at the northern end of the Bay of Naples, there were two lakes, Lucrinus and Avernus, which were joined by canals to each other and to the sea. Here the new fleet was assembled in absolute security. Freed slaves were instructed in oarsmanship for a whole year, and in the manipulation of a new device (invented by Agrippa himself) whereby grapnels were shot from catapults to facilitate the holding and boarding of an enemy ship.

During Octavian's naval preparations, Antony was already on his way back to the East. His wife Octavia came with him as far as the island of Corfu, but using the argument that she was once again pregnant and sea travel would be dangerous to her health, he sent her back to Rome. When Octavian heard about this, he was enraged. It was as though Antony were telling him, *Have your sister back. I don't want her or her children.*

On reaching Antioch, Antony summoned Cleopatra to come there and meet with him. "His passion for Cleopatra," wrote Plutarch, "which everyone [including Cleopatra herself] thought had been lulled, now broke out anew, and finally, like the stubborn and rebellious beast of the soul, of which Plato speaks, he flung away all sensible counsel and sent Fonteius Capito to bring her to Syria."

Antony and Cleopatra spent the winter of 37 B.C. in Antioch. It was a regal city, third in line to Rome and Alexandria, and as the capital of Syria it possessed many elegant works of mosaic art in its homes, buildings, and monuments. To reach the city, which was considerably inland from the sea, Cleopatra's galleys had to ease first into the bustling harbor of Alexandretta. As she was transported in a carriage across the wide square of the city, she noticed the many obelisks that lined both sides of the main street. At the extreme outskirts of Alexandretta, they were confronted by a huge mountain range over which they had to climb to reach Antioch. Hillmen and mules were waiting for them at the foothills of Mt. Silpius. Cleopatra and her attendants were mounted on mules, and the entourage proceeded into the heart of the mountains, led by the hillmen on their scrawny ponies, while her soldiers protected the rear from any attack by robbers and plunderers. Behind them, Alexandretta had already disappeared from view. Thick layers of ice coated their path as they moved across a wide sun-drenched plateau. The footing became perilous for the animals, and the hillmen had to lead them by hand through a tunnel of deep gorges that glistened with gigantic mirrors of ice. Within an hour, they reached a small mountain village that clung like an eagle's nest to a precipitous cliff. Clay huts hugged narrow terraces that were arranged in symmetrical steps as a protection against the winds lashing at them overhead. It was now unbearably cold. The hillmen wanted to stop and rest, build a fire, but the soldiers commanded them to continue until they struggled up yet another incline and at last came to the summit. Far below them lay the sun-bleached city of Antioch.

The place was exactly as Cleopatra had envisioned it—a broad sprawling plain spreading itself along the brown shores of a swollen lake, the Orontes River cutting its silvery path into Asia Minor under the heedful eye of Mt. Casius, clouds of white birds circling over the red-tiled roofs, thin spirals of smoke from a thousand ovens—and all around, everywhere, the encroaching mountains. She could not understand why the Romans, until Caesar, had expressed a boundless contempt for Antioch. Indeed, this was a splendid city, ideally situated, massive mountains protecting the fertile valleys, woods, and freshwater streams.

Antony and Cleopatra spent the rest of the winter here. They dined at endless banquets, enjoyed the theater, the baths, made love; and in the spring of 36 B.C., Antony, accompanied by Cleopatra, set out with his legions on a final march against the Parthians. She had hoped to remain at his side throughout the operation, but she got no farther than the Armenian frontier town of Zeugma when she realized she was pregnant. At Antony's insistence, she reluctantly made her way back to Alexandria, the slow, tedious route taking her through Damascus, across the Sea of Galilee, and along the river Jordan to Jericho and a meeting with Herod. The Jewish historian Josephus, writing a full century after the event, and as a biased client of the emperor Vespasian, claimed she attempted to seduce Herod, but this could hardly be true since she despised Herod and he felt the same way toward her, especially after Antony had assigned to her the choicest portions of Herod's territory: the balsam-producing groves of Jericho. Furthermore, she couldn't have been that seductive to Herod while carrying Antony's child. Equally unlikely is Josephus's claim that Herod planned to murder Cleopatra and was dissuaded by his counselors who begged him to do nothing rash, for Antony would never countenance it.

"What actually did happen," wrote the historian Appian, is that Cleopatra agreed to lease to Herod that part of Judaea which Antony had given her for the sum of two hundred talents a year. This pleased Herod and he escorted her and her entourage as far as the frontier town of Pelu-sium, after which she made her way safely back to Alexandria and settled down in her Royal Palaces to await the birth of her child, a son, who would be given the name Ptolemy Philadelphus.

The enemies of Parthia had always invaded the country from the west across the desert, but Antony decided to launch a surprise attack from the north. The scheme required much planning and organization, a skill Antony lacked. Another problem, a major one, was the necessity of se-crecy and hiding the army with its 60,000 legionaries, 10,000 horsemen, and 30,000 soldiers from the eastern provinces. Behind this huge force trailed a long line of siege weapons and engines of war, including a bat-tering ram 80 feet in length.

Soon after this, Antony began sending dispatches to Cleopatra in Alexandria, imploring her to come to his aid and bring him money so he could pay his complaining soldiers. Momentarily, Cleopatra's hopes were crushed. By this time, she had expected Antony to return to her in glory after having defeated the Parthians and opened the road through Persia to India and the East. The Romans would then hail him as their conquering hero, and the unpopular Octavian would be cast into oblivion.

From Zeugma, Antony marched to the plateau of Erzeroum and re-viewed his enormous army, which had grown even larger with the addi-tion of 13,000 cavalry and foot soldiers supplied by Artavasdes, king of Armenia, plus a strong force provided by King Polemo of Pontus. The heavy engines of war were dispatched, together with the contingents from Armenia and Pontus, toward Media along the valley of the Araxes, while Antony's forces took the more direct route across northern Assyria into Media.

The news of his approach in such force not only alarmed the Parthi-ans, but filled northern India with fear, and indeed, made all Asia uncom-fortable. It was generally supposed that he would march in triumph through Persia, and carry his arms, like Alexander the Great, into India, where Cleopatra's ships, coming across the high-sea trade route from Egypt, would meet him with money and supplies.

Toward the end of August, Antony reached the city of Phraaspa, the capital of Media Atropatene, and waited there for the arrival of his siege train with its engines of war and accompanying soldiers. He had hardly settled in Phraaspa when he received news that his second army had been attacked and defeated, that his entire siege train had been captured, that the king of Armenia had fled with the remnant of his forces back to his own country, and that the king of Pontus had been taken prisoner. Nevertheless, Antony bravely decided to launch the attack on Phraaspa, but before he could begin, the Parthian army, fresh from its victory at Carrhae against the kings of Armenia and Pontus, arrived at Phraaspa and began harassing Antony's forces without really engaging them in open battle. These delaying tactics proved disastrous. Antony now faced the possibility of conducting a war at a time when the mountain passes of Parthia would soon be heavy with snow. Already his army was destitute and despondent; and their provisions were rapidly running out.

In desperation, he sent a message to the Parthian king, requesting that all Roman prisoners be returned, together with the Eagles (the symbols of Roman arms and prowess) taken in the Battle of Carrhae. In return, Antony promised to lift the siege and depart from Parthia.

The king, refusing these terms, declared that if Antony withdrew from Parthia, his retreat would not be molested, and to this, Antony had no choice but to agree. It was a terrible loss not getting his prisoners back, but losing the Eagles was a gross insult, for if he had been able to return to Rome with them, his whole campaign would have been justified in the eyes of the people.

The Parthians did not keep their word.

As the weary and starving legionaries crossed the snow-covered mountains, they were mercilessly attacked by the fierce Parthian tribesmen, who ambushed them at every pass, and even followed at their rear to cut off stragglers. The intense cold, the lack of food, and the extreme weariness of the troops, caused the number of these stragglers to increase rapidly; and besides the thousands of men who were thus cut off or killed in the daily fighting, a greater number perished from exposure and want of food. At one period, so great was the scarcity of provisions that a loaf of bread was worth its weight in silver. The Roman historian Dio Cassius writes that, at this time, large numbers of men, having devoured a certain root which seemed edible, went mad and died. "He who had eaten of this root remembered nothing in the world and employed himself only in moving great stones from one place to another, which he did with much earnestness and industry; and thus through all the camp there was nothing to be seen but men grubbing upon the ground at stones, which they carried from place to place, until in the end they vomited and died."

Throughout this long and terrible march, Antony behaved with remarkable bravery and endurance. Not only did he share every hardship with his men, but when camp was pitched at night, he went from tent to tent, talking to the legionaries and cheering them with encouraging words. The respect that his soldiers felt for him as their leader, their obedience and goodwill, and the degree of loyalty, by which every man—whether good or bad, officers or private soldiers—chose honor and favor from Antony rather than life and safety, was something even the greatest generals could not have commanded. There were many reasons for this: Antony's nobility of birth, his eloquence, his simple manners, his largesse, the very way he treated his soldiers, making even the wounded and the sick as eager to serve him as those who were well and strong.

On one occasion, during their difficult march toward Armenia, the Romans formed their famous *testudo* (tortoise) as a defense against the Parthians who rushed down from a steep hill to attack them. The shield-bearers wheeled about, enclosing the lighter-armed troops within their ranks while they themselves dropped on one knee and held their shields out in front of them. The second rank held their shields over the heads of the first, and the next rank likewise. This tactic produced a most striking appearance, like the roof over a house. It was particularly effective against arrows, which merely skimmed off the Roman shields harmlessly.

The Parthians, seeing the Romans dropping on one knee, thought they were exhausted, so they laid aside their bows and came in at close quarters with their spears, at which point the Romans suddenly sprang up with a battle cry, killed the foremost of the enemy with their javelins, and put the rest to rout.

At last, after twenty-seven days of cold and famine, during which they had beaten off the Parthians no less than eighteen times, Antony's forces crossed the river Araxes into Armenia. Antony made a review of his troops here and was distressed to learn that he had lost a large number of legionaries and cavalry, most of whom had died from exposure and illness. Although the Parthians had now been left behind, the Romans still had to face the severe winter and a long march through Armenia into Syria, which involved more difficulties. By the time they reached the coast, another 8,000 men had perished.

They went into winter quarters at a small town north of Sidon called the White Village, where Antony eagerly awaited the arrival of Cleopatra. Throughout the entire retreat from Parthia, he had managed to keep up the morale of his troops and hold them together by his strength and courage, but now he felt so ashamed at his failure, so unhappy at the thought of Cleopatra's reproaches for his defeat, he turned in despair to the false comfort of wine, and daily drank himself into a state of oblivious intoxication. But even here, in the midst of his drinking, he would spring up from the table and run down to the seashore to scan the horizon for a sight of her sails.

He and his men were in this deplorable condition, haggard and unkempt, clad in rags, when at last Cleopatra's fleet was sighted off the coast of the White Village.

Although Antony failed dismally with the Parthians, Octavian, aided by the military genius of Agrippa, had just achieved a remarkable naval victory in his campaign against Sextus Pompeius. The battle took place near Mylae off the east coast of Sicily. The two opposing fleets were equal in numbers, three hundred on each side. Agrippa's heavy ships seized one after another of Pompeius's, and in the hand-to-hand combat that ensued, Pompeius's forces suffered heavy casualties. Many of the sailors attempted to flee but were driven ashore on the treacherous limestone coast and captured. Only seventeen ships managed to escape, and as they rounded into the Strait of Messina, Pompeius, having already abandoned his army, climbed aboard one of the galleys and set sail for Alexandria to throw in his lot with Antony.

The troops that Pompeius left behind surrendered to Octavian, who was now in possession not only of Italy and the West, but also of Sicily and Sardinia. Throughout those morbid weeks in Alexandria, Cleopatra did her utmost to restore Antony's spirit and rejuvenate his hopes of becoming master of the Roman world. She constantly uplifted his sagging morale by reminding him that he had her at his side, also his children, Alexandria, and potentially all the wealth of the East. She remained close to him as he reassembled and equipped his legions, offered him the Egyptian fleet, which was second to none, and even reassured him that he would in time return to Parthia and gain his elusive victory.

After a brief sojurn on the island of Mytilene, Sextus Pompeius set out for Alexandria, hoping to join forces with Antony, but in the meantime

Antony, after learning that Pompeius was engaged in a secret correspondence with the Parthians, now resolved to capture him and put him to death. The order was carried out by Marcus Titius, the nephew of the governor of Syria, who effected Pompeius's arrest in Phrygia on the Asia Minor coast, then executed him in Miletus shortly thereafter.

This act did not meet with the approval of the Roman people, who still respected the son of the great Pompey; but with Octavian it was a far different matter. Antony had executed his most dreaded enemy, and in appreciation Octavian decreed that statues to Antony be erected in the Forum. Adding to this, he granted Antony the equal right to hold banquets with his wife and family in the Temple of Concord, which may have seemed an insignificant honor, but Octavian was really looking out for his sister Octavia, and in essence was saying to Antony: *This is where you belong, in Rome with your wife and family—not in Egypt!*

Antony, however, had no desire to leave Cleopatra and the East. Now more than ever, he was determined to erase the memory of his bitter defeat and strike back at the Parthians. Fuel was added to this obsessive impulse by the sudden arrival in Alexandria of the king of Pontus, who had been captured by the Parthians when they attacked the siege train, and was held a prisoner throughout the winter by the king of Media. The long pact between Media and Parthia had suddenly been broken and, through the king of Pontus, the king of Media informed Antony that they should form a new alliance against their common enemy, the Parthians. Antony was overjoyed, but not Cleopatra. Her reasons were twofold: she was afraid that Antony might suffer another humiliating defeat, perhaps the final and most degrading of all; and secondly, she wanted him at her side in Alexandria because she had just learned that Octavian, always the cunning politician, had sent his sister to Athens for a reunion with Antony.

Unlike Caesar, who rarely allowed his emotions to get in the way of politics, Antony was an easy victim of Cleopatra's charms. She now pretended to be dying of love for Antony—dieting to make her body more slender, opening her eyes wide with love whenever he drew near, and languishing or fainting whenever he left. She often took great pains to be seen in tears, which she would swiftly wipe away after everyone was gone.

Her friends and courtiers did their part also, pointing out that Octavia had only married Antony as a political act urged by her brother, whereas Cleopatra had chosen to be his mistress out of love. At any rate, Antony decided to postpone the campaign against the Parthians until the next spring. He had learned from bitter experience that autumn was not the season to be ensnared in the biting cold and deep snows of the Parthian mountains.

Octavia, deciding there was no further reason for her to remain in Athens, returned to Rome and immediately put her foot down on any attempt by her brother to capitalize on the affair. She refused to leave her husband's house as Octavian had ordered her to do, and she even begged him to ignore Antony's treatment of her, saying that it would be infamous if the two rulers of the world should plunge it into civil war for the sake of a woman. She confirmed her words by her deeds and lived in her home just as if her husband were still there, caring not only for her own children, but also for those that Fulvia had borne Antony. Beyond this, she even received any friends Antony sent to the capital, and helped them obtain an audience with her brother. Little did she realize, however, that she was inadvertently damaging Antony by her conduct, making him even more hated by the Romans for wronging such a fine woman.

On the surface, it seemed apparent that Cleopatra had won, but Octavian was the real victor. He had outmaneuvered his rival for the second time and was now in a position of great strength. Antony paid no heed. Abandoning his plans to attack the Parthians, he returned to Alexandria, and in Rome the gossipmongers had a field day: "Was this the man who claimed descent from Hercules? Was this the God of War, this caricature of a man gone soft and enslaved by a woman?"

The Romans mockingly associated Antony and Cleopatra with the legendary Hercules and Omphale, the queen of Lydia, who had kept the hero in bondage to her for three years, making him perform women's tasks about her palace. Propertius, a Roman poet of the first century B.C., wrote an elegy on the subject, and subsequently drinking vessels unearthed in Italy depicted the implied legend: Hercules riding in a chariot drawn by centaurs, attired in a Greek woman's dress, while maidservants held a parasol over his head. Another servant waved a fan, as others brought him the traditional emblems of the housewife: a spindle and a skein of wool. To stress the point even further, Omphale drove the chariot and wore the hero's helmet and lion skin. In her left hand, she held the club of Hercules, and with her right, she reached out to grasp the hero's vast wine bowl.

Being the butt of such cruel Roman jokes greatly affected Antony, and once again he fell into a deep depression from which Cleopatra eventually released him. They spent the waning months of 35 B.C. quietly in Alexandria, enjoying the theater, dining, and playing dice. Unlike his first winter in Alexandria, there were no drunken escapades for Antony, no orgies.

In the spring, he at last launched his campaign, and although he let it be known that it was to be against the Parthians, he in fact decided on an easier objective: the kingdom of Armenia. Accordingly, he led his forces into Armenia and took King Artavasdes prisoner. His army looted, raped, desecrated the ancient temples, melted down statues of the gods for their gold and silver, and hauled away the entire royal treasure. It wasn't a grand victory, but at this moment in Antony's career, he badly needed something to improve his morale.

Meanwhile, in Rome, the people expected him to return to the capital city and celebrate his conquest of Armenia in the usual grand fashion: free banquets, public entertainment, games and spectacles. Octavia too anticipated his return, hoping that he would once and for all cast aside Cleopatra and resume his life with her and the children.

⟨ⱬⱡⱡⱡⱠ⟩

But Antony had no intention of returning to Rome. That autumn, he decreed that his Triumph should be celebrated not in Rome but in Alexandria, something that had never happened before in Roman history. Only the Senate, after an investigation of all the records of the campaign, had the power to issue a Triumph, the highest honor that Rome could confer upon any man. For Antony to decree himself this honor, and far worse, to hold it in the capital of a foreign country, was the greatest insult against Rome, her people, and the entire nation. Antony was well aware of this, but he was not to be dissuaded. He knew that the main wealth of the empire was to be derived from the East, not Gaul or obscure Britain, nor even mineral-abundant Spain. The countries of the East were rich in gold, silver, gems, linen and sailcloth, Tyrian dyes, glass, and papyrus; more importantly, their institutions of learning were far better than any to be found in Italy. Alexandria had a further advantage over Rome: from Alexandria, a march of six hundred or eight hundred miles brought one to Antioch or Tarsus; whereas Rome was nearly three times as far from these great centers. The southern Peloponnesus was, by way of Crete, considerably nearer to Alexandria than it was to Rome by way of Brundisium (Brindisi). Ephesus and other cities of Asia Minor could be reached more quickly by land or sea from Egypt than they could from Rome. Furthermore, Rhodes, Lycia, Bithynia, Galatia, Pamphilia, Cilicia, Cappadocia, Pontus, Armenia, Crete, Cyprus, and many other great and important lands were all closer to Alexandria than Rome.

Octavian seized this opportunity to capitalize on the public resentment against Antony by skillfully emphasizing the non-Roman character of the East, with its princes, potentates, kings, "and at their command, a Queen, followed by a dog-like, devoted Antony, a Roman who had lost all shame."

Despite this current of ill feeling, Antony defiantly proceeded with the celebration of his Triumph. Leading the procession was a body of Roman legionaries bearing on their shields the large letter *C,* which some claimed stood for Cleopatra, and others for Caesar, either of which was an offense in Roman eyes, for only Octavian, by benefit of Julius Caesar's will, had the right to bear the name of Caesar. If, on the other hand, the name stood for Cleopatra, it was unthinkable that Roman legionaries would bear the initial of a foreign monarch, as though they owed allegiance to her and not to Rome.

The Roman troops were followed by select units of the Egyptian army, contingents from allies and client states of the Roman Empire, and also by the Armenian soldiers taken as prisoners, including Artavasdes in golden chains, accompanied by his wife and children. Lined up behind these came the usual procession of carriages laden with the spoils of war: captured insignia and emblems, and the Armenian treasury. These in turn were followed by deputies from the various vassal cities in the East, each bearing a golden crown awarded to Antony.

Finally came the victor himself, in his elegant chariot and dressed not as a general of Rome, but in the guise of Dionysus, carrying the god's thyrsus (a reed tipped with a spear point and with a pinecone at the top), and wearing the god's garland of ivy. The procession made its way through the main streets of Alexandria so that the majority of the inhabitants could enjoy the splendor that Antony and his queen were conferring upon them and upon Egypt. The spectacle started from the Royal Palaces at Lochias and moved solemnly through the Forum, onward into the wide thoroughfare of Canopus and past the hill of Pan, until eventually it reached the Serapium, the elaborate temple to the principal god of the city, Serapis. He became the Greek god of Alexandria, whose great cult statue, with its golden head and jeweled eyes gleaming from its darkened shrine, stood out as one of the chief glories of the city.

Waiting for the procession to reach the high ground before the Serapium, Cleopatra stood surrounded by her court officials and the important dignitaries of Alexandria. She was seated on a golden throne, with the priests of Serapis on each side of her, all waiting for Antony to make his way into the temple. After dismounting from his chariot, Antony greeted her, then went into the temple and performed his sacrifice to Serapis, the god who had brought him victory. By this act, he deliberately insulted Rome, the Motherland, and the gods of the Roman people.

It was customary for all royal prisoners to be put to death, but Cleopatra was lenient to Artavasdes, who declined to kneel in homage before her and instead merely addressed her by name. Both Antony and Cleopatra respected Artavasdes' nobility of bearing, and for this he and his family were not harmed and even treated with honor. Cleopatra certainly was aware that Artavasdes was no barbarian king, but a man of considerable refinement, a poet and a playwright; and Antony (unlike "Octavian the Executioner") was rarely cruel or vindictive.

A vast banquet was given to all the inhabitants of Alexandria, and later that afternoon an extension of the celebration was held in the Gymnasium near the tomb of Alexander the Great. On a silver dais erected in the center of the stadium, two golden thrones were set, with four smaller golden thrones around them. Antony and Cleopatra took their seats on the two thrones, while the four others were occupied by the thirteen-year-old Caesarion, Cleopatra's twins by Antony (Alexander Helios and Cleopatra Selene), and the little two-year-old Ptolemy Philadelphus, also Antony's child. Seated there as Dionysus and Isis, Antony and Cleopatra were making it known to the world that the Empire of the East was not to be governed by Rome, but ruled from Alexandria, and that they now considered themselves sole potentates of the eastern half of the empire.

In the presence of city dignitaries, the army, and the immense crowd of Alexandrians, Antony delivered his address, and Cleopatra was proclaimed queen of Egypt, Cyprus, Libya, and the southern part of Syria. Caesarion was named co-regent of these areas, and given the title king of kings.

Caesarion was the very image of his father Julius Caesar, and might possibly have made an excellent ruler of the whole Roman world. It is curious to think of Antony conferring upon Caesar's son by Cleopatra so grandiose a title, but it must be borne in mind that the whole episode was no more than a piece of statecraft and the execution of a carefully conceived plan to remove from Octavian the richest part of the empire. Caesarion sat proudly in Roman dress, but Antony's male children by Cleopatra wore the costumes of the countries they were one day to govern. Thus, Alexander Helios was arrayed in the Persian style of clothing that was also worn in Armenia and Media: trousers, a flowing cloak over a sleeved tunic, and a tiara on his head from which hung (like an Arab burnous) a cloth flap to cover the neck. His infant brother (Ptolemy Philadelphus) was dressed in Macedonian costume—with the boots of Macedonia, a purple cloak, and the Macedonian cap with a diadem around it.

From a political standpoint, the most important part of this ceremony was Antony's bestowal of honor to Caesar's son in preference to his and Cleopatra's own children. By this act, he was declaring that "Octavian was no more than a usurper, and that this child of Caesar's flesh and blood was the rightful inheritor of all the Western Empire as well as the East."

But it was Cleopatra who gained the most, for this surely was the greatest day of her life. She was not only confirmed as the queen of the Eastern Empire, but she was now universally acknowledged as King Antony's wife and the mother of his children.

❦

"To the Romans, the ocean remained an object of terror rather than of romance." From the time of their battles with Carthage, the Romans considered legionary service to be an honorable duty, whereas service at sea was no more than a necessary evil. For this reason, Rhodes and Pergamum (both important naval states of Rome) provided a large part of the Roman navy. Sailors were also supplied from Syria and Lebanon. Up to the age of Caracalla, there were no Roman citizens among the naval personnel in the Battles of Misenum and Ravenna.

In Cleopatra's time, the Mediterranean was traversed regularly by oared vessels and also by large sailing ships, some weighing up to 1,000 tons. Among these were the Egyptian grain ships that made regular sailings between Alexandria and Italy. Cleopatra was familiar with all of them, at least thirty different types, as she gazed out at the harbor from her palace on the promontory of Lochias. There were *barides*, the big Egyptian cargo-bearers; *camarae*, small open boats that could hold about twenty-five men; *celoces*, the fast cutters that were used as dispatch boats for fleet communications; *cercuri*, war galleys from the isle of Corfu; and *corbitae*, the large Roman vessels that depended almost entirely upon sail. One of these was on record as having carried as many as six hundred passengers. In addition, there came from Syria and Phoenicia the cargo-carrying *gauloi* (tubs), and from the Adriatic the *lembi*, small swift warships which, unlike war galleys, had no ram on their bows. The light and exceedingly fast vessels used for scouting and shadowing duties were known as *speculatoriae* (spies). Their sails and ropes were dyed blue, the color of the seawater; and even the wax with which the hull was painted was similarly colored, while the soldiers and sailors aboard them likewise dyed their clothes.

The main warship was the *bireme*, propelled by two banks of oars. This vessel had changed very little since its evolution during the great Battle of Salamis in Greece. For a short period of time the *trireme*, with three banks of oars, superseded it, but the bireme proved to be just as fast and much more maneuverable.

Some of the vessels in Cleopatra's navy were designed for "vain pomp," but the warships that she was about to contribute to Antony's cause, together with their experienced Greek crews, were vastly superior to any others. They were large, heavily timbered biremes, equipped with fighting castles from which arrows and other projectiles could be hurled at the enemy, while grapnels could be cast by catapults to secure the opposing ship alongside.

After his naval victory over Sextus Pompeius, Agrippa decided to build a lighter type of warship. Named the *Liburnian*, after a district in Illyria on the Adriatic, this ship had evolved over the centuries under the guidance of local builders who were famous for their skill in seamanship and navigation. Although they were built with two banks of oars, they were designed principally for speed and maneuverability, either under oar or canvas. In the stormy Adriatic, where the bora (north wind) can at times blow at 100 knots, the *Liburnian* was unchallenged as the finest warship of its time. Like all biremes, it had a long underwater ram constructed at the bow for punching a hole in the enemy's side. Its huge square sail enabled the ship to reach a speed of 6 knots or more, while at the same time giving the oarsmen a respite from their strenuous task. Most sea travel at this time was confined to the months between spring and autumn.

During the winter of 32 B.C., Cleopatra's fleet of warships was refitted and made ready for battle. Octavian's strength seemed to be far superior in quality than that of Antony. In numbers, they were about the same, although Octavian's troops had not suffered the defeat that Antony endured against the Parthians. Most of Octavian's soldiers were native-born Romans, whereas Antony, apart from a few Roman legions, had to contend with a heterogeneous collection from foreign provinces and client states.

These two men who were about to challenge each other in battle were worlds apart in their private lives. For all his faults as drinker and buffoon, Antony was known as sensitive and kind, and generous to extremes. By contrast, Octavian tended to be sly and cunning, forever secretive. They were both promiscuous in their sexual habits, but Octavian indulged in innumerable affairs and on many occasions would send his servants out into the streets of Rome to find women for his pleasure. He even took the wives of his friends away from dinner parties and brought them to his sleeping chambers if he found them attractive.

The following spring, Antony and Cleopatra went to Ephesus, one of the most illustrious Greek cities on the Asia Minor coast. After months of preparation assembling his army and his fleet, Antony was now ready for his confrontation with Octavian. Cleopatra felt very much at home in Ephesus. The patron goddess of the city was Artemis, who had long flourished in Asia and dominated nearly all the Mediterranean world. Until it was burned, her shrine, the Artemision, with its 60-foot columns, was one of the wonders of the ancient world, along with the two Egyptian marvels, the pyramids and Pharos Lighthouse. It seemed unlikely that Antony would lose. He had all the wealth of the East at his command, and the queen of the richest country in the world was his wife. On top of this, he had the best sailors from Egypt and Asia Minor, and all the shipbuilding resources of Greece. He also had 50,000 Roman legionaries and 80,000 infantry and cavalry from the eastern provinces. In addition, even more ships were being built on the neighboring island of Cos and throughout the chief ports of Asia Minor. Cleopatra herself had brought her huge Egyptian fleet, plus large sums of money to pay the troops and to buy grain, clothing, and arms. She willingly staked her entire fortune, knowing that the impending battle between Antony and Octavian was essentially a war between the East and the West: between Rome, which had cruelly exploited its provinces and client states, and Alexandria, which had become the center of Hellenistic culture and civilization.

The Roman historian Dio Cassius believed that the real cause of the war between Antony and Octavian was Antony's recognition of young Caesarion's legitimate right to Julius Caesar's inheritance. Assisting Antony in this ultimate challenge against Octavian were the richest and most powerful rulers of the East, including the kings of Cappadocia, Cilicia, Paphlagonia, and Pontus, King Amyntas of Galicia, King Mithridates of Commagene, Kings Sadalas and Rhoemateles of Thrace, and King Bogud of Mauretania. They all hastened to Antony's side in rebellion against the dominance imposed upon them by Rome; and through Antony's association with Cleopatra, they now felt confident that a new power would rise up in the East, which would eventually enable them to rule the entire world. Along with these powerful rulers from the East, Antony had the solid support of four hundred senators from Rome who regarded him as the protector of Caesarion. In fact, it was strongly believed in Rome that the document that decreed Octavian the heir of Caesar was not the dictator's last testament, but that he had made a later will in favor of Caesarion. Thus, to the Roman people, Antony was fighting to carry out Caesar's wishes to overthrow the usurping Octavian.

Throughout the year of 32 B.C., Octavian allowed Antony to take up a firm position in Asia Minor and even encouraged him to make the first move. However, Antony was not yet ready. He had to assemble a strong force from many nations, making it necessary to enlarge his fleet so that he could transport them to battle. This meant more delays. Nevertheless, both Antony and Cleopatra were so confident of victory they decided that this was the ideal time for a great celebration; and they set sail for the island of Samos.

After all the kings, dynasts, tetrarchs, nations, and cities between Syria, the Mareotic Lake, Armenia, and Illyria had been ordered to send or bring their equipment for the war, the fun-loving friends of Antony, including actors and actresses, musicians, entertainers, and clowns, were invited to appear in Samos. While most of the world was suffering under war and sickness, this one island in the Aegean resounded with the music of flutes and harps. The theaters were filled, and choruses competed against one another. Every city of the known world sent an ox for sacrifice, and kings vied with one another in entertainment and gifts.

Toward the end of May, Antony and Cleopatra, together with their assembled forces, finally sailed for Athens, where once again sports and entertainment took up most of their time. Numerous banquets were given, both by Antony and Cleopatra, during which the behavior of Antony was often crass and undignified. On one state occasion, he caused considerable excitement by going across to Cleopatra in the middle of the meal and rubbing her feet, a ministration performed only by a slave.

Cleopatra, well aware that Octavia, through her beauty and intelligence, had captured the hearts of the Athenians, wasted no time in making herself popular with all the important citizens of the city, and when this was achieved, she informed Antony that it was now the appropriate moment for him to send the formal letter of divorce to his wife. But Antony, who had heard all this many times before, was uncertain about making a final breach with Octavian. Besides, his Roman friends came to him in alarm, pointing out that his brutal treatment of Octavia, who had won Rome's sympathy by her quiet and dutiful behavior, would turn from him a great number of his supporters in Italy, and would be received as a clear indication of his subservience to Cleopatra. In his younger days, Antony would have faced this challenge with a different mind and a much lighter heart, but now the power of his will had been undermined by excessive drinking and lovemaking. Moreover, since he was nearly fifty and Cleopatra only thirty-eight, he had become increasingly dependent upon her in all things.

At this time, two defectors from Antony's army (Titius and Plancus), who had had their own falling-out with Cleopatra, arrived in Rome and immediately began to spread rumors about Antony. Plancus in particular related that Antony was so gravely under Cleopatra's magical spell that he insisted that the Ephesians hail her as queen, and when this was done she forced him to present her (for the Library in Alexandria) the entire library of Pergamum, consisting of more than 200,000 volumes. Titius, not to be out done, informed Octavian about the contents of Antony's will. The document, as was customary, had been lodged with the Vestal Virgins who, in their role as symbols of purity, guaranteed the will's inviolability until Antony's death. Fearing that this could convince the Senate and the Roman people, Octavian sent notice to the Vestal Virgins and demanded that the will be handed over to him, but they refused, saying they were not allowed to do so. In a fit of rage, Octavian went personally to the Vestal Virgins and seized it, after which he read it aloud to the full Senate. At first, they objected, maintaining that Octavian had obtained it illegally and furthermore that it would not be right to hold Antony accountable for his dispositions after death while he was still alive.

The contents of the will astonished the Senate. Antony had not only confirmed the "Donations" of the Eastern Empire but also the legitimacy of Caesarion as Caesar's rightful heir to the whole empire. Another clause in the will sealed the case against Antony: if he were to die, his body was to be conveyed in solemn procession through the Forum, and after this it was to be shipped to Cleopatra and buried in the Mausoleum at Alexandria alongside Alexander the Great.

The Senate fully realized the implications. Rome, after all, was the capital city and should be the proper burial place for its heroes and distinguished citizens, but with this document Antony was now breaking away from a noble tradition and intended to be buried like a Ptolemy in Rome's rival city of the East.

⌖

Antony now decided to wait for Octavian to attack him, chiefly because he had the utmost confidence in his great fleet to destroy Octavian's forces before they could land on the shores of Greece. He also felt that Octavian's army (and all of Italy herself) would be devastated by still another war, but in Greece and Asia Minor it would make hardly any difference. While Italy would starve, Egypt alone could supply enough wheat to feed Antony's whole army. Egypt also would provide money for regular payment of the troops, whereas Octavian did not know where to turn for funds. Confident that he would not have to fight a big battle on land, Antony subsequently felt it safe to leave four of his legions at Cyrene, another four in Egypt, and three in Syria. His army in Greece consisted of 100,000 foot soldiers and 12,000 cavalry.

In late autumn, Antony and Cleopatra advanced from Athens with the whole army and went into winter quarters at Patras, which stood near the mouth of the Gulf of Corinth on the Achaian side, about two hundred miles from the Italian coast. The fleet meanwhile was sent farther north to the Gulf of Ambracia, which had a large natural harbor with a narrow entrance; outposts were placed at Corcyra (modern Corfu), some seventy miles from the Italian coast.

Constrained by the restlessness of his army and the difficulty of providing food and supplies for them during the winter, Octavian sent a message to Antony asking him not to postpone the confrontation but to come over to Italy and fight him at once. He even promised not to oppose Antony's disembarkation and to battle him only when he was quite prepared to meet him with his full forces. Antony replied by challenging Octavian to engage him in single combat. Octavian refused, whereupon Antony invited him to bring his army over to the plains of Pharsalia (where Julius Caesar and Pompey the Great had fought seventeen years before) and to fight him there. This offer was also refused by Octavian, and thus the two massive armies settled down once more to glare at one another across the Ionian Sea.

News reached Antony and Cleopatra at Patras that Octavian, while making his official sacrifices to the gods before the outset of hostilities, had employed the ritual observed before a campaign against a *foreign* enemy. He had stood before the Temple of Bellona in the Campus Martius and, clad in the robes of a Fetial priest, had thrown the javelin as a declaration that war was about to be undertaken against an alien enemy.

Antony's fleet in the Gulf of Ambracia encountered many hardships during those winter months. The supplies had run out, and disease and starvation destroyed nearly a third of the rowing slaves and sailors. To fill their places, Antony ordered his officers to press into service every man on whom they could lay their hands. Peasants, farmhands, harvesters, plowboys, donkey drivers, and even common travelers were seized and thrust into the ships, but still their complements were incomplete, and most of them were unfit for battle.

Octavian, well informed of this turn of events, ordered a segment of his fleet to make an initial thrust against Antony on the south coast of Greece. This force seized the town of Methone and from all appearances seemed to be seeking a landing place for the main army. Antony marched down at once and prepared to hold the coast against the expected attack, but while his attention was turned in that direction, Octavian slipped across the sea from Brundisium and Tarentum, to Corcyra, and from there to the mainland, marching down through Epirus toward the Gulf of Ambracia, thus menacing Antony's ill-manned fleet lying in the harbor.

Antony sped northward in haste and arrived at the southern promontory of Actium in March 31 B.C. Almost at the same time, Octavian had reached the northern promontory on the opposite side. Antony quickly drew up his ships in battle array, manning them as much as possible with his best legionaries, and forcing Octavian to abandon any thought of immediate battle. This afforded Antony time to settle himself on the southern promontory of Actium, where he assembled an enormous camp; and a few days later he was joined there by Cleopatra.

Cleopatra made her presence known immediately after she arrived at Antony's camp with her attendants and princes. Now more than ever, she was determined to remain at Antony's side, to be there when Octavian was defeated, and to sail with the conquering army to Rome, where the queen's throne awaited her. As the weeks dragged by, with both armies restlessly camped at their positions across the entrance into the harbor of Actium, Octavian's brilliant general Agrippa deployed a small force just to the south of the Ambracian Gulf and seized the towering island of Levkas, which commanded the whole area to the south. Not only was Antony's fleet blockaded, but his army's supply source was now totally cut off. Clothing, food, weapons, and reinforcements had to be transported over narrow roads and craggy mountain paths from the south. These deprivations brought more anguish and suffering to the encamped forces, opening the door for diviners and soothsayers who profited from dire predictions: word came from Athens that a famous statue of Dionysus, with whom Antony identified himself, had crashed to the ground during a violent storm; and in Patras, almost at the same time, the temple of Hercules, Antony's supposed ancestor, was struck by lightning.

Antony, as well as his army, looked upon these unfavorable portents with alarm. To break the long stalemate, Antony decided to slip past the point of Actium with all his fleet, destroy Octavian's ships, and set sail for Rome, leaving most of his army behind. With his fleet gone, and the bulk of Antony's forces still in command of the surrounding countryside, Octavian would then be starved into surrender.

No doubt this plan of battle originated with Cleopatra, since Antony was a soldier and not a sailor. They were now fully into summer. The hot sun scorched the gulf as swarms of mosquitoes invaded the surrounding swamps. By the thousands, the defections began: first with the Galatians and their commander, who went over to Octavian's camp. Domitius Ahenobarbus followed, also deserting Antony for Octavian. Along with most of the other kings and rulers of the East, he had voiced strong opposition to Cleopatra's role in the campaign, and even went so far as to tell Antony that her presence was fatal to his cause. Torn between his love for Cleopatra and his regard for his friends and supporters, and compelled furthermore by Octavian to play the waiting game, Antony succumbed to drinking heavily once again.

The combination of the wine and the summer heat, the friction between Cleopatra and his other advisors, led to violent quarrels between him and the queen. Canidius, the commander of Antony's land forces, advised him to send Cleopatra back to Egypt, and for a while Antony gave this serious thought. A story circulated later suggested that during these hectic weeks Antony believed she was prepared to poison him, and he became so suspicious of her he never touched his food or drink unless it was first tasted by a condemned criminal. Cleopatra, after hearing from a friend that Antony believed she was planning to murder him, decided to teach Antony a lesson he'd never forget.

One night at dinner, she filled her goblet out of the same wine jar from which he had been drinking, and having herself drunk some of the wine, she handed the cup to Antony as if in reconciliation. He eagerly raised it to his mouth, was about to place his lips where the queen's lips had rested a moment before, when she took the wreath of flowers from her hair and dipped it into the wine. Again Antony lifted the cup, but suddenly Cleopatra dashed it from his hand and said the wine was poisoned. He laughingly replied that she was mistaken, since she herself had just drunk from the same cup. Cleopatra calmly explained that the wreath, which she had dipped into the wine, was poisoned, and that she had chosen this means of showing him how baseless his fears were. As Plutarch wrote: "You see," she said, "I could have killed you at any time."

No matter how distressed Cleopatra felt over Antony's obvious degeneration of character and mounting hostility toward her, she realized full well that she needed him; otherwise her goal of entering Rome with her son Caesarion would not materialize. Moreover, the Roman people would never accept her as their queen unless she was accompanied by a victorious Antony and his legions.

It was now late summer and Antony's forces had been blockaded for four months. Octavian, content to play the waiting game and careful not to be at too close quarters, had fortified himself in a position several miles back from the entrance to the Gulf of Ambracia and proceeded to build a wall down to the shore of the Ionian Sea, thus preventing Antony from interfering with the landing of equipment and supplies from Rome. Fearing the advent of winter, Antony quickly called a council of war and it was decided (largely through the insistence of Cleopatra) that the fleet had to break away, sail out of the gulf, and engage Octavian's fleet in open waters. The officers and soldiers heatedly opposed this idea, arguing that they had not come all this distance to do battle on the sea. "Let Antony give up Cleopatra's projected naval battle," the officers exclaimed, "and order the Queen to go back quickly with her ships to her own country."

They knew full well that Cleopatra was the moving spirit in this war. She had supplied the money, and it was against her that Octavian had declared war. She was in supreme command of all the forces, not Antony; and every senator, every vassal king, and every general was furiously resentful of her, particularly because she was a woman.

Cleopatra, of course, paid no attention to these objections, nor did the reluctant Antony, and the situation deteriorated rapidly. After several disputes, more desertions followed. A Roman senator and a chieftain from Arabia were caught and brought back to Antony's camp, where they were executed in front of all the troops as a deterrent to any other defectors. But even this could not stop them. There were more betrayals among the kings; and Amyntas and Delotarus also went over to Octavian. Quite apart from this, since Antony's naval forces seemed to be of little use and always too slow to be of much help, the best thing would have been for him to turn his attention to his army. Canidius urged him to abandon the sea to Octavian, who had gained considerable knowledge of naval affairs in the Sicilian War. It would be far best for Antony, who was so experienced in land battles, to make use of his many legionaries and not to distribute them among the fleet and thus fritter away their strength.

Antony was well aware of this, but his hands were tied. He had attempted on several occasions to lure Octavian into a land battle but had failed; and he was no match for Cleopatra's strong persuasions. She prevailed with her opinion that the war should be decided with ships, and thus the decision was accordingly taken to prepare for a breakout by sea. Orders were then issued for ships to be manned by the legionaries and for those vessels which were unserviceable to be burned.

In a final attempt to dissuade Antony from Cleopatra's plan, a veteran centurian came up to him and, pointing to the many scars he had suffered in Antony's service, cried out: "General, look at these wounds! Why have you now decided to put your trust in miserable pieces of timber rather than in our swords? Let Egyptians and Phoenicians fight upon the sea, but give us the land where we know how to stand and fight, and either conquer or die!"

On August 28, 20,000 legionaries and 2,000 archers boarded the ships in preparation for battle the next day. These vessels were much larger than those of Octavian, some having as many as ten banks of oars. With such a sea force, and tens of thousands of legionaries stationed on land, it seemed indeed that victory for Antony was close at hand. On the following day, however, the sea was extremely rough and the battle had to be postponed. It was a violent storm and all plans of breaking Octavian's blockade had to be put off for the next four days, all of which placed such a heavy strain on Antony's forces that two important generals deserted to Octavian's lines, taking thousands of soldiers with them. One of the generals, Dellius, informed Octavian about Cleopatra's plan of attack and Octavian immediately prepared for battle, embarking eight legions and five praetorian divisions on his ships of war.

The storm finally abated on September 1, and in the evening Antony went from ship to ship encouraging and inspiring his men for battle. The next morning the weather had cleared and the sea was calm. Quite surprisingly, not only Cleopatra's fleet, but all of Antony's ships put out to sea, with their masts, spars, and rigging aboard. By overloading his ships this way, Antony was placing himself at a grave disadvantage.

Antony had a curt but unconvincing explanation for this: when his shipmasters asked him to let them leave their sails behind, he ordered that they should be put aboard, saying he did not want a single one of his enemies to be allowed to escape. This was absurd. Sea battles of that period were entirely dependent upon the strength of the rowers to bring their vessels into action. No one fought under sail. The battle was either determined by the rams of the galleys or by a landing engagement fought by the legionaries in ship-to-ship action.

Another argument supporting the suggestion of flight was that Antony had at last determined to sever ties with Cleopatra and had secretly ordered all her private treasure to be hauled aboard before the fleet got under way. Certainly, the crewmen who carried the queen's possessions to the ships were aware of still another, and this time, more serious dispute between the two. They had parted that morning with much anger and bitterness. Cleopatra told Antony how much she resented his order for her departure to Egypt, and added that she didn't trust him anymore, accusing him of abandoning her and Caesarion, calling him a coward and a traitor. "In her bitter anger, she exclaimed that she was leaving him with delight, having found him wholly degenerate, and that she hoped never to see him again."

Thus they parted, each to their flagships. Antony was visibly stung by her words. His boyish nature, impulsive and quickly repentant, could not bear so painful a scene with the woman to whom he was truly devoted, and as he proceeded out to battle, he was consumed with the desire to ask her forgiveness. As Plutarch related, the thought of being separated from her in anger troubled him; and, already a little drunk, the contemplation of his approaching loneliness reduced him to tears.

The battle was initiated by the advance of Antony's left wing. Agrippa immediately attempted to outflank it with his right wing, and as Antony's other vessels moved forward, a general attack was launched. When the two enemies at last engaged, there was no ramming or charging of one ship into the other because Antony's vessels, with their great bulk, were incapable of the speed to make the stroke effectual. On the other side, Octavian's ships dared not charge, prow-to-prow, into Antony's, which were all armed with solid masses and spikes of brass; nor did they attempt to ram their sides, which were so strongly built with great squared pieces of timber, fastened together with iron bolts, that their own bows would certainly have been shattered. In many ways, the engagement resembled a land fight, for there were always three or four of Octavian's vessels around each one of Antony's, pressing upon them with spears, javelins, poles, and many instruments of fire.

From her galley a short distance away, Cleopatra surveyed the appalling scene. The anxieties that had plagued her during the last few weeks as to her husband's intentions regarding her position and that of her son Caesarion were now displaced by the more frightful thought that he would meet his end. Her anger against him for his vacillation, her contempt for the increasing weakness of his character, and her misgivings in regard to his ability to direct his forces in view of the growing intemperance of his habits, were now combined in the one staggering certainty that defeat and ruin awaited him. Far worse, he had told her to go back to Egypt, had ordered her to take herself off with her fleet at the end of the battle.

But it was not from a riotous scene of victory that she was to retire, nor was she to carry over to Alexandria the tidings of her triumph. Instead, she would have to sail away from the spectacle of the utter destruction of her dreams and free herself by flight from a man who, no longer champion of her rights, had become a disgusting encumbrance.

Late in the afternoon, a strong wind kicked up from the north, blowing straight from Rome toward distant Egypt. The sea grew rough and the angry waves thrashed against the sides of the queen's flagship. As the wind whipped against her face, the thought struck her that the moment for her departure was now imminent. Antony had ordered her to go; there was no further reason for her to remain. In another hour he would be captured or killed, and she too would be taken prisoner, to be marched through the streets of the Capitol.

Quickly, she ordered a signal to be given to her scattered ships and, hoisting sail, she passed through the warring vessels and made off downwind, followed by her damaged fleet. From his own flagship, Antony had a clear view of her departure and became overwhelmed with remorse and despair. For the past several years, he had relied entirely upon her, and even in his most degenerate state she was always at his side to console and advise him. Suddenly, his army and fleet were not important to him any longer. There was no hope of victory now. Disgrace and ruin stared him in the face; and the sooner he fled from the horror of defeat, the better would be his chance of retaining his life.

It was here that Antony showed to all the world that he was no longer driven by the thoughts and motives of a commander. As soon as he saw Cleopatra's ships sailing away, he abandoned all the men who were fighting and laying down their lives for him, and followed after her.

Transferring from his flagship to a lighter, faster galley, Antony quickly caught up with the retreating Egyptian fleet. He drew up alongside Cleopatra's flagship and was taken on board, but he did not see her, nor was seen by her. Instead, he went forward into the bow and sat down by himself in silence, holding his head in both hands.

For several hours, Cleopatra remained in her cabin, refusing to see him or speak to him. After it had grown dark, the steady beat of the oars of several galleys was heard behind them, and just then the hull of a vessel loomed out of the darkness. The shouts and commotion across the water aroused Antony, and for a moment he hoped that the pursuing ships were bringing him a message from Actium, and that perhaps the battle had turned in his favor.

Moving to the prow of the flagship, he shouted across the dark sea: "Who is this that follows Antony?" A loud voice echoed through the darkness: "I am Eurycles, the son of Lachares, come to revenge my father's death."

Lachares was from one of the noblest Maniot families in the Peloponnesus and Antony had caused him to be beheaded for an alleged robbery. Enraged at Antony, Eurycles fitted out a galley at his own expense and vowed to avenge his father, and as he stood upon his deck, ready to hurl a lance at Antony, his galley charged into an Egyptian vessel that was sailing close to the flagship, and the blow turned Eurycles' galley away. In the darkness and confusion, Cleopatra's captain successfully managed to escape.

Long after the danger was passed, Antony sat himself down once more in the prow, nor did he move from that part of the ship for three whole days. Hour after hour, he sat staring out to sea, his hands idly folded before him, his mind dazed in despair. By his own folly, he had lost everything, and he had carried down with him all the hopes and all the fortune of Cleopatra. "It is surprising that he did not at once put an end to his life, for his misery was pitiable."

When at last the port of Taenarus (the mythical entrance into Hades) was reached at the southernmost tip of the Greek peninsula, Charmion, Iras, and others of Cleopatra's serving women induced the queen to invite Antony to her cabin, and after much persuasion she and Antony consented to speak to each other and later to sup and sleep together.

As the queen's flagship lay at anchor in Taenarus, several vessels sailed into the harbor, bringing survivors from Actium, who reported to Antony that his fleet was entirely destroyed, more than 5,000 of his men killed, but that his army still stood firm and had not surrendered. His sagging spirit was temporarily revived. He and Cleopatra rewarded the fugitives with a large sum of money, numerous dishes and cups of gold and silver; Antony also wrote letters in their behalf to his steward at Corinth to provide for them until the end of the war. At first, these defeated officers refused, but Antony pressed them to accept the gifts and cheered them with wishes of goodness and health.

Finally, the Egyptian fleet put out to sea and set sail for the coast of Egypt, arriving at Paraetonium, that desolate spot some 160 miles west of Alexandria, where a small Roman garrison was stationed. While Cleopatra proceeded to Alexandria, Antony decided to stay in Paraetonium for a few weeks in hiding. The place was dreary and the damp heat of September depressed him. The slow-breaking waves beating on the scorched beach like a tolling bell were stark reminders of the waning moments of his life.

Throughout these long fitful days, he wandered along the beach accompanied only by two friends: Aristocrates, a Greek rhetorician, and Lucilius, a Roman soldier who, while fighting on the side of the enemy at Philippi, had heroically prevented the capture of Brutus and had been pardoned by Antony as a reward for his courage.

During Antony's stay at Paraetonium, one of his naval vessels put into the little port and brought him the tragic news of Actium: after his escape, the battered remnant of his fleet had continued the fight until sunset, then sailed back into the Gulf of Ambracia. They were invited to Octavian's camp the next day and asked to surrender, along with their army, but not one of them believed that Antony had fled, and consequently they refused Octavian's offer. The next day, several of the vassal kings laid down their arms, and after another week, Canidius abandoned his forces and fled— part of his legions scattering into Macedonia, and the rest surrendering on September 9, together with the fleet. Jubilantly, Octavian then sailed to Piraeus, where he received the surrender of every city in Greece except Corinth. A general massacre followed, and in every district of Greece, the townspeople struggled to save their lives, heaping honors upon the conqueror Octavian, erecting statues to him and praising his name.

Shortly after this, a messenger reached Antony from Rome and informed him that the legions he had left in North Africa had gone over to

Octavian. Dejected and trying desperately to summon up the courage to kill himself, he was restrained by his two faithful friends, who persuaded him to sail at once for Alexandria and seek comfort in the arms of Cleopatra.

Unlike the despondent Antony, Cleopatra was still determined to salvage her plans for herself and for her son Caesarion. For the second time in her life, she had played for the highest stakes and lost. But the one thing she had not lost was her perseverance and courage. She knew by now (and had probably known for a long time) that Antony was a pitiful drunk. She had three children by him and saw him as the man most likely to inherit the Roman Empire and establish with her the Greco-Roman dynasty that would rule the world. But these aspirations were blown away at the Battle of Actium. She had now lost all faith in Antony as a leader and hoped that like all defeated generals of that time he would fall upon his sword and kill himself.

Antony sank into even deeper despair in Alexandria. The fond memories of his first visit as a young cavalry officer, that radiant Alexandrian winter he spent with Cleopatra, and the plans they made together for the ultimate defeat of Octavian, now compounded his misery and brought about a complete physical and mental collapse. He forsook the city and the company of his friends, and built a dwelling for himself near Pharos, on a mole which he had specially constructed near the water. He lived there for months, an exile from all humanity, emulating the example of Timon of Athens, who had been wronged and ill-treated by his friends and had shut himself off from the rest of the world.

The place was appropriately named the Timonium, and here Antony remained in dejection until Cleopatra inveigled him out of his solitary and pointless seclusion. Throughout her life, she proved to be a fighter and a great leader, suppressing riots and opposing factions, making certain that the people knew that she, Cleopatra the queen and Isis incarnate, the descendant of the Ptolemies, was still firmly in command of her country; and although all seemed lost at this point, she nevertheless resolved that, by reviving Antony's spirit and morale, she might be able to reach some agreement with the conquering Octavian and thus possibly ensure the throne of Egypt for her son Caesarion.

Consequently, the Society of the Inimitable Livers was restored, but it was given a new name: the Club of Those Who Die Together. Cleopatra did not fear death. Ever since she was a child, she had known it in all its familiar forms. Her golden city of Alexandria foretold it from the early morning rays that anointed the Sun Gate to the dark descending shadows around the Moon Gate. Everywhere she stood, she was reminded of it: the Mausoleum where Alexander the Great lay buried, the countless other tombs, the Serapium, pyramids, and obelisks. Indeed all of Egypt knew death, even prepared for it, and if Antony feared it, she had to revive his spirits so that he could face the last enemy as he once faced countless others throughout his life.

Thus she set about preparing for her own death in a calculated and methodical way. As was customary with all Egyptian rulers, she had an impressive mausoleum built to house her remains and then proceeded to test various methods for killing herself, for she was determined never to walk, as her sister had done, a defeated and chained victim at a Roman Triumph. And so she began collecting all sorts of deadly poisons and testing them out on prisoners who were under sentence of death to see whether they were painless or not. She observed that the speedier poisons made death more painful, while the milder poisons were not quick enough, and accordingly she and her physicians conducted experiments on animals. In the end, she found that the bite of an asp alone induced a quiet sleep, without spasms or pain, and while the mind remained gently relaxed, the victims could not be aroused or restored.

It was ironic that despite these elaborate plans for her eternal rest, Cleopatra still labored strenuously for the earthly survival and security of her children. She sent an ambassador to Octavian, proposing that she would resign the throne of Egypt if he allowed Caesarion to inherit it. At the same time, Antony humbly made a request of his own, asking that he be permitted to live as a private citizen, if not at his Timonium in Alexandria, then in Athens.

Octavian made no reply to Antony's appeal, but he sent word to Cleopatra that she would receive honorable treatment on the condition that she either expel Antony from her kingdom or have him put to death. Still loyal to Antony, she refused to consider Octavian's proposal. Hoping to bring about a final schism between her and Antony, Octavian then sent Thyrsus, a very personable man, to the court at Alexandria to conduct secret discussions with the queen. Cleopatra treated the emissary in a polite manner, but Antony, who was not invited to these discussions, angrily had Thyrsus hung up, flogged, then sent back to Octavian. Cleopatra was not upset by Antony's behavior, because deep down she was playing for time. She did her best to relieve Antony of any causes for complaint or suspicion, paying elaborate court to him, and while she observed her own birthday in a modest manner as was suitable in view of the circumstances, Antony's was celebrated in a most luxurious and splendid way. Many of those who came to the banquet arrived poor and went away rich.

At this time, Octavian was in Asia Minor, preparing for a final assault. Forewarned about his plans and fearing for the safety of her son, Cleopatra sent Caesarion and his tutor away from Alexandria. They traveled south by ship up the Nile as far as Copros, and from there they planned to cross the desert and proceed to the Red Sea port of Berenice, which was Egypt's main trading center with Arabia and India. Cleopatra still nursed the flimsy hope that Antony might defeat Octavian in a final battle, and if so, Caesarion could be called back to Alexandria. Should Antony lose, Caesarion would then have to make his way onward, into Arabia or India, where he would be received as Queen Cleopatra's son and still be able to salvage his aspirations for the future.

In May 30 B.C., Octavian marched into Syria from Asia Minor, and all the legions stationed there surrendered to him. King Herod of Judaea had already deserted Antony, and after Octavian's General Gallus captured the garrison town of Paraetonium on the western frontier of Egypt, the road to Alexandria now lay open and the city was vulnerable to attack from both sides. Anticipating the worst, Cleopatra had all her royal riches taken into her mausoleum: gold, silver, emeralds, pearls, ebony, and ivory. In addition, large quantities of inflammable materials were stacked everywhere, for she was determined that the ancient treasures of the Ptolemies should not fall into the hands of this upstart Octavian. As for Caesarion, she was almost certain she would never see him again. All that remained for her was the prospect of dying in a manner befitting a queen.

Pelusium, the garrison town on the eastern branch of the Nile, fell quickly to Octavian. Though Plutarch and the historian Dio Cassius maintained that Cleopatra turned against Antony and handed the town over to Octavian, the assumption is unlikely. What would be the gain if she allowed Octavian to advance at will into Egypt? She had already ignored Octavian's offer to have Antony exiled or murdered, and had also sent her son away from Alexandria as a measure of safety. Her meticulous preparations for death illustrate that she knew the end was near.

Antony made a bad situation worse. His nerves frayed from one disaster after the other, he accused Cleopatra of having betrayed him by arranging secretly with Seleucus, the commander of the fortress at Pelusium, to surrender in the hope of placating Octavian. She denied the accusation and, to prove she was telling the truth, she caused the wife and children of Seleucus to be arrested and handed over to Antony, so he might put them to death if it were shown that she had had any secret correspondence with Seleucus.

Antony's suspicions were not allayed. In a desperate move, he attempted once again, as he had done at Actium, to reduce the whole contest between himself and Octavian to the level of the Homeric encounters in the Trojan War by sending his enemy a challenge to single combat, which of course Octavian rejected. When this failed, Antony dispatched his emissary Euphonius to Octavian once again, accompanied by his young son Antyllus and with vast sums of money, to appease Octavian and initiate plans toward a reconciliation. Octavian kept the money, paid no heed to the pleas of Antyllus on behalf of his father, and angrily sent the emissaries back to Alexandria. Cleopatra was shocked to hear that Antony could fall so low as to attempt to buy off his enemy with gold, *her gold*.

Octavian's troops made a tumultuous entry into Alexandria on the night of August 1. Complete stillness had fallen upon the starlit city, and the sea and wind had dropped. Throughout that day, and well into the night, the city was very quiet, and everyone was fearful of the worst. Suddenly, the loud echo of music was heard, and a sweet harmony from many musical instruments, together with the shouts of a huge number of people. There were loud Bacchic cries as dancers dressed as satyrs leaped into the dark night. "At first," wrote Dio Cassius, "it appeared as though a massive throng of boisterous revellers was leaving the city, making their way through the center of Alexandria and heading toward the Gate of the Moon, inside of which Octavian's legions were encamped. Then abruptly it all gave way to such a stifling silence, it seemed to those present that the god to whom Antony had always likened himself, and to whom he was most attached, was at last deserting him."

At dawn the following morning, Antony led his forces out of the eastern gates of the city and assembled them on the high ground between the walls and the Hippodrome overlooking the sea. From this vantage point, he was able to watch his fleet sail out from the Great Harbor and head toward Octavian's ships, which were in formation near the shore several miles east of the city. To his dismay, the Alexandrian vessels made no attempt to deliver an attack on the enemy as he had ordered them to do. Instead, they saluted Octavian's fleet with their oars and, on receiving a similar salutation in response, joined up with the enemy and sailed with them toward the Great Harbor.

In despair, Antony turned from his elevated vantage point and saw the whole of his cavalry behind him galloping suddenly over to Octavian's lines. Left only with his infantry, he realized he was no match for the enemy, and he fled back into the city, shouting and crying for everyone to hear: "She has betrayed me! Cleopatra has betrayed me!" He stormed into the palace with his confused officers, smiting his brow and calling down curses on the woman who had delivered him into the hands of the enemy for her gain.

Fearing that he might cut her down with his sword, Cleopatra, together with her servants Iras and Charmion, escaped through the empty halls and corridors of the palace, and at length crossed the deserted courtyard and reached the mausoleum adjoining the Temple of Isis. Once inside, they shut the bolts of the massive door and the two servant women huddled around Cleopatra, wailing and moaning their fate. But she would have no part of this. Chiding them, she sent a messenger to Antony, informing him that she had killed herself, thus hoping to prompt him to suicide.

The messenger reached Antony in the palace, where he still raged over the desertion of his fleet and cavalry, spewing out his wrath on Cleopatra for betraying him. Eventually, the full significance of the situation penetrated his brain, and he came to the realization that there was no place left for anger or suspicion. "Now, Antony," he cried, "why delay any longer? Fate has taken away the only thing for which you still wanted to live." And with this, he rushed into his bedchamber and tore off his armor.

Earlier that same day, he had made his servant Eros solemnly promise to kill him if all should be lost, and now as he gave Eros that instruction, the slave drew his sword as though he intended to do as he was bid, but instead turned sharply around, drove the blade into his own breast, and fell dying upon the floor, whereupon Antony bent over him and shouted hoarsely: "Well done, Eros! Well done! You have shown your master how to do what you had not the heart to do yourself." With this, he picked up the sword, drove it upward into his breast below the rib cage, and fell back upon his bed.

In great pain, he implored the Egyptian servants who had gathered around him to put him out of his misery, but when they realized that he was not yet dead, they rushed out of the room in horror. One of the servants brought the news to Cleopatra, and a few moments later her secretary Diomedes came to Antony and informed him that the queen had not yet killed herself and that she desired his body to be brought to her.

Gasping for life, Antony hastily ordered the servants to carry him to Cleopatra. They lifted him in their arms, placed him on an improvised stretcher, and hurried toward the mausoleum, where a crowd had already gathered around the great door. Looking down from her window above, Cleopatra saw the servants bringing her husband to her, but she was afraid that some of them, seeking a reward, would seize her and carry her alive to Octavian as soon as they entered her stronghold. It would also be a difficult task for her to pull back the bolts of the door, which in her excitement she had managed to drive deep into their sockets.

Below her window, Antony lay on the ground, groaning and entreating her to let him die in her arms. Frantically, she let down ropes and cords, then she and her two women, the only persons she had allowed to enter the mausoleum, drew him up. For Cleopatra and the crowd below, this was a sad spectacle indeed, to see Antony covered all over with blood, expiring, thus drawn up, clutching at the ropes with what little strength he could muster.

It was no easy task for the women to haul up the mortally wounded husband of Cleopatra, but with the help of Antony's servants below, who brought ladders and assisted, they at last succeeded, dragging him first through the window, then carrying him to the bed. With fitful moans, Cleopatra wept, calling Antony her lord, her husband, and her emperor, while at the same time trying to stanch the blood that flowed from his wound.

Momentarily, Antony came to his senses, and with a last bold attempt to remain faithful to his model Dionysus, and also to soothe Cleopatra's wild lamentations, he asked the servant women to bring him wine, either because he was thirsty or because he knew it would hasten his death. His last hope was that Cleopatra would not pity him.

He died in her arms, "the gold Alexandrian sunlight pouring in through the window embrasure, and the sea-wind stirring the dust along the marble floor."

⟨∞⟩

Octavian made his formal entry into Alexandria shortly before sunset of that same day, when all the marble buildings and temples, the Mouseion, the Serapium, the Hippodrome, and the palaces of the Lochias promontory were turning ruby-red. Standing beside the conquering hero in his chariot, to the astonishment of the citizens, was the Alexandrian philosopher Areius. In essence, Octavian was demonstrating to the populace that he was a civilized and gentle man, not a cruel warlord. As he mounted a rostrum to address them, they all fell prostrate on the ground, but he commanded them to rise, assuring them that he in no manner held the people of Alexandria responsible for the war.

Octavian's benevolent mood changed the instant he entered the palace and took up quarters in those same halls where Cleopatra had fashioned herself and Antony after Isis and Dionysus, and where she had lain with Julius Caesar and had given birth to his son Caesarion. Moving swiftly, Octavian dispatched a party of soldiers to seize Caesarion before he managed to escape from the port of Berenice. At the same time, after being informed by Theodorus, the tutor of Antony's eldest son Antyllus, that the youth had taken refuge in the temple Cleopatra had erected to Julius Caesar, Octavian gave orders to have him killed. Immediately, Antyllus was dragged from the altar, out of the temple, and beheaded. In the struggle and wild confusion, Theodorus somehow managed to steal a very valuable stone that Antyllus wore on a chain around his neck, and when the theft was reported to Octavian, he gave orders for the tutor to be crucified. Various members of Cleopatra's court, along with her most fervent followers, were also put to death. The philosopher Areius hardly needed to remind Octavian that "a Caesar too many is not a good thing," not while his horsemen were speeding across the desert in pursuit of Caesar's only son. As for Antony's other children, they were to be spared and taken back to Rome and raised as if they were Octavian's own.

Meanwhile, Antony's body was being prepared for burial, and although mummification was still practiced in Alexandria by both Greeks and Egyptians, no attempt was made to embalm the corpse. Out of respect to the dead general, Roman officers and foreign potentates requested to perform the funeral rites at their own expense, but in deference to Cleopatra's wishes, Octavian ruled that only her orders were to be honored.

Thus, Antony was buried with every mark of royal splendor and pomp, in a tomb Cleopatra had prepared for him not far from her mausoleum. She followed him to his grave, a tragic, piteous little figure, surrounded by her lamenting ladies; and while the priests burned their incense and uttered their droning chants, the queen's fragile hands ruthlessly beat her breast as she called upon Antony by his name.

After the funeral, she returned to her quarters in the mausoleum, racked with high fever. The incessant blows to her breast had caused severe ulcerations and inflammation. Over and over again, she was heard to exclaim in delirium: "I will not be exhibited in his Triumph. Never!"

She refused all food and repeatedly begged her physician Olympus, who was now constantly at her side, along with her two trusted servants Iras and Charmion, to be allowed to die and pass quietly out of the world. Octavian heard about her increasing weakness and warned her once more that unless she made an effort to live he would not be lenient to her children. The threat worked. Her maternal instincts induced the necessary struggle for her recovery and she obediently accepted the medicine and stimulants the physician Olympus prescribed for her.

On August 28, as she lay on her pallet bed in the upper room of the mausoleum, her servants rushed in to tell her that Octavian had come to pay his respects. It was an unexpected visit, and on his arrival, she sprang up from her bed, having nothing on but a flimsy robe, and flung herself at his feet, her hair and face looking wild and disfigured, her voice trembling, her eyes sunken and dark. The marks of the blows she had rained upon herself were visible about her breast. Yet, for all this, her charm and boldness of character remained beautiful as ever.

Octavian mercifully assisted her to her bed and sat down beside her. The later Roman historians asserted that even at this moment she tried to seduce Octavian, but this was a sick and vanquished woman Octavian beheld. Antony was just beyond fifty when he killed himself, and she was thirty-nine, an old woman by Egyptian standards.

At this point, she rose from the bed and brought to Octavian a number of letters written to her by Julius Caesar. "You know very well," she exclaimed, "how much I was with your father; and certainly you are aware that it was he who placed the crown of Egypt upon my head. Here, please read these letters. They are all written to me with your father's own hand."

Octavian of course was flattered by her remarks. He always spoke of Julius Caesar as his father, and even called himself "Caesar." Going back to her bed, she agreed to place herself entirely in his hands in return for his clemency, and then offered to hand over to him, without reserve, all her treasure and property. Her chief steward was quickly summoned and instructed to furnish the complete list of her jewelry and valuables now deposited with her other papers in another room of the mausoleum. The steward ran his eyes over the list and, hoping to ingratiate himself with his new master and realizing that loyalty to Cleopatra no longer paid, volunteered the information that various articles were omitted from the list, and that the queen was purposely hiding these for her own advantage.

Hearing this, Cleopatra sprang from her bed, seized the steward by the hair, shook him and furiously slapped his face. Octavian, who could not refrain from laughing, finally restrained her and led her back to her bed. Olympus, her physician, disclosed the details of this sad incident:

> "Really, it is very hard," Cleopatra shakingly informed her visitor, "when you do me the honor to come and see me in this condition, that I should be accused by one of my own servants of setting aside some women's trinkets—not so as to adorn my unhappy self, you may be sure, but so that I might have some little presents to give to your sister Octavia and your wife Livia, that by their intercession I might hope to find you to some extent disposed to mercy."

Even in her deplorable state, Cleopatra was still the golden-tongued diplomat. However, she was not deceived by Octavian's promise of leniency. There was something about his words and manner that convinced her that he planned to exhibit her in Rome, and that he had no intention of allowing her son Caesarion to reign in her place. Sure enough, before the day was over, a messenger came to the mausoleum and broke the news that, after finding her now fully recovered from illness, Octavian had decided to ship her immediately to Rome with her two children. As for Caesarion, Octavian was now firmly convinced, largely through the advice of his Alexandrian philosopher friend Areius, that it would be unwise to leave at large one who claimed to be the rightful successor of the great Julius Caesar, and thus he decreed that Caesarion be killed as soon as possible.

It was this alarming news that drove Cleopatra to do away with herself; this and the frightening vision of Octavian's Triumph in Rome, where she and her children would be the main exhibits. She would be led in chains up to the Capitol, exactly as she had watched her sister Arsinoe paraded in the Triumph of Julius Caesar.

Highly distraught, and determined now more than ever to end her life, she sent a message to Octavian requesting his permission to visit Antony's tomb. This was granted to her, and the next morning, August 29, she was carried in her litter to the grave, accompanied by her women and her physician Olympus. She threw herself on Antony's gravestone, passionately kissing it, all of her past quarrels with him now forgotten in her desire for his companionship in the netherworld. She then stood up, placed wreaths of flowers on the grave, entered her litter, and was carried back to the mausoleum, only to discover that Octavian had ransacked the place, confiscating her entire wealth, even her most cherished jewelry and valuables. Eventually, she calmed down, ordered her bath to be prepared, and after being washed and scented, her hair carefully plaited around her head, she had herself arrayed in her formal robes as queen of Egypt and the goddess Isis, then reclined on a couch for a sumptuous dinner. After this, she wrote a brief letter to Octavian, asking that she be buried in the same tomb with Antony. As soon as the letter was dispatched, she ordered everyone to leave the mausoleum with the exception of Iras and Charmion. All the doors were then quickly closed and the sentries mounted their guard outside the mausoleum.

Moments later, a peasant carrying a large basket of figs asked to be allowed to enter the mausoleum, saying he was bringing the fruit at the queen's request. The guards made a hasty inspection, lifting the leaves that covered the fruit and remarking on the fineness of the figs, whereupon the peasant laughed and invited them to take some, which they refused to do. After several loud knocks, the door was opened and an attendant took the basket of figs from the peasant and brought it to Cleopatra, who fitfully exclaimed, "So, here it is!"

Meanwhile, Octavian had received her message and realized at once what had happened. At first, he thought about going to the mausoleum himself, but he changed his mind and sent some officers to try and prevent Cleopatra from killing herself. When they arrived, they found the sentries oblivious to any impending doom. Quickly, they burst open the door, ran up the stairs to the upper chamber, and found the dead Cleopatra stretched upon her bed of gold, arrayed in her Grecian robes, the royal diadem of the Ptolemies tilted awkwardly over her brow. On the floor at her feet, Iras too had breathed her last, and Charmion was tottering at the bedside, trying to adjust the queen's crown. One of the Roman officers shouted angrily, "This is a fine deed, Charmion!"

"Yes," replied Charmion, turning her ashen face toward the officer, "it is a very fine deed indeed, and befitting the descendant of so many kings."

Those were her last words, and she too fell to the floor beside Iras and her dead queen. The asp hidden under the leaves in the basket was never found, although one of the sentries stated that he saw the track of a snake leading from the mausoleum and running over the sand toward the sea. It is unknown how Iras and Charmion died, but there were many poisons in Egypt, drugs that could easily be concealed in combs and jewelry.

Octavian issued orders for the queen to be buried with full honors beside Antony, and without wasting any time he attended to the nagging problem of Caesarion by sending a message to him in Berenice, promising that if he returned to Alexandria he would not be harmed. The tutor of Caesarion, Rhodon, counseled the young man to trust Octavian and, acting upon this advice, the youth returned to Alexandria, only to be immediately executed.

The last of the Ptolemaic pharaohs of Egypt, the son and only real heir of the great Julius Caesar, was now no longer an obstacle to Octavian's ultimate goal of reigning supreme on the throne of Rome. Cleopatra's two other children in Alexandria, Ptolemy and Cleopatra Selene, were shipped off to Rome, and messengers were dispatched to Media to seize Alexander Helios and bring him there also.

Thus, Cleopatra passed into legend. History, and particularly Roman history, has maligned her as an infamous woman, a seductive temptress capable of every deceit and treachery, whereas in fact she proved to be a woman of remarkable courage and political ingenuity. From the age of eighteen until her death, she not only fought to free her country from Roman mastery, but as a devoted mother, she painstakingly endeavored to ensure the crown of Egypt for the son of her first lover Julius Caesar. Like Alexander the Great, she too deserved to be buried in his glorious city.

In the centuries that followed, the death of Cleopatra captured the imagination of many creative minds, particularly Shakespeare:

CLEOPATRA: Give me my robe, put on my crown. I have
Immortal longings in me; now no more
The juice of Egypt's grape shall moist this lip.
Yea, Yea, good Iras; quick. Methinks I hear
Antony call; I see him rouse himself
To praise my noble act; I hear him mock
The luck of Caesar, which the gods give men
To excuse their after wrath; husband, I come;
Now to that name my courage prove my title!
I am fire and air; my other elements
I give to baser life. So, have you done?
Come then, and take the last warmth of my lips.
Farewell, kind Charmian; Iras, long farewell.
    (kisses them. Iras falls and dies.)
Have I the aspic in my lips? Dost fall?
If thou and nature can so gently part,
The stroke of death is as a lover's pinch,
Which hurts and is desired. Dost thou lie still?
If thus thou vanishest, thou tell'st the world
It is not worth leave-taking.
CHARMIAN: Dissolve, thick cloud, and rain; that I may say
The gods themselves do weep.
CLEOPATRA: This proves me base;

If she first meet the curled Antony
He'll make demand of her, and spend that kiss
Which is my heaven to have. Come thou mortal wretch
   (to the asp, which she applies to her breast.)
With thy sharp teeth this knot intrinsicate
Of life at once untie; poor venomous fool,
Be angry, and dispatch. O! couldst thou speak,
That I might hear thee call great Caesar ass
Unpolicied.

CHARMIAN: O, eastern star!

CLEOPATRA: Peace, peace!
Dost thou not see my baby at my breast,
That sucks the nurse asleep?

CHARMIAN: O, break! O, break!

CLEOPATRA: As sweet as balm, as soft as air, as gentle—
O, Antony!—Nay, I will take thee too.
   (applying another asp to her arm, dies.)
What should I stay—

CHARMIAN: In this vile world? So, fare thee well.
Now boast thee, death, in thy possession lies
A lass unparallel'd. Downy windows, close;
And golden Phoebus never be beheld
Of eyes again so royal! Your crown's awry;
I'll mend it, and then play.
   (enter the Guard, rushing in.)

FIRST GUARD: Where is the queen?

CHARMIAN: Speak softly, wake her not.

FIRST GUARD: Caesar hath sent—

CHARMIAN: Too slow a messenger.
   (applies an asp.)
O! come apace, dispatch; I partly feel thee.

FIRST GUARD: Approach, ho! All's not well; Caesar's beguil'd.

SECOND GUARD: There's Dolabella sent from Caesar; call him.

FIRST GUARD: What work is this? Charmian, is this well done?

CHARMIAN: It is well done and fitting for a princess
Descended of so many royal kings.
Ah! soldier. (dies.)

          (*ANTONY AND CLEOPATRA*, ACT V, SCENE 2)

Cleopatra's eulogy was sung by the Roman poet Horace:

> *Indeed she preferred a finer style of dying;*
> *She did not, like a woman, fear the dagger*
> *Or seek by speed at sea*
> *To leave her Egypt for distant shores.*
>
> *But gazing on her desolate palace*
> *With a soft smile, unflinchingly accepted*
> *The angry asp until*
> *Her veins had drunk the deadly poison deep;*
>
> *And thus more determined, fiercer than ever,*
> *Perished. Was she to grace a haughty triumph,*
> *Dethroned, paraded by*
> *The rude Liburnians? Not Cleopatra!*

(ODES, I, 21ff.)

PART FOUR

THE SOUL

OF THE CITY

ALEXANDRIA'S REMARKABLE ABILITY to recover from apparent disaster revealed itself during the years of Roman rule (30 B.C.–A.D. 311). Just when it seemed that the once-great city of the Ptolemies was destined for oblivion, confined within the narrow limits of a typical Roman province and on the verge of losing her real identity, she embarked on the discovery of another kingdom—that of the spirit.

Quite amazingly, her diverse population focused its energies on religion at the same time and was now more determined to find a solution to a more serious problem than the one posed by the Roman occupation: the existence of God and His relationship to man.

Soon after Alexandria was founded, the Jews had begun emigrating there, and their customs and language were absorbed in a new world of Greek. To meet the Jews' religious needs, the Hebrew Scriptures had to be translated, and legend suggests that seventy rabbis were shut up by Ptolemy Philadelphus in seventy huts on the island of Pharos, from which they simultaneously emerged with seventy identical Greek translations of the Old Testament: the famous Septuagint.

The Alexandrian Jews differed greatly from the conservative Jews at Jerusalem, and although both worshiped Jehovah, the Alexandrians found it difficult to identify him as their God. To them, *wisdom* was far more important then *worship*.

One such Alexandrian was the unknown author of an apocryphal book called *The Wisdom of Solomon*. It was written in Greek and it revealed a wide knowledge, not only of Stoic, Epicurean, and Platonic philosophy, but of Egyptian rites as well. This mysterious writer solved the problem concerning God and man in a truly innovative yet Alexandrian way: by conceiving an intermediary between Jehovah and man whom he called Sophia, or Wisdom.

> Wisdom is more moving than any motion; she goeth through all things by reason of pureness. Being but one, she can do all things, and in all ages entering into holy souls she makes them friends of God, and prophets. She is more beautiful than the sun and all the order of stars; being compared with the light, she is found beyond it. For after this, cometh night, but vice shall not prevail against wisdom.

The Jewish school of Alexandria reached its greatest fame under Philo Judaeus, who lived in Alexandria during the early years of Christianity, when the city dominated the cultural and philosophical life of the Roman Empire. Born of a sacerdotal tradition but untrained in Hebrew, he acquired, like most Alexandrian Jews, the usual religious instruction through the Septuagint version of the Scriptures. He came from several generations of wealth. His father enjoyed Roman citizenship, and his brother Alexander held the high government office of alabarch at Alexandria (which meant that he was responsible to the Romans for the collection of taxes), and could very well have been the Alexander "of the kindred of the high priest" mentioned by St. Paul in the Acts of the Apostles.

Alexander was unquestionably the foremost Jew of Alexandria and indeed one of the richest men in the ancient world. Such wealth could hardly be acquired in a single generation, particularly wealth that had strong political and social ties. When Herod Agrippa was in dire financial straits during his early years as emperor, Alexander lent him two hundred thousand drachmas because he admired the fiery spirit of Agrippa's wife Cypros. Great as this amount may have seemed, it was but a small portion of Alexander's fortune. He came to Herod's assistance still another time by assuming the total cost of the silver and gold plates that adorned the nine gates of the rebuilt Temple at Jerusalem. His son Marcus married Berenice, daughter of Herod. Another son, Tiberius Julius Alexander, abandoned his religion for a political career that proved to be even more brilliant than his father's. He was first appointed epistrategos of Egypt by Claudius, then procurator of Palestine in A.D. 46. Under Nero, he became prefect of Egypt. During one of the riots, he was responsible for turning the Roman legions upon the Jewish uprisers; more than 50,000 of them were killed.

He played a key role in supporting Vespasian's rise to the throne, and in the great siege and destruction of Jerusalem was subordinate commander to Titus. In Rome, a statue of Tiberius Julius Alexander stood at a prominent place for many years.

His brother Philo, however, was not interested in government. Educated in Greek, philosophy, geometry, poetry, and music, he dedicated himself entirely to spiritual and cultural pursuits. A typical Alexandrian, he never relied on the literal meaning of things and looked for mystical and allegorical interpretations. As he himself put it:

> There was once a time when, by devoting myself to philosophy and to contemplation of the world and its parts, I achieved the enjoyment of that Mind which was truly beautiful, desirable, and blessed; for I lived in constant communion with sacred utterances and teachings, in which I greedily and insatiably rejoiced. No base or worldly thoughts occurred to me; nor did I grovel for glory, wealth, or bodily comfort, but seemed ever to be borne aloft into the heights with a rapture of soul, and to accompany sun, moon, heaven and universe in their revolutions.

Despite his relative spiritual seclusion and investment in the sublime, Philo could not escape from the world around him. When the emperor Gaius Caligula, in his madness, provoked a pogrom that threatened to destroy all the Jews in Alexandria, Philo, who was known and respected as "the learned Jew," "the Platonist," "the Pythagorean," was appointed to head a diplomatic legation to the emperor in Rome and plead the cause of justice and mercy.

Despite his religious and philosophical fervor, Philo was nevertheless an Alexandrian in that he remained constantly in touch with the teeming life of the city, attending the theater, games, celebrations, festivals, and athletic contests. He had a keen love for boxing and wrestling; his knowledge of training and nutrition was sound and scientific. He knew that a good boxer had to be in excellent physical condition and not rely solely on his skills, and that a trainer of athletes should insist that they chew their food thoroughly.

He was a frequent spectator at chariot races, and a vivid chronicler. He described one event when some onlookers became so emotional they broke down the barriers, dashed onto the course, and were killed by the stampeding horses. He also observed the outburst of passion by an audience at a play of Euripides when an actor recited a stirring passage in praise of freedom.

He had an acute ear for music and was temperate in his habits. Whenever he was invited to a banquet, he had to watch himself vigilantly—"take reason along," as he himself explained—"otherwise one could very easily become a slave to the pleasures of food and wine." He had respect for money but did not worship it. His wife felt the same way. At state functions and formal dinners, she was often chided for not wearing the usual gold ornaments typical of wealthy women of the time. Her curt reply pleased Philo: "The virtue of a husband is a sufficient ornament for his wife."

It was quite inappropriate for someone with Greek philosophical background to display a low opinion of women. However, while Plato and the Stoics firmly emphasized women's equality, Philo believed they should be kept in the interior rooms of the house and allowed out only under strict supervision and the most favorable conditions. Though his remarks reflected the general restrictions of society at that time, he carried this attitude to extremes. "In nature," he maintained, "men take precedence over women. The female is incomplete and in subjection, and belongs to the category of the passive rather than the active."

Although Philo much admired Phintys, a Pythagorean woman philosopher, he parted company with her over a statement she made: "A woman may and should have virtues of mind and body equal to those of a man."

In the matter of sexual relations, Philo insisted they be permitted only for procreation. "Men seek pleasure when they mate with their wives, not to begat children and perpetuate the race. They are like pigs and goats in quest only of enjoyment. If a woman was barren she ought properly to be divorced, since intercourse with her could produce no children." The only instance when a woman had a right to divorce a husband was when the husband bore false witness that, on marrying her, he found her not to be a virgin. A man lost his right to divorce on any ground after such a false accusation if she chose to continue living with him, but she was free to leave him if she wished.

Despite an entrenched sexism, Philo's legacy is important for other reasons. Having devoted himself from his youth to a life of study and contemplation, he in time amassed a great number of works, most of them scriptural commentaries. Veins of discursive allegory course throughout all his writings, and in many instances entire chapters are devoted to mystical interpretation. Nevertheless, he was loyal to the Mosaic law and believed that every word in the Greek text of the Old Testament was inspired and correct. It was not unusual for him to wrestle hour upon hour over one word, seeking its deeper allegorical meaning.

He had a sound training in Greek and freely quoted the dramatists, poets, historians, and philosophers. At times, he was torn between the Jewish and the Greek. The two traditions blended in his mind so completely that he read Plato thinking it was Moses, and Moses thinking it was Plato. Despite all this, he was a Jew and never ceased to be a Jew. His Jewish piety influenced his love and admiration for everything Greek. He spiritualized and justified the festivals and laws of Moses, embellishing them with the superb ethics espoused by the Greeks. For Philo, the Torah lost its Jewish character and became a mystical vessel of Greek thought. With this departure from Judaism, it was only natural that he accept the pagan idea of salvation: the release of the spirit from the flesh so that it could return to God, its ultimate source.

Philo contended that the Greek philosophers must in some way have been influenced by the Torah, and to carry out these presuppositions he relied heavily on allegorical interpretation. This was nothing new. The allegorical method of interpreting Scripture had been practiced long before in the rabbinical schools of Palestine. Using this method, Philo was able to create some of the most profound doctrines of philosophy from the simplest stories of the Pentateuch. His doctrine of God begins with the idea that God is a Being absolutely bare of quality. To predicate any essence of God would be to reduce Him to the sphere of finite existence, and this raised a problem: it excluded the possibility of any active relation of God to the world and to mankind. To resolve this, Philo, guided throughout by Plato, and concurring indeed that the absolute perfection of God would be violated by any direct contact with imperfect finite beings, offered the possibility of a connection between God and the world through an infinite multiplicity of divine Ideas, by whose mediation an active relation of God to the world is brought about. As did Plato before him, he called these ideas the thoughts of God, possessing a real existence and having been produced before the creation of the finite world. However, in distinction to Plato, Philo named these ideas Forces, which bring unformed matter into order and are the agents of all God's activity in the world. This modification of the Platonic Ideas is due largely to Stoic influence, especially where Philo gives to these ideas the name Logos, for to the Stoics, God was the Logos, the reason that operated in the world.

At the same time, Philo identified the Ideas with the daemons of the Greeks and the angels of the Jews, who were servants and messengers of God, and through whom He communicated with the finite world.

Philo's doctrine of man was also mainly derived from Plato. Philo saw man as dualistic in nature, with a higher and lower origin. Of the pure souls that inhabit ethereal space, those nearest the earth are attracted by sensible beings and descend into their bodies. These souls are the God-ward side of man. But on his other side, man is a creature of sense, and thus has in him a source of evil, which makes his body a prison, a coffin and grave for the soul which seeks to rise again to God. At this point, the Stoics leave man to his own resources, but Philo directs him toward the merciful assistance of God, and thus with God's help, even in this life, the truly wise and virtuous are lifted above their earthly existence.

> Where was my body before I was born, and where will it go when I have died? And what has become of this self? Where is the babe that once I was, the little boy, the stripling, the young adolescent, the youth, the young buck, the adult, the man? Whence came the soul and where will it go? Can we tell what its essential nature is? And when did we come to possess it? Before birth? But then we did not exist. After death? But then we shall not exist.

In Philo's reasoning, there remained yet one further step: the complete liberation from the body and the return of the soul to its original condition. Since it came from God, it now must rise back to Him. Natural death, however, brings about this consummation only to those who, while they lived on earth, kept themselves free from any attachment to sensual things. All the others must at death pass into another body, and although Philo never expressly mentioned it, transmigration of souls was indeed the necessary consequence of his philosophical premises.

It was primarily in the realm of allegory that Philo excelled. He used it in his speech and in his writing. Alexandria was a source of consternation to the Romans. Not one day passed without some disturbance, political or social. In most cases, the Romans, knowing full well that their citizens had been subjected by one conqueror after the other for many centuries, possessed the good sense to look the other way and allow the arguments and squabbles to eventually run their course. But when the problem was religious, this approach did not work, especially with the Jews. Most of the other nations under the yoke of the Romans readily accepted the notion that Venus was the same as Astarte, Aphrodite as Isis, Apollo as Osiris, but to even suggest to the Jewish mind that Yahweh could be identified with Zeus meant a battle to the death. The volatile issue of assimilating and sharing in the Roman way of life came to a supreme test during Philo's life. Much as he deplored arguments and uprisings, he felt it was his duty to calm the Jewish populace of Alexandria, and at the same time curb his own anger, at the thought of participating in any form of pagan worship demanded by the emperor Gaius. For this reason, he decided to travel to Rome and confront Gaius personally. It was a difficult and dangerous mission, but he accomplished it nobly.

In his own account, *On the Embassy to Gaius,* Philo, who was an old man when he made the journey to Rome, introduced startling evidence of Jewish persecution. The Romans, after all, were fascists. They had no constitutional sanction for their totalitarian authority, and they assumed their power through assassinations and civil wars. From each conquered nation they demanded full submission and prompt payment of exorbitant taxes. In every corner of their wide empire, a constant thorn in their side was the Jewish nation. Their frustration with the Jews reached its highest point during the days of Tiberius (42 B.C.–A.D. 37). Sejanus, the most influential Roman in Tiberius's court, initiated measures that were designed to destroy the whole race, and after the death of Tiberius, Gaius was more than eager to fulfill Sejanus's plan.

> The character of Gaius is extremely capricious towards all, but particularly toward the Jews. He hates us bitterly, and in many cities, particularly Alexandria, he has seized the synagogues and filled them with images and statues of his own form. And in Jerusalem, the temple which has hitherto been untouched and held worthy of preservation from all violation, he has tried to change and transform to a shrine of his own, to be called that of *Gaius, the new Zeus manifest.*

Philo, more than any other Jew of the time, knew that if Gaius were allowed to defile the temple with statues and pagan worship, it would be more devastating than if it were completely torn down and destroyed: "For in the destruction of the temple there is reason to fear that Gaius will also order that the general name of our whole nation be abolished. If that be the case, we will perish. But a glorious death in defence of our laws is another form of life."

Philo's words embody the basic spirit of Judaism, a spirit that has kept it intact over the centuries despite continuous defamations and persecutions. Philo lived and died in Alexandria, the city he loved and revered. A prolific writer, his life and work reveal that he was thoroughly a Jew and desired to be nothing else, for Jewish *philosophy*, or the knowledge of God and of things human and divine as contained in the Mosaic Scriptures, was to him the true and highest wisdom.

Six hundred years before this, Plato had taught that the world is an imperfect copy of an ideal universe, and although he had also taught many other things, it was this doctrine that the "New Platonists" of Alexandria adopted and pursued to sublime and mystic conclusions.

The first school of Neoplatonism was founded in Alexandria by Ammonius Saccas (c. A.D. 175–250), who began life as a porter in the docks and as a Christian, but he abandoned both pursuits for the study of Plato. Very little is known about his teaching, but he produced scores of famous pupils, most notably Plotinus.

Even his closest friends could not fathom Plotinus. He never revealed the day he was born because he did not want them to celebrate the occasion with sacrifices and feasts. But more importantly, he was ashamed of being confined within a mortal body. He once remarked, "The descent of my soul into this detestable vessel is an event so unfortunate and appalling, I care not to discuss it." He scorned any talk about race, parents, or native country, preferring to be a man of the universe, unchained to time or place. He was also an impetuous child. Up to the age of eight, though he was already going to school, he kept asking his nurse to bare her breasts so he could suck. He stopped this practice only after his father told him he was a little pest and should be ashamed of himself.

Plotinus came to Alexandria when the city was still basking in cultural glory and reputation. The head of its superb philosophical school was Ammonius Saccas, whose fame had spread so rapidly throughout the world, students flocked to Alexandria to study with him, but being selective, he chose only a few each year and demanded that they wear a philosopher's cloak throughout the course of study and hold secret everything they learned. Plotinus was enraptured with Ammonius. "This is the man I've been seeking from eternity," he later wrote.

Longinus and Origen were also students of Ammonius at this time, and with the latter, Plotinus struck an enduring friendship. After classes, they would take long walks along the Heptastadion and wrestle over Plato, Socrates, and Christ. Time had little meaning for them. Their minds clove to each other with such intensity that their discourses often carried them into the early morning hours. Origen was a brilliant scholar, and at the age of eighteen he had just succeeded Clement as dean of Alexandria's widely acclaimed theological school.

Since their common bond was Plato, the two hit it off instantly, and not one subject escaped their scrutiny. During this period, every person in Alexandria—Christian, pagan, and Jew—wallowed in fatalism. Charlatans cast long and seemingly knowledgeable looks toward the stars and foretold detailed events to gullible ears; vendors of horoscopes stood on every street corner; soothsayers flourished. Plotinus, of course, scorned all this. He felt that the stars did not cause human events but merely announced them. "How could we possibly say the stars determined the course of our lives when this had already been ascertained? Did we dare admit there was another force pulling against that which already had been decreed?"

Even from the time he was a child, Origen was a master of allegory. To him, a tree was not merely branch and leaf, but creation—life giving birth in the spring and dying in autumn splendor. More importantly, man was not placed on earth merely to stare at the four walls of the universe. "He should take each moment and hold it tenderly in his hands, compare it with other moments, with earth and sky, planets, constellations—examine what other possible meaning it may hold, what other purpose or end."

After completing his course of study with Ammonius Saccas, Plotinus traveled to Persia to take part in a military expedition, but his real purpose was to acquaint himself with Persian and Indian philosophy. His plans almost met with disaster, and Plotinus was very nearly relieved of the disgrace of having a mortal body. After an escape, he made his way to Rome, where he was to remain until his death. While there, he opened his own philosophical school, and at the age of forty-nine began writing his famous *Enneads*. Like Ammonius Saccas and Origen, he too was a Neoplatonist, but as a mystic, his thoughts carried him much further, into uncharted spiritual and philosophical worlds: God the Creator was not one but three. However, Plotinus was not referring to the Christian trinity. He believed that as humans, we are all imprisoned with feelings of frustration that originate solely from the body and its passions. As long as the mind is held captive inside such a material body, it must of necessity be subjected to evil and suffering. Thus the body becomes a tomb for the mind. But a far greater tomb is the world, and since the mind earnestly desires to escape from its imprisonment but cannot, tension is the subsequent result. This tension between the mind's existence in a material world and its deep yearning for the eternal is like a man plunged in mud from head to feet, causing his original beauty to be marred by ugliness. In order to become beautiful again, he must undertake to cleanse himself through the gradual ascent of his mind from Here to There—from the lower region into which the mind descended, to the higher region: the fulfillment of its spiritual destiny.

For Plotinus, the ultimate cause of the Universe is the One. He is the Agathon, which transcends all being, and since He is the source of life, He must consequently be beyond the material as well as the spiritual. He is absolutely One and absolutely Good. For this reason, He has nothing whatsoever to do with the existing world. As for the creation of the universe, it proceeded from the One like water pouring out of a fountain. From this overflow was generated the second stage of the creative process: the intelligible world of thought, which alone created the third stage: that of the mind. Everything we comprehend through our senses comes from this mind. It creates animals, trees, stones, oceans, the prophets of Israel, the gods of Greece and Rome. Thus, Plotinus saw the Creator as Good, Divine, and Mind: Three in One. Not only do all things overflow from Him, but they also strive to return to Him.

But could a struggling and weak humanity actually attain this goal? Plotinus of course was speaking of a spiritual journey, whose objective could not be reached "by that inane practice of taking God into one's mouth, or worshipping the bones of saints and martyrs." If one was to be sincere in his quest for the eternal truths, he had to withdraw into his own mind and see himself as beautiful, act as a sculptor who planned to create a statue by cutting away, smoothing down, carving deeply until a face was formed. When he too realized that he was a perfect work, that his being was wrapped in purity, that nothing could shatter his inner strength—when he discerned himself abiding in perfection—then he had to take still another step. If his eyes had not been blurred by vice—if he was whole and strong, if his mind was beautiful, was pure—he believed that he would behold a sight never before envisioned by man: *he would see himself as God!*

It was Plato who first taught that the material world was an imperfect copy of the intelligible, and whereas the prophets promised that man might eventually see God, Plotinus claimed that man could *be* God. For many, his theories contradicted one another: Greek philosophy and eastern mysticism seasoned with a dash of Christian dogma and Hebrew theosophy. They also failed to answer a very important problem, particularly for the Alexandrians: the existence of evil. But to this, Plotinus was quick to respond that sooner or later we must all realize that evil is a deficiency of good. Poverty, disease, and crime cannot disturb the man of virtue. Moreover, war among animals and men is not entirely evil since both multiply so rapidly they would perish if they did not destroy each other. Even the most wicked have their place within the cosmos, for in the universal drama, the bad as well as the good are called upon to play the roles assigned to them. "Mankind," he said, "must stop viewing the world as a tiny corner of earth made expressly for itself. The world is immense and overflowing with competing minds, which of necessity are evil because they are chained to bodies. To attain the *Highest Vision,* these minds must eventually separate themselves from all material bondage."

Throughout his lifetime, Plotinus refused to eat meat. He often suffered from a disease of the bowels but would not take an enema. He also avoided the baths, and instead had himself massaged every day at his home. His closest friend and physician, Amelius Gentilianus, once urged him to sit for a painter so that a portrait could be made. Plotinus erupted. "Is it not enough to have to carry the image in which nature has encased me, without leaving behind me a longer-lasting image of the image, as if it were something genuinely worth looking at?"

For many years, Plotinus accepted students but, true to his promise to Ammonius, wrote nothing. Since he encouraged his students to ask questions, the course of instruction was lacking in order and produced mostly an endless stream of pointless chatter. Nevertheless, his fame as a philosopher drew scores of people to his classes, including members of the Senate.

Along with their husbands, many women came to his classes. They often brought their children and entrusted them to Plotinus with the assurance that he would be a holy and godlike guardian for them. In some cases, they assigned all their property and possessions in exchange for rearing their children. Thus his house was filled with young lads and maidens, to whose education he gave serious thought and dedication. He even attended to the accounts of their property when their trustees submitted them, and he assumed that they were always accurate. Although he shielded his students from the worries and cares of ordinary life, he never relinquished his love for philosophy and the academic life.

Yet he had his enemies. One of them, Olympius of Alexandria, another former student of Ammonius, adopted a superior attitude toward Plotinus out of envy. His attacks soon reached the point of trying to invoke an evil spell on Plotinus, but when he realized his attempts had recoiled upon himself, Olympius gave up, stating that "the soul of Plotinus has such great power it is able to ward off all forms of evil." Through his great mystic power, Plotinus had somehow been aware of Olympius's cruel scheme. In truth, he did possess from birth something more than other men. When his trusted friend Amelius took to religion and became unbearably ritualistic, he tried to tug Plotinus along with him on a pious visit to the feast of the gods at the temples of the New Moon, but Plotinus rigidly objected. "The gods ought to come to me, not I to them."

Even in his later years, he had a surpassing degree of concentration and penetration into others' thoughts. After a valuable necklace was stolen from an honorable widow living in his house, all the slaves of the house were assembled before him. He peered at each of them carefully, then, pointing to one man, said, "This is the thief." At first, the man persisted in his denial, but finally he confessed and gave back what he had stolen.

Plotinus was also gifted in foretelling how each of the children who lived with him would turn out: that Polemon for instance, who was his favorite, would have a short life. And he actually did. On another occasion, when his dearest friend Porphyry was contemplating suicide, Plotinus unexpectedly appeared and told him this lust for death did not stem from any rational decision but from an indisposition, and urged Porphyry to go away for a holiday. Porphyry obeyed and took off for Sicily, never again to consider self-destruction.

Gallienus, who was joint emperor with Valerian beginning in A.D. 253, and sole emperor from 260 to 268, so greatly honored and venerated Plotinus that he created a city community of philosophers in Campania and invited them to settle there and live according to the laws of Plato. At first, Plotinus gave serious thought to the invitation, but was prevented by the jealousy and spite of his opponents.

When he finally began to write, he was weak and gray with age. He could never bear to go over his work twice, and even to read it through once was too much for him. As he wrote, he did not form the letters with any regard to appearance or divide the syllables correctly, and he paid no attention to spelling. He was only concerned with thoughts and ideas. If it weren't for the assiduous editing of Porphyry, the *Enneads* and all the other works of Plotinus would be lost in confusion.

Encouraged by Porphyry, who now was not only his right hand but also his eyes, Plotinus kept writing to the very end of his life. Many teachers and philosophers wrote to him continually, requesting copies of his works. One was Longinus, whom Plotinus considered to be a scholar but certainly not a philosopher. Writing to Amelius in Sicily, Longinus begged him to come to Phoenicia and bring all of Plotinus's works with him. An extremely severe critic who subjected all the works of his other contemporaries to drastic examination, Longinus gave an astute appraisal of both Plotinus and Amelius. In the preface of his book *On the End: By Longinus in Answer to Plotinus and Amelius,* he revealed how at first he despised Plotinus, admitting that this was due to the fact that he had misjudged the Plotinus manuscripts he had received from Amelius. Apparently, he didn't understand Plotinus's unusual manner of expressing himself and now he wanted to correct matters.

More than any other place, Plotinus loved and revered Alexandria. The city was constantly in his thoughts, particularly the halcyon days he spent with Ammonius Saccas. He was never to return to Alexandria. Much as the idea would have repelled him, chronographers were able to ascertain the exact dates of his birth and death. According to his physician Eustochius, Plotinus was sixty-six years old when he breathed his last in Rome, at the end of the second year of the reign of Claudius. By tracing back sixty-six years from this date, the chronographers concluded that his birth occurred in the eleventh year of the reign of Severus, A.D. 204.

Clement of Alexandria was no Desert Monk. He lived in the midst of the city, moved among its crowds, knew its intellectual elite, and loved them all in Christ. He knew, however, that in order to reach these people, he had to do it in a cultivated and intelligent way; otherwise they would never accept his teachings. And so he adopted the unique idea of leading them into Christianity through the wide portals of Greek philosophy, particularly Plato.

> Clement's wisdom has no equal because he is the first of his kind: the first to embrace with his whole heart the new and dangerous vocation of teaching Christianity to the intellectuals and society people of a great cosmopolitan city.

Born in Athens, Clement was an educated pagan and no doubt initiated into paganism's mysteries. He traveled all over the world, from one philosophical school to the other, seeking the one true doctrine, the one true teacher. He finally found him in Pantaenus of Alexandria, "the Sicilian Bee," whom Clement called "the last of my teachers in time and the first in power."

It was in Alexandria that Clement became a Christian and eventually established a school. With his wide knowledge of Greek culture, his philosophy, his urbanity, and his simplicity, he welcomed all comers to his school of Christian philosophy. It was not a college of theology, and it appealed less to the simple catechumens seeking baptism than to the cultured pagan, the intellectual, the artist, the poet, the scientist, the lawyer, the man of business, or the government official who might be curious about the new doctrine. To these, Clement addressed no mere apology, but a Christian philosophy of life and a preparation for Christian experience at the deepest level.

In his teaching and in his writings, Clement by no means attempted to put Plato and the Bible on the same level. "In Clement, there is no shadow of compromise. He knows very well the difference between revelation and metaphysics, and he knows well enough the poverty and the unfulfillment of philosophy without religious faith."

One of Clement's three surviving works—*The Protreptikos,* or *The Ex-*

hortation to the Greeks (which dealt with the awakening of the pagan soul)—
contains a pertinent diatribe against the antiquated gods:

ZEUS IS DEAD

Zeus is snake no longer, nor swan nor eagle
Nor erotic man.
He does not fly as god, nor chase boys
Nor make love, nor fight;
Yet there are now far more lovely women
Sweeter than Leda, more seductive than Semele.
Where then is that eagle? Where that swan?
Where Zeus?
He and his wings have mouldered;
He has, no doubt, not repented of loving and not
    learned temperance.
The myth is unveiled; Leda is dead.
And you are looking for Zeus? Look not in heaven
But on earth. The Cretans, in whose island he lies buried,
They will tell you of him. Listen to Callimachus:
The Cretans, Lord, have built thy tomb.
For Zeus, like Leda, is dead.
Dead as a swan, dead as eagle, as erotic man,
And dead as serpent!

Clement regarded Christianity as the one true philosophy. The ancient philosophers sought through their teachings to attain a nobler and
more virtuous life, which was also the aim of Christianity; but in
Clement's judgment, the chief difference between the two was that the
Greek philosophers had only glimpses of the truth, that they attained only
fragments of the truth, whereas Christianity revealed the absolute and
perfect truth. All the stages of the world's history were but preparations
leading up to this full revelation. He stressed, above all, that God's care for
mankind was not confined to the Hebrews alone; also that the worship of
the heavenly bodies was given to man at an early stage, so that he might
rise from a contemplation of these sublime objects, to the worship of the
Creator. As the schoolmaster, or *paidagogos,* Greek philosophy was the perfect preparation of the Greeks for the new religion.

In essence, Clement was a bit shaky in his statement about how Plato got his wisdom or his fragments of Reason. At times, he assumed they came directly from God, like all good things, but he also was fond of maintaining that many of Plato's best thoughts were borrowed from the Hebrew prophets; and he made the same statement in regard to the wisdom of the other philosophers. Clement regarded the Father as the Absolute of the philosophers, and the Son was the Reason and Wisdom of God. Beyond this, he believed that the Son of God really became incarnate, though he speaks of Him almost invariably as the Word and attaches little value to His human nature.

Clement fervently believed that the Christian must act like someone who has but has not. He has to accept the world as a good gift of God but remain detached from it as a pilgrim and sojourner. A Christian woman should be restrained in dress, which did not mean that she be slovenly or dowdy; and she was only allowed cosmetics if she was married to a pagan husband, in which case she needed them to hold him. Dyed or false hair was to be deplored, and baths were a luxury to be treated with moderation. There was to be no compromise with the world in military service, and the true Christian should avoid the use of oaths. Physical exercise and sport were good in moderation for the sake of physical health but should not be pursued for personal pride. Fishing, on the other hand, was quite appropriate for a Christian gentleman, since it had apostolic precedent. There was to be no compromise with the eroticism of pagan society, and the Christian should avoid dance music that provoked sensuality. In choosing a signet ring, the Christian was expected to have a seal that fitted his belief—like a dove, or a fish, or a ship, or an anchor—and not symbols that suggested idolatry, or erotic passion, or drink. Lastly, the Christian life was a ceaseless conflict with the downward pull of passions, and the disciple must learn to rise through the moderation of Aristotelian ethics to achieve the *apatheia* (passionlessness) of the Stoics, a calm tranquility of silent worship, which is a life of continual joy in prayer.

Clement was a man of scholarship and culture who found in Christianity the best rewards life can offer, and a religious vantage point from which one can observe and study the contemporary intellectual scene. He was a lay teacher of Christian philosophy and a trusted figure of whom Alexandria was proud. His entire character and personal achievement constituted in themselves an answer to a thesis of the pagan philosopher

Celsus, which claimed that between Christianity and the Hellenic tradition there could be no reconciliation.

In Clement's own appraisal, "The Old Testament and Greek philosophy are tutors that bring the world to Christ, and they are both tributaries of the one great river of Christianity. The idea of God was implanted in man at Creation and breathed into Adam. Man thus belongs to God and is made for the contemplation of God, which is what distinguishes him from animals."

Clement owed much to the Stoics. Except for his censure of their approval of suicide, and his criticism of their notion that mercy is an emotional weakness that the wise man must suppress, he openly welcomed the body of Stoic teaching. The Christian, called to travel light in this world and to possess it as if he had it not, could find much in common with the Stoic, for whom only inward moral virtue was necessary to happiness. On this basis, Clement deliberately set out to adorn his Christian ethic with Stoic and Platonic teaching. Like most philosophers before him, he reasoned that the ethical ideal of Plato's assimilation to God as far as possible was identical in meaning with the Stoic ideal of life according to nature. As a result, it was no great step for Clement to identify both the Platonic and Stoic ethical teachings with the Christian doctrine that man must shape himself to correspond to his Creator's purpose, and that the measure of his departure from this purpose is sin. "Plato, Aristotle, and the Stoics, were wise and clever men who discovered many truths for themselves under the beneficent hand of God's providence. To deny that philosophy is God's gift is to deny Providence and the image of God in Creation."

On the other hand, Clement rejected the Platonic doctrine that the sun, moon, and stars are invested with divine souls responsible for their perfect orderly motion, and are in fact gods. To him, the stars were powers that fulfilled the command of their Creator, their prime duty being to mark the passage of time, whereas comets, thunderbolts, and other such celestial portents, were purely physical phenomena and must be given an entirely naturalistic explanation.

Clement's sex ethic also owed much of its inspiration to the Stoics, who combined a vindication of marriage with an austere condemnation of self-indulgence and "unnatural" practices, such as abortion and homosexual vice. Like the Stoics, Clement insisted that there should be nothing to be ashamed of in the body. Marriage was ordained by God, "who made man male and female, and knew what He was about when He did so." To beget children was not merely a duty to society but it also cooperated with the work of the Creator.

While some could be called to celibacy as part of their vocation to a higher spiritual life, it was wrong to regard celibacy as inherently nearer to God than the married state, as if sexual intercourse involved a moral defilement. In fact, Clement believed that the married man had greater opportunities for sanctification than the celibate, since he faced the daily exasperations that came to him from his wife, his children, and his household responsibilities.

As for wine, it was a good gift of God to be received with thanksgiving, but drunkenness was disgusting and wrong. The modest consumption of a glass or two of wine at an occasional dinner party, especially by older people whose blood is thin and cooler, was not only permissible but sanctioned by the authority of Plato, by Christ in the miracle of Cana, and by St. Paul, who exhorted Timothy to take a little wine for his stomach's sake.

The whole moral philosophy of Clement can be summed up in his firm conviction that Christ was the true philosopher and teacher, who guided and formed his students in every aspect of the Christian life. Without the light of this teaching, man was little more than a fowl fattened in the dark for the butcher's knife, and his life was without significance. But in Christ, everything came to life, and even the most simple and ordinary task acquired a spiritual and supernatural dimension.

Clement best exemplified the effects of the Alexandrian spirit. Through his efforts, Christianity was liberated from blind belief and superstition, and bolstered by its new link to a strong philosophic tradition. During the persecution of Severus, he left his beloved Alexandria and traveled to Cappadocia to stay with a former pupil, Alexander, who had just been ordained a bishop. Later, when Alexander was raised to the see of Jerusalem, Clement followed him there, and shortly after, he returned to Athens, where he died in comfortable old age.

⟨⟩

Clement's work was carried on by his greatest pupil, Origen, the strangest and most adventurous of the Early Church Fathers, who like Clement also believed that Christianity was the heir of the past and the interpreter of the future. He was the most distinguished and most influential of all theologians of the ancient church, and as the father of theological science, he created a solid system of dogma and laid foundations for scientific criticism of the Old and New Testaments. In achieving this, he owed much to Justin, Tatian, Pantaenus, and Clement, all of whom had labored at the problem of finding an intellectual expression and a philosophical basis for Christianity. By working to reconcile science with the Christian faith, philosophy with the Gospel, Origen did more than any other man to win the Old World to the Christian religion.

He was born in Alexandria and as a boy displayed evidence of remarkable talents. His father, Leonidas, a teacher of Greek, gave him an excellent education; and from his Jewish mother he obtained a thorough knowledge of Hebrew, often clamoring to sing the Psalms with her. He was the eldest of seven sons and, during adolescence, attended the lectures of Pantaenus and Clement in the School of Alexandria. By the age of seventeen, he had attained such fame that his father was distinguished as "Leonidas, the father of Origen."

His full name was Origenes Adamantius, and because of his unusual strength and powerful body, he was also called "brazen-boweled." In the ninth year of Severus's reign (A.D. 202), his father, refusing to deny Christ, was dragged out of their house and taken to the Caesarium. While his mother and six brothers cowered, Origen insisted on accompanying his father to martyrdom, and when his mother realized that he was serious, she took his sandals and hid them. But he was not to be dissuaded. Rushing barefoot after the soldiers, who kept beating his father, he yelled out to him, beseeching him not to renounce his faith because of them. With the sun descending over the Necropolis, he looked on as his father was beheaded. After the crowd dispersed, Origen made his way through the maze of columns and entered the inner chamber of the Serapium, where rows of torches burned. On the floor, in two large mounds, he saw the dead: their heads tossed into one heap, their bodies into another.

As was customary, the Roman authorities confiscated all the property of Leonidas, leaving the family destitute. Through the intercession of a friend, Origen remained in Alexandria, earning his bread by teaching and copying manuscripts. For a short period of time, he was supported by a woman of rank named Paula, but when Clement left his post as dean of the theological school, Origen, at the age of eighteen, was chosen to succeed him. The school was under the strict jurisdiction of the bishop Demetrius, with whom Origen was to clash on many subsequent occasions.

It was during this time that Origen decided to castrate himself for spiritual reasons.

> While he was performing the work of instruction at Alexandria, he did a thing which gave abundant proof of an immature and youthful mind, yet withal of faith of self-control. For he took the saying, "There are eunuchs who make themselves eunuchs for the kingdom of heaven's sake" in too literal and extreme sense . . . thinking to fulfill the Savior's saying and also to prevent all suspicion on the part of unbelievers (for, young as he was, he discoursed on divine things with women as well as men), he hastened to put into effect the Savior's word.

(EUSEBIUS, *ECCLESIASTICAL HISTORY*, VIII, 1–8)

Another theory suggested that Origen never did castrate himself, but that he created the rumor to conceal his homosexuality. Furthermore, he was accused of sustaining himself on exotic drugs from the East; otherwise he would have gone mad in his struggle to remain celibate in the midst of the beautiful young women who flocked to his classes. Nevertheless, nearly everyone in Alexandria, and even his former students in the far corners of the empire, believed that Origen had committed this rash act even though he refused to admit it. Nevertheless, to avoid becoming slovenly and fat—telltale signs of a eunuch—he embarked on a strenuous program of fasting and intense exercise.

In his teaching, meanwhile, things continued smoothly. Origen gave instructions in Greek grammar, science, philosophy, and the exegesis of sacred Scriptures. He divided his pupils into two groups. He took the more advanced, while Heracles, whom he had first met at the lectures of Clement, took the elementary group. Along with these duties, Origen further immersed himself in a thorough study of Plato, the Stoics, and the Pythagoreans. His manner of life was ascetic; the sayings of the Sermon on the Mount and the practical maxims of the Stoics were his guides.

In the spring of A.D. 215, Origen learned that Clement had settled himself in Athens and he dispatched a letter to his revered teacher. As he had frequently done when he was Clement's student, Origen wrote frankly about his theological views.

Although Bishop Demetrius kept him occupied at the school, Origen still found the time to make several journeys, the last of which was to Arabia, where he was called in compliance with a request brought to Bishop Demetrius by a soldier of an Arabian prince, asking that Origen be permitted to visit that country and deliver a series of philosophical lectures in the presence of the prince. While there, Origen had the good fortune to meet with Hippolytus, a Roman scholar and philosopher.

On his return to Alexandria, he again devoted himself to study. He now held that the Father and the Son were two distinct essences, two substances and beings. "Christ should not be the object of supreme worship; nor should prayer be addressed to Him, but offered only to the God of the universe, to whom Christ himself prayed." Consequently, Origen placed Christ at an immense distance from the Father, and called it profane even to suppose an equality or union between the Father and any other being.

Moreover, Origen could not dislodge himself from the inclination that all beings were endowed with reason and were produced long before the foundation of the physical world. At first, they were pure intelligences glowing with love toward their Maker, but since they were entirely free, they also had to possess the capacity of virtue and vice. Choosing between the two estranged them from the Creator and caused their original love for Him to fade. In time, they were reduced to varying ranks of beings and placed in the bodies of the stars, where they were given the task of enlightening and adorning the universe.

Origen believed that all beings would be restored to virtue and happiness, without being subjected to a trial of fire as the North African theologian Tertullian maintained. For Origen, the only fire that could burn vice was the flame of conscience. Their own consciences would remind them of their sins. In this manner, all would be chastised, but their sufferings would have an end, because every living being would be returned to purity and love, after death.

During this time, a wealthy Roman named Ambrosius became Origen's patron, and it was through his efforts that Origen was able to amass his voluminous writings. At one time, the number of his works was estimated to be over several thousand. "Which of us," asked Jerome in awe, "can read all that Origen has written?"

Ambrosius supplied seven stenographers for Origen. They worked every day for many years, taking his rapid dictations, then passing them to fourteen calligraphers, who proceeded to make copies. At first, Origen had refused to work under such conditions, but Ambrosius insisted:

"From this day on, you will write, record everything on papyrus. That way you will never be misquoted or attacked by ignorant men."

"But I am a teacher, not a writer," Origen protested.

Ambrosius was unyielding. "I will not permit you to dissipate your life in fruitless endeavors. You have mountains of lecture notes. I have seen them with my own eyes: commentaries on philosophy, poetry, ethics, logic, the Scriptures. What do you accomplish by bouncing them from one head to another? Put them into books and they will be remembered into eternity."

Ambrosius was to be Origen's "taskmaster" until his death. Along with his writing, Origen continued as dean of the theological school for twenty-eight years, a period broken only by travel for scholarly and theological reasons. In Rome, he listened to the sermon of Hippolytus "The Praise of Our Lord and Savior," then traveled again to Arabia, where a high Roman official desired to hear his lectures. After this, he went to Antioch in response to a most flattering invitation from Julia Mammaea, the mother of Emperor Alexander Severus.

Seventy-five years before the birth of Origen, a book written by the pagan philosopher Celsus, *The True Word*, so devastated Christianity with its attacks that it threatened to put an end to the new religion. All the early apologists, including Justin, Irenaeus, Polycarp, and Ignatius, made no effort to respond to Celsus's charges, and for many decades Christianity seemed destined to crumble into a meaningless sect of fear and superstition, relegated only to the poor and uneducated. Deciding that it was time to refute Celsus's charges, Origen wrote perhaps his greatest work, which remarkably has survived in its entirety. It is appropriately titled *Against Celsus*. Half the book is devoted to a full account of Celsus's views, and with unusual honesty, Origen lays them before the reader without much distortion. It was Celsus's chief purpose to address himself to the Jews who converted to the new religion. He could not understand what madness possessed them to leave the Law of their fathers and accept a fool who called Himself the Messiah. Why couldn't the Roman and Greek world recognize this Messiah? His own followers weren't convinced; otherwise they never would have betrayed and deserted Him. If He could not persuade those who daily saw and spoke with Him, how could He convince generations that followed? As for His resurrection, the same could be said of many charlatans. Zamolxis told the Scythians he had come back from the dead. So Pythagoras told the Italians. Rhampsinus claimed he played dice with Ceres in hell, and even showed a golden handkerchief that Ceres had given him. Orpheus, Protesilaus, Heracles, and Theseus—all were said to have died and risen again.

> "And who saw your *Messiah* after he arose?" Celsus mocked the Jewish converts. "An hysterical woman who had the reputation of a harlot, and some of his own companions who dreamed of him and were deluded by their enthusiasm? All the world was witness to his death, yet only a few friends witnessed his resurrection."

In this diatribe, Celsus proceeded to attack the person and character of the Messiah, saying that He was born in a small Jewish village and that His mother was a poor woman who earned her bread by spinning. Her husband Joseph divorced her because she committed adultery with a soldier named Panthera, but Joseph agreed not to abandon her. After the child was born, they brought Him to Egypt, where eventually He mastered the healing arts. Soon after this, He returned to Palestine and began claiming He was God. "The story of his divine parentage," ridiculed Celsus, "was taken from the myth of Danae. Who was it that saw the dove descending upon him in the Jordan River? Who heard the voice declaring him the Son of God?"

Celsus conceded that this Messiah might have cured diseases, restored dead bodies to life, fed multitudes with a few loaves of bread, "but were these not the common tricks of Egyptian wizards, performed every day in the market places for a few obols? They too drive out devils, heal sicknesses, call up the souls of the dead, provide suppers, cover tables with platters, and make things seem what they are not. We do not call them Sons of God. They are rogues and vagabonds!"

According to Celsus, the thief, the burglar, the poisoner, the robbers of temples and tombs—these were the Messiah's proselytes. Did He look upon the just man who remained steadfast from the cradle in the ways of virtue? Why should sinners have preference with Him? Was it not a known truth that persons with a proclivity to evil had so formed their habits they were notoriously past cure and neither punishment nor tenderness could save them?

Furthermore, God would never come down to earth to judge mankind. Why should He do this? He already knows all things. The everlasting order of His universe does not need to be judged or set right. He is all-perfect and all-blessed. If He leaves His present state to come down as a man among men, He must pass from blessedness to imperfection, from good to evil. Change is only the condition of mortality; God cannot change and still remain Himself. He cannot seem to change while He remains unchanged, for then He is a deceiver.

Celsus likened the Jewish converts to ants creeping out of a hill, or frogs sitting around a pool, or a congregation of worms on a dung heap, all of whom claimed that the secrets of God were revealed only to them:

Who are you, that you should demand such high privileges? History knows you as a colony of Egyptian slaves who revolted and then settled in a corner of Palestine. In your own account of yourselves, you assert that God made man with His own hands and breathed life into him. He then put him to sleep, took out one of his ribs and made a woman out of it. Having thus created them, He gave certain orders which a serpent tempted them to disobey. And then there was a deluge, and a miraculous ark in which all manner of living things were assembled, with a dove and a raven to act as messengers. The history of your patriarchs follows: children singularly born, brothers quarreling, mothers plotting, a story of Lot and his daughters, which is far worse than the banquet of Thyestes, one of the lads goes to Egypt where he interprets a dream and becomes ruler of the country . . . on and on it goes.

Celsus asserted that, like Euripides, the new religion claimed that the day and night were ministers of man. But why more of man than of ants, to whom night brought sleep; and day, food? Was mankind lord of the animals because it captured and devoured them? Did they not equally chase and devour mankind? Would a higher place be claimed for man simply because he lived in cities and ruled himself by laws? So do ants and bees. They too have their rulers, their wars, their victories, their captured enemies. They too have their cities, their division of labor, laws of punishment, cemeteries for their dead.

Celsus insisted that the universe was no more made for man than for the lion, the eagle, or the dolphin. One created being is not better than another, because all are but parts of a great and perfect whole, whose constant care lies in the hands of the Creator. He does not forget it, or turn away from it when it becomes corrupt. He is never angry with it; never threatens to destroy it.

Lashing out at the Jews again, Celsus derided the tenacity of their traditions, especially when they pretended to have sole possession of divine knowledge and refused as unclean a communion with the rest of mankind. Indeed, their dogmas pertaining to a God in heaven were hardly unique, for the Persians too sacrificed on the hilltops to Dis, by whom they meant the circle of the sky. It mattered little whether this being was named Dis or Most High or Zeus or Adonai or Sabbaoth or Ammon.

As for the customs of the Jews, "they should be aware that the Egyptians and Colchians were circumcised before them. The Egyptians furthermore did not eat swine's flesh nor the flesh of many animals; the Pythagoreans touched no meat at all."

Through Moses, God promised the Jews prosperity and earthly dominion. He bade them to destroy their enemies, sparing neither old nor young. He even threatened them with destruction if they did not obey Him. Yet their false Messiah condemned riches, condemned earthly dominion, counseled them to care no more for food or raiment than the ravens or the lilies of the field, and even invited them to turn the other cheek if they were smitten on one. Either Moses was wrong, or their false Messiah was.

Lastly, Celsus warned the Jewish converts that they dreamed of an illusive world, like an Elysian field, where all riddles would be solved, all evil put away, and God seen in His full glory. But these promises of their Messiah, Celsus reminded them, were words of flesh, not of reason. Then only could they see God when they closed the eyes of the body and opened the eyes of the mind, and if they sought further proof, they should avoid those quacks and conjurers who promised to show them ghosts:

> Put away your vain illusions, your magic formulas, your lion and your Amphibius, your God-ass and celestial doorkeepers in whose names you allow yourselves to be persecuted and impaled. Did not Plato

say that the Architect and Father of the universe is not easily found? If you must have a new doctrine, at least adopt an illustrious name that is better suited to the dignity of a divine nature than that of your impudent *Messiah*. If Heracles and Aesculapius do not please you, there is Orpheus. He too died of violence. There is also Anaxarchus who was beaten to death and mocked. *"Pound on,"* he yelled to his tormentors. *"You can pound the sheath of Anaxarchus, but himself you cannot pound!"*

Celsus's final words cut deeply into the heart of the Jews.

> You audaciously believe that you are God's chosen people, and yet you do not have one yard of ground to call your own. You are persecuted and are only safe when you keep concealed. If you are found, you are executed.

Origen bore all these arguments in mind before he decided to reply to Celsus's charges. If Christianity truly proceeded from God, why should it fear one man? In the passage of time, what harm could Celsus's words do? Did not the aged wise man of the Jews, Gamaliel, stand up before the Council in Jerusalem when Peter and the other apostles were threatened with execution, and did he not say, "Ye men of Israel, refrain. Let them alone, for if their teaching be of men it will come to nought. But if it be of God, ye cannot overthrow it, lest ye fight against God!"

Nevertheless, his taskmaster Ambrosius insisted that Origen write a book and respond to Celsus's charges. At first, Origen was reluctant, but after much prodding, he finally undertook the project. In his book, he expounded the fact that the evidence of truth concerning any religion was not the testimony of one or more persons who saw or thought they saw some indication of a supernatural presence. The real evidence was the power with which a religion could cope with moral disease, lift it out of self-indulgence, into more virtuous spheres. The new religion effected this in a manner that no creed or system of philosophy had ever accomplished. Origen asserted that

> . . . the highest speculations of the Greeks were mere theories, because they still continued to nourish ancient beliefs, still persisted in sacrificing a cock to Aesculapius. Their beautiful syllogisms may have converted a few students into philosophers, but the crude words of Scripture trans-

formed multitudes, making the coward a hero, and the wicked good. Unlike the Greeks, the Jewish people never found delight purely in games, nor the theater, nor horse races. Their women never sold their beauty, and from their earliest years they were taught the blessing of spiritual realities. They always believed in the immortality of the soul, and are indeed wiser than those philosophers who, after their most learned utterances, continually fall back upon the worship of idols and demons.

Long after he had written *Against Celsus,* Origen was hounded by worries of failure and defeat. Celsus was probably right when he claimed that the Scriptures were echoes of Greek tradition, that the idea of Satan originated in Pherecydes, that the story of Babel was a plagiarism from Aloidae, and that the Christian concept of heaven was revealed first in Plato's world of Ideas; but later theologians all concurred that Origen gave the most powerful argument against Celsus and, with this book, established his unshakable reputation and fame.

The following year, Origen left Alexandria and traveled to Jerusalem to visit his friend Alexandros. His benefactor Ambrosius was in Rome on business matters, and since Origen had no money for the long journey to Palestine, he contracted to feed and water the mules, put up the tents, and help prepare the meals for a caravan that was headed for Antioch. After passing through Gaza, he left the caravan and headed eastward across the desert alone.

Three days later, he reached a small village. He stayed the night in a dung-filled stable and left at daybreak before anyone awoke. As in Gaza, he noticed skulls of camels nailed to the doors of all the houses for protection against evil spirits. Just before nightfall, he reached the town of Marissa, where he found a water spring near a small grove of almond trees. Their fruit hung heavy on the branches, and after he satisfied his hunger, he remembered that it was in Marissa that the God of the Jews smote thousands of Ethiopian invaders. In the morning, he filled his haversack with almonds, then went to the spring and refilled the waterskins. By midday, he was in Eleutheropolis, and at dusk he stood on a high ridge overlooking the Valley of Elah, where David slew Goliath.

Throughout the next day, he struggled across bleached hillsides and burning sand, while ravens kept a vigilant watch overhead. The night turned bitterly cold. He awoke the following morning, hungry and numb with pain, but he set out once more, his eyes pointed toward the east. When it seemed that the world was but a huge log on a lake, spinning furiously and without purpose under his feet, he came upon a magnificent sight: rising high above him on a golden plateau stood the table of God— Jerusalem.

In Palestine, Bishops Alexandros and Theoctistus received him warmly and arranged for him to deliver public lectures in the church at Caesarea. In the East at that time, particularly in Asia Minor, it was not unusual for a layman, with permission of the bishop, to address the people in church. But in Alexandria, this custom had been abolished, and when Bishop Demetrius heard about it, he expressed his disapproval and recalled Origen to Alexandria. There was another reason for Demetrius's drastic action: he had become increasingly jealous of Origen's fame and reputation.

The event in Caesarea brought about an open rupture. This was soon augmented by Origen's reluctant ordination as presbyter by his two bishop friends in Palestine, which Demetrius took as an infringement of his sole rights as bishop of Alexandria. He immediately convened a synod, where it was resolved to banish Origen from his beloved Alexandria. But even this did not satisfy Demetrius's displeasure. He ordered a second synod, composed entirely of bishops, and they determined that Origen should be deposed forthwith from the presbyterial status. This decision was subsequently communicated to all the foreign churches.

Demetrius sought to justify the action by referring to Origen's self-castration and his objectionable doctrines. However, no formal excommunication was ever decreed, since it was deemed sufficient to have him demoted to the position of layman. The sentence was approved by certain churches, but particularly that of Rome. Even Heraclas, his former friend and teacher at the school in Alexandria, turned against him, and by so doing was chosen to succeed to the bishopric of Alexandria when Demetrius died.

Origen had no wish to cause a scandal and, obeying the synod's decision, he never returned to his beloved Alexandria. Settling in Caesarea, he continued with his writings, but without the use of scribes and calligraphists, the amount of work was significantly reduced. He also inaugurated a school in Caesarea whose reputation soon rivaled that of Alexandria. Enthusiastic students sat at his feet, and the methodical instruction that he imparted in all branches of knowledge became famous throughout the world.

But here again his activities were interrupted by more journeys: to Athens, Numidia, and twice to Arabia, where he was called to combat the Christology of a former student, Beryllus, bishop of Bostra, who accepted Christ's divine nature but sought to strip away His humanity. After a warm greeting, Origen asked Beryllus:

> "You want to cast away Christ's entire human nature?"
>
> "Yes," replied Beryllus.
>
> "His suffering and death?"
>
> "Yes."
>
> "But what does this leave?"
>
> "Exactly what He had from the very beginning, His divine nature."
>
> "But if Christ has no humanity," said Origen, "He holds no interest for me. I cannot imitate a God. No one can. But I will follow a virtuous man to the ends of the earth."

Since he had earlier dealings with the house of Emperor Alexander Severus, Origen now entered into a correspondence with Emperor Philip the Arabian and the empress Severa. Through all the situations of his life, Origen preserved his equanimity, his keen interest in science, and his indefatigable zeal for the instruction of others.

The year A.D. 250 found him in Tyre, and during the persecution of the Roman emperor Decius (A.D. 201–251), he was arrested, imprisoned, and maltreated. Somehow he managed to survive. Every morning, guards dragged his rigid body outside and whipped him with heavy straps. They then fastened an iron collar around his neck and distended his feet on a cruel instrument that left him almost crippled. Fitfully, he withdrew into his childhood and imagined himself walking down Canopic Way toward his martyrdom as thousands cheered. While deep in his fantasies, the guards came again and tortured him with even deadlier force. Remembering the words of Plotinus, he tried to convince himself that suffering had its virtue, that it obliterated the face of time until whole eons fell away like dead leaves from a tree.

The death of Decius freed him from prison. He was taken by cart from confinement to the house of Photius, a presbyter in Tyre, who also had been imprisoned in the same dungeon. Photius's wife nursed his wounds, fed him, and soon he was able to walk as far as the agora with the help of a cane. Within one month, he was hobbling along the shore, one hundred yards each day, still trying to prove to himself and to the world that he would never be branded by the telltale signs of a eunuch.

One morning a former student Dionysius delivered Origen a message. Dionysius had just succeeded Heraclas to the bishopric of Alexandria. Origen took the letter with him and slowly began a painful trot along the sea. He went no more than fifty yards when he felt a powerful stab in his chest. Dropping to his knees, he waited for the pain to subside, but the burden in his chest was unbearable. He scooped up a little water from the sea and tossed it over his face. He tried to get on his feet but could not find the strength. Dionysius's letter was still clenched in his hand. With great effort, he brought it close to his eyes and read:

Dionysius to Origen:
Beloved Master, it is my sincere wish that you return to Alexandria, where your name is once again spoken with respect and admiration.

He tore the message to shreds and watched the sea carry them away. Again he tried to get up but failed. In despair, he put his thoughts on Tyre. It was not unlike Alexandria, built on an island with a long causeway connecting to the mainland. And yet, they were not the same; not with those huge billows of purple smoke pouring out of Tyre's dye factories, polluting the sky.

Origen died in A.D. 253, one year shy of seventy. Along with an immense output of books, he had devoted twenty years of labor to the *Hexapla* and *Tetrapla* alone. In these two imposing volumes, he placed the Hebrew text of the Old Testament side by side with the various Greek versions, examined their mutual relations in detail, and tried to find the basis for a more reliable text of the Septuagint. His exegetical endeavors extended over the whole of the Old and New Testaments. They were divided into scholia, homilies, and commentaries. Only a very small portion of his work has been preserved in the Greek original, but in Latin translations a large number have survived. The most important are the homilies on Jeremiah, the books of Moses, Joshua, and Luke, and the commentaries on Matthew, John, and Paul's Epistle to the Romans.

With grammatical precision and critical discernment, Origen combined the allegorical method of interpretation with the logical corollary of his conception of scriptural inspiration. He distinguished a threefold sense of the Scripture: a grammaticohistorical, a moral, and a pneumatic. Above all, he set up a formal system of allegorical interpretation that remains to this day, making the sacred writings an inexhaustible source of philosophical and dogmatic wisdom, and encouraging the student to read his own ideas into any passage chosen.

Of his dogmatic writings, only one remains in its integrity: *On First Principles.* The work is the first attempt at a scientific dogmatic to accommodate the needs of the ancient church. The material was drawn solely from Scripture and formed into an intellectual and speculative system of theology. In it, Origen discusses God, man, the earth and its creatures, evil, the soul, free will, and salvation. Each of these areas embraces, although not in a strictly comprehensive way, the whole scheme of the Christian view of the world from different points of view and with different contents.

The controversies that hounded Origen throughout his lifetime grew even more intense after his death. The cruelest attack was launched by Bishop Epiphanius in the fourth century. There were many others, their cause strengthened when Jerome, influenced by the surging tide, turned against his once-honored teacher.

It was not so much the relation between faith and knowledge as defined by Origen that critics singled out, but rather some isolated propositions, such as his doctrines of the preexistence of souls, of the body and soul of Christ, of the resurrection of the flesh, and of the final restoration, in which all souls would be saved, even that of the devil, "for God is a God of love and would never want the eternal damnation of any of His creatures."

With typical Alexandrian aplomb, Origen also asserted that, after the Crucifixion, Christ continued His work of salvation throughout the planetary system, beginning first with Venus.

By the sixth century, the disputes erupted into open battle, and blood was shed over the gentle Origen's name. Under the jurisdiction of Emperor Justinian, he was anathematized by the Fifth Ecumenical Council at Constantinople in 553, and soon thereafter all of his writings were systematically sought out and destroyed. The loss was immeasurable. Fortunately, some Latin translations survived—those of Hilary, Jerome, and Rufinus of Aquileia.

Well into the Middle Ages, Origen's grave near the cathedral in Tyre was still identified for visitors. It is remarkable how long his name has lingered over the ruins of that ancient city. Even to this day, natives of Lebanon reverently point toward the place where he presumably lies buried.

∽∾

In the freethinking society of Alexandria, it was an easy matter to formulate new opinions and even radical beliefs about the existence of God and His relationship to man. Hilary, bishop of Poitiers, wrote in the fourth century:

> It is a thing equally deplorable and dangerous, that there are as many creeds as opinions among men, as many doctrines as inclinations, and as many sources of blasphemy as there are faults among us; because we make creeds arbitrarily, and explain them as arbitrarily. The Homoousion is rejected, and received, and explained away by successive synods. The partial or total resemblance of the Father and of the Son is a subject of dispute for these unhappy times. Every year, nay, every moon, we make new creeds to describe invisible mysteries. We repent of what we have done, we defend those who repent, we anathematize those whom we defended. We condemn either the doctrine of others in ourselves, or our own in that of others; and, reciprocally tearing one another to pieces, we have been the cause of each other's ruin.

One such doctrine greatly disturbed and almost caused the downfall of the struggling early church. It was perpetrated by a young deacon named Arius. Some say he was Libyan by birth, others Alexandrian, but he lived his entire adult life in Alexandria.

He was tall of stature, handsome, intelligent, well-mannered, austere in character, but with an unyielding pride and quarrelsome disposition. Even as a young presbyter, he was twice excommunicated by Bishop Peter of Alexandria for defending the cause of the schismatic Meletius. Neander, in his church history, stated that the mind of Arius was acute and well versed in the arts of debate, but destitute of depth, a contracted intellect without the intuitive faculty.

Arius was educated in the school of Lucian of Antioch, which favored a free grammatical and rationalistic exegesis, in opposition to the allegorical and spiritualistic method of the Alexandrian school. His principal work, called *Thalia* (The Banquet), which he wrote during his stay with Eusebius of Nicomedia, was a defense of his beliefs in an entertaining popular form—half poetry, half prose—and with a predominantly flowery style.

His doctrine provoked one of the most powerful and tenacious quarrels in the history of the church, regarding the question of the divinity of Christ and His relation to the Father. Although the debate led to a series of violent controversies that shook the Roman Empire during the fourth century, it ultimately resulted in a more complex knowledge of and symbolical statement on the doctrine of Christ's divine nature. Above all, it was by no means a fruitless logomachy that revolved around a Greek Iota, for indeed it entered into the very heart of the Christian religion: Arius maintained that Christ was inferior to God the Father; that He was a created being and dissimilar in all things to the Father.

Therefore, in the marketplaces of Alexandria, on the streets, and in the barbershops, the main topic of conversation was not politics, but whether the Son was inferior to the Father. On many occasions, there were fierce outbreaks and blood was shed, even killings, all because of Arius and his teachings. He insisted that the Father alone was God. He alone was unbegotten, eternal, wise, good, unchangeable. He was separated by an infinite chasm from man, and there was no real mediation between them. God did not create the world directly, but only through an agent, the Logos, who was himself created for the purpose of creating the world. The Son of God was preexistent before time and the world, and before all creatures—a middle being between God and the world, the perfect image of the Father—the executor of His thoughts, the Creator of the world of matter and of the spirit. Christ was a creature, the first creature of God, through whom the Father called other creatures into existence. He was made, *not in the essence of the Father*, but out of nothing. He was therefore not eternal, and there was a time when he was not. Neither was He unchangeable, but subject to the vicissitudes of a created being. The Son did not perfectly know the Father, and therefore could not perfectly reveal Him. He was essentially different from the Father.

Arius supported this doctrine with passages directly from Scripture, such as "The Father is greater than I," though other scriptural passages, which taught directly or indirectly the divinity of Christ and his equality with the Father, refuted his claim. In addition, these Scriptures maintained that the conception of a created Creator, who existed before the world, and yet Himself began to exist, was self-contradictory and untenable. There could be no middle being between Creator and creature; no time before the world, since time itself was part of the world. And if the Son was but a creature himself, man still remained separated from God, because no creature could redeem other creatures and unite them with God. If Christ was not divine, man too could not be a partaker of the divine nature and be called a child of God.

Arius, however, contended that no matter how far the Son surpassed other created beings, He remained Himself a created being. In his view, it was blasphemy when he heard Alexander, the bishop of Alexandria, proclaim in public that "God is eternal, and so is his Son." The church historian Theodoret suggested that Arius made these statements because "he was chagrined that Alexander, instead of himself, was appointed to the see of Alexandria, and that his heretical attitude was attributed to discontent and envy."

Nevertheless, the controversy fermented for years, continuing into the reign of Constantine. At first, the emperor viewed the dispute with indifference, but when he realized it was getting out of hand, he addressed a moderating epistle to the contending parties, in which he attributed the origin of the heresy to a trifling and subtle question concerning an incomprehensible point of law. At the same time, Constantine lamented that the Christian people, who had the same God, the same religion, and the same worship, should be divided by such inconsiderable distinctions; and he seriously recommended to the clergy of Alexandria the example of the Greek philosophers, who could maintain their arguments without losing their tempers. This evasion by Constantine should have been the most effectual method of silencing the dispute, but the current of opinion throughout the populace was so powerful and impetuous that the emperor's epistle was ignored.

Arius was not without his army of adherents, even outside Alexandria. Many of them, now bishops, had been fellow students in the school of Lucian at Antioch and were not inclined to let him fall without a struggle. In a letter to Eusebius of Nicomedia, Arius requested his help and ended with the words "Be mindful of our adversity, thou faithful comrade of Lucian's school."

Excommunications and counterexcommunications followed, each reaching the ears of Constantine, who as sole emperor saw in the one Catholic Church the best means of counteracting the movement toward disintegration in his vast empire; and he also realized how dangerous dogmatic squabbles such as these might be to its unity. Therefore, he was left with no recourse except to obtain a general decision. This took place in the First Ecumenical Council, which convened at Nicaea in A.D. 325. After various turns in the controversy, it was finally decided (against Arius) that the Son was of the same substance (homoousios) as the Father, and all thought of His being created or even subordinate had to be excluded.

Constantine accepted the decision of the council and resolved to uphold it. Arius, who refused to subscribe to the Nicene Creed, was excommunicated once again and banished to Illyria. Eusebius of Nicomedia, who accepted the creed but not its anathemas, was exiled to Gaul. Bishop Alexander, having been previously exiled, now returned to Alexandria in triumph, accompanied by his fiery young deacon Athanasius.

In A.D. 330, Arius was recalled from banishment, and once again fierce riots erupted in the streets of Alexandria. Through Constantine's firm insistence, Bishop Alexander reluctantly assented to receive him once more into the bosom of the church. On his way to the church preparatory to the act of admission, Arius was attended by a crowd of partisans acting like guards, and they paraded him through the heart of the city, attracting the notice of all the people. As they approached the place called Constantine's Forum where a column of porphyry had been erected, Arius was seized with stomach cramps. Socrates (A.D. 380–450), the overzealous church historian, recounted the event with characteristic energy:

> . . . a terror arising from the consciousness of his wickedness seized him, accompanied by a violent relaxation of the bowels. In his distress, he inquired if there was a convenient place nearby, and he was hastily directed toward the rear of Constantine's Forum. Soon after this, a faintness came over him, his bowels protruded, together with the evacu-

ations, followed by a copious hemorrhage and the descent of the smaller intestines; moreover portions of his spleen and liver were carried off in the effusion of blood, so that he almost immediately died.

For a long period of time, everyone in Alexandria avoided the spot where Arius died, until a rich follower bought the place and built a house on the site so that there would be no perpetual memory of his violent death.

Five months after his return from the Council of Nicaea, Bishop Alexander died, and on February 8, A.D. 326, Athanasius, the new bishop, resolved to continue Alexander's battle against the Arian heresy. He had just turned thirty-three. Unlike Arius, he was sickly thin, frail, and unattractive. Yet even as a young boy, he showed remarkable qualities of self-confidence that often bordered on precociousness, as the following incident indicates.

Bishop Alexander one day looked down from the window of his house near the sea and saw a group of boys on the beach playing at an imitation of church ceremony. After watching them some time, he began to think that their game was touching a bit too closely on things sacred, so he summoned them before him in the presence of several members of the clergy. They ascertained that one of the boys, named Athanasius, had acted the part of a bishop, and as such had baptized some of his companions who were as yet unchristened. After consulting with his fellow clergymen, Alexander resolved to recognize the baptisms as valid, and commended not only the boy-bishop but also the other boys, who had acted as ministrants.

In his early twenties, Athanasius became a deacon to Alexander and took residence in the bishop's house, serving as his companion and secretary. This position involved great advantages. The seat held by Alexander as successor to St. Mark, and occupant of the Evangelical Throne, was second in the Christian hierarchy, and although the terms "archbishop" or "patriarch" were not as yet in use, bishops were frequently designated by the title of *papas* (pope, or dear father). Their power throughout the churches of Egypt, Libya, and Pentapolis was by ancient custom almost monarchical, extending over a hundred or so episcopal sees who revered their judgments just as the decisions of the see of Rome were revered in Italy. Therefore, to be admitted to the intimacy of *Pope* Alexander was for Athanasius a high privilege, and to live as a son with a father, under the roof "of one beloved for the sweetness of his disposition," provided him with the best opportunities for growth in ecclesiastical affairs. From childhood, he had lived in a city that was an emporium for the interchange of ideas and philosophies, where different nationalities jostled each other, and different streams of thought ran side by side.

He was familiar with all the forms of paganism practiced in the East, particularly Egypt, where Osiris was annually lamented and Isis, Apis, and the Nile still adored. He saw Judaism, in its most stubborn and self-asserting mood, established within two of the five regions of Alexandria, and no doubt heard echoes of the Neoplatonism of Plotinus, Clement, and Origen. In all probability, he may even have fallen in with the Manicheans; and his studies of grammar and rhetoric introduced him at an early age to Homer and Aristotle. His acute logical ability predisposed him to consider such hypotheses as pantheism and materialism. Thus he became an enthusiastic supporter of the argument linking the idea to the Creator, and an active participant in the search for the proof of the soul's instinctive yearning for immortality. Sulpicius Severus, the Christian writer and native of Aquitania (c. 363–425), noted that Athanasius added Roman law to his other studies, but all these, it is evident, were subordinated to the great object of becoming a scribe instructed only on the kingdom of heaven.

Christian theology constituted his chief interest, and for this lifelong interest his antecedents had laid a strong foundation. At close hand, he had seen what a pagan persecution was like, especially when carried on by Maximin II; and as a boy of fourteen, he had been taught and inspired by teachers who were soon to seal their beliefs with blood. Even after the persecution was over, he would be confronted with constant evidence of the severity of the struggle that Christianity was still called upon to wage. The Alexandrian mockeries that Hadrian had found so biting were now targeting a religion which proclaimed an Incarnation and a Cross, and whose votaries had but lately been killed themselves.

As a theologian, Athanasius had strong ideas about what was right, and as a politician, he knew how that good could be enforced. The first years of his episcopate were tranquil, but slowly the conflicts and controversies that would surround him began to appear.

The Council of Nicaea had by no means solved the problem of Arius, and subsequently his friend Eusebius of Nicomedia, by rapidly regaining his influence over the emperor Constantine, was now successful in obtaining a decree demanding that Arius's name be readmitted to communion. Athanasius rebelled against the idea, but since he was no particular favorite of the emperor, his accusers were allowed to attack him at will, charging him with cruelty and sorcery. A more serious accusation inferred that Athanasius had unlawfully put to death Arsenius, a Melitian bishop in the Thebaid.

Athanasius was able to clear himself of these charges, but the hatred of his enemies never abated, and in the summer of 335 he was peremptorily ordered to appear at Tyre, where a council had been summoned to sit in judgment on his conduct. Sensing the prejudice of the council to condemn him, he fled to Constantinople to appeal in person to the emperor. At first, he was refused a hearing, but his perseverance was rewarded by the emperor's agreeing that his accusers at least be brought face-to-face with him in Constantine's presence.

Accordingly, the leaders of the council at Tyre, the most conspicuous of whom were Eusebius of Nicomedia and his namesake of Caesarea, were summoned to Constantinople, where instead of repeating their old charges they now seized upon a more effective and political charge: that Athanasius had threatened to stop the Alexandrian wheat ships bound for Constantinople. Believing the testimony of the accusers, Constantine refused to grant Athanasius the opportunity to respond, and banished him to Trèves in Gaul. This first exile of Athanasius lasted a year and a half, but at the death of Constantine, and the accession of Constantine II, he was allowed to return to Alexandria, in June A.D. 337.

He reached the city on November 23, and as he himself wrote, "the people ran in crowds to see my face; the churches were full of rejoicing; thanksgiving were everywhere offered up; the ministers and clergy thought the day the happiest in their lives."

The euphoria was short-lived. Once again Arius's stolid friend Eusebius of Nicomedia revealed his powerful influence at court, and the old charges against Athanasius were revived. A further charge accused him of tampering with the decision of a council. On March 18, 339, the exarch of Egypt confronted him with an imperial edict by which he was deposed and a Cappadocian named Gregory was nominated bishop in his place. On the following day, after tumultuous scenes, Athanasius fled, and four days later Gregory was installed with the aid of the soldiery.

Athanasius journeyed immediately to Rome to lay his case before the western church. Subsequently, a synod was assembled at Rome in the autumn of 340, and the great council declared him guiltless, but the decision did not immediately favor him. In fact, the bold action of the western bishops incited the Arian party in Alexandria even more, and when Constans succeeded Constantine II as emperor, Athanasius was permitted to return to Alexandria. "Once again," wrote Gregory of Nazianzus in his panegyric on Athanasius, "there were enthusiastic demonstrations streaming forth like another Nile, to meet him afar off as he approached the city."

The six years Athanasius spent in the West were filled with activity, during which he made long journeys throughout Italy and Gaul, and even as far as Belgium. Everywhere he went, he labored strenuously for the Nicene Creed, making such powerful impressions through his personality and zeal that the faithful in all these countries were quite willing to lay down their lives, not only for the Orthodox faith, but for Athanasius as well.

After the death of Constans, Constantius became sole ruler of both East and West, and with the help of counselors, who were more subtle than discerning, he endeavored to unite all the bishops under a general creed of belief. However, his efforts failed and he decided to use force. "My will is your guiding line," he stated in the summer of 355 to the bishops assembled at Milan in response to his order of enforcement. His most defiant opponents, Liberius of Rome, Hilary of Poitiers, and Hosius of Corduba, were exiled. Soon several unsuccessful attempts were made to expel Athanasius, prevented only by the support of the populace. On the night of February 8, however, when Athanasius was holding the Vigils, soldiers and police broke into the cathedral church of St. Theonas. In his treatise *Against the Arians*, Athanasius recounted the scene: "I was seated upon my chair and the deacon was about to read the psalm, the people to answer: 'For His mercy endureth forever.' The solemn act was interrupted; and a panic arose."

That night, when the Syrian troops invaded the Church of St. Theonas, Athanasius sat on his throne and awaited his death with a calm dignity. As shouts and screams interrupted the public worship, he spurred his trembling congregation to their religious confidence by chanting one of the psalms of David, which celebrated the triumph of the God of Israel over the Egyptian tyrant. Suddenly, the doors were flung open and arrows sprayed the people. Many were killed. With drawn swords, the soldiers rushed forward into the sanctuary, the gleam of their armor reflected by holy luminaries that burned around the altar. Athanasius, in a noble gesture, refused to desert his episcopal throne until the remainder of his congregation left in safety.

Concealed by the night's darkness and confusion, he managed to escape and find asylum at a remote monastery on the western outskirts of Alexandria. He had always championed the cause of asceticism and monachism, and throughout his episcopate he maintained close personal relations with Antony the Hermit and Pachomius, the founder of monasteries. Thus the monks received him warmly, providing him a sanctuary to write and think. During his exile, he occupied his time writing long diatribes defending his cause, as well as two treatises: *The Life of Antony* and *Discourses Against the Arians.*

Within months, Julian succeeded Constantius to the imperial throne and, professing indifference to the controversies of the church, permitted all the exiled bishops to return home. In February A.D. 362, Athanasius once more seated himself upon his throne in Alexandria, to the relief of the people.

He flung himself into his episcopal labors with renewed effort, but before he could assemble his bishops, he was deposed, for the fourth time, by the Arian sympathizers. As a faithful crowd gathered around him weeping, he consoled them: "Be of good cheer. It is but a cloud; it will pass."

His forecast proved true, and several weeks later Julian's brief career of pagan revival had ended. In early September 363, Athanasius journeyed to Rome once again in response to a letter sent to him by Jovian. The new emperor praised him for his Christian fidelity and encouraged him to resume his good work. He returned to Alexandria on February 20, 364, but again his period of repose was short. In the spring of 365, after the accession of Valens to the throne, troubles once more arose and he was compelled to seek safety and concealment from his persecutors. However, this lasted only a few months. In February 366, he resumed his episcopal duties and remained undisturbed until his retirement from the office of archbishop, after which he once more traveled to the desert and lived with his society of monks, who faithfully served him as guards, as secretaries, and as messengers. Throughout, he remained diligent in pursuit of heresy. He often came back to Alexandria to supervise ecclesiastical matters, but always under complete secrecy, for his followers still feared for his life.

He was once hidden in a dry cistern, which he had scarcely left before he was betrayed by a woman slave. In another test of his celibacy, he was concealed in the house of a virgin, only twenty years of age, celebrated throughout the city for her exquisite beauty. In her old age, she narrated the story to the fourth-century Roman author Palladius, remembering how surprised she was by the appearance of the archbishop in loose undress. Shuffling toward her, he had confessed that he had been directed by a celestial vision to seek her protection, assured that he would be safe under her roof. A pious girl, she hid him in the best place she could and didn't tell anyone that she harbored a fugitive in her bedchamber.

During his stay with her, the girl supplied him with books and provisions, washed his feet, managed his correspondence, and concealed "from the eye of suspicion that familiar and solitary intercourse between a saint whose character required the most unblemished chastity, and a female whose charms might excite the most dangerous emotions."

Athanasius spent the last years of his life in relative peace until May 2, 373, when, after having consecrated one of his presbyters as his successor, he died quietly in his own house near the sea. His labors were well rewarded. The church accepted as final his opinion on the nature of Christ and, in gratitude, recognized him as a doctor and canonized him as a saint. A large church was built in Alexandria to commemorate his name. It stood on the north side of Canopic Way in the shadows of the Great Library.

⟨∞⟩

About twenty years later there flourished Hypatia, daughter of Theon, the renowned mathematician of Alexandria. Her name was derived from the Greek word *hypatos*, meaning "the most high" or "the greatest." She was initiated early in her father's studies, including philosophy and mathematics at the University. A brilliant student, she later assisted her father in his voluminous writings on Euclid and Porphyry. Then, in the Christian year 400, after a long period of lecturing at the University, she became the recognized head of Neoplatonic studies. Students from every corner of the world competed for her classes. But in addition to her searing intelligence, her eloquence and rare beauty made her remarkable and legendary for her time.

Though she was the author of numerous commentaries on geometry and the astronomical canon of Ptolemy, these works were destroyed by the patriarch Cyril and his army of fanatical monks. Their titles—combined with the admiration expressed by Synesius in his letters—indicate that she devoted most of her efforts to astronomy and mathematics. Synesius had even consulted her on an astrolabe and a hydroscope. As for her philosophical opinions, she embraced the intellectual rather than the mystical side of Neoplatonism and was a follower more of Plotinus than Porphyry.

It is believed that Hypatia's murder was the result of an incident involving the Jews. The Roman prefect Orestes, although a Christian, had assembled a party of supporters whose numbers included not only Christians and high government officials, but also the esteemed Jewish leaders of the city, many of whom had been students of Hypatia. On the contending side stood the patriarch Cyril and his staunch adherents, including the orthodox faithful of the city and the hundreds of Nitrian monks under his jurisdiction.

Everyone in the city loved and glorified Hypatia. She was bestowed with many civic honors and was considered one of the pillars of Alexandria. Cyril, on the other hand, was scorned and mocked from the day he was chosen patriarch. Envious of Hypatia's fame, he began spreading rumors about her, vicious lies portraying her as a witch with powers of sorcery and black magic. His propaganda was enough to convince many of the people who harbored superstitious beliefs of this nature. Cyril and his followers claimed that the first person victimized by her spells was the prefect Orestes, who had curtailed his daily devotions as a Christian and was often seen in her company, along with many of the Jewish citizens.

Cyril's assault on non-Christians began with the Novations, a small, harmless sect not known for trouble. He expelled them from the city, closed their places of worship, confiscated their belongings, and excommunicated their bishop. All without apparent cause.

He next focused his attention on the Jewish citizens. Capitalizing on the behavior of certain individuals, some of whom attended the theater to watch performances instead of celebrating the Sabbath. Cyril stationed his agents in the theater to keep watch on them, rankling the crowd. Orestes attempted to dispel the tension but was unsuccessful. To make matters worse, the Jews accused Orestes of allowing Cyril's informers to spy on them and create trouble.

Cyril called upon the Jewish leaders to stop antagonizing and mocking the Christians of the city, only further riling the Jews. In retaliation, they began raiding Christian homes and launching secret attacks. One evening the Jews ran through the streets of the city shouting that the Church of St. Alexander was consumed in flames. The Christians hurried to save their church, but when they arrived, the Jews attacked and killed many of them. The ruse and loss of life incensed Cyril, and he ordered his army of supporters to the Jewish Quarter of the city, where they plundered the synagogues, set fire to Jewish homes, and chased many of them out of Alexandria.

Orestes lifted his voice against the marauding clergy but was immediately silenced. As he passed through the streets with a small column of soldiers, a band of 500 Nitrian monks yanked his carriage to a halt. He pleaded with them, saying he was a Christian, but his protests were answered with a volley of stones, several of which were thrown by a fanatic monk named Ammonius. The stones found their mark and Orestes fell unconscious in the street. A few brave citizens of Alexandria hastened to his rescue, then seized the monk Ammonius and beat him to death.

After Orestes and the soldiers departed, Cyril commanded the body of Ammonius to be raised from the ground and transported in solemn procession to the cathedral. The name of Ammonius was changed to Thaumasius (the Wonderful), and his tomb was decorated with the trophies of martydom.

Hypatia spent her entire life in Alexandria. Her learned studies on the philosophy of Plato and Aristotle became known throughout the world, and no doubt her intimate friendship with the Roman prefect Orestes caused the patriarch Cyril to believe she was using her influence with the civil authorities to undermine the church's position in Alexandria.

Cyril's feelings were passed on to the clergy, and on a day during the holy season of Lent, Hypatia was pulled from her carriage, stripped naked, dragged to the cathedral, and butchered by a young reader named

Peter and a fanatical mob of Christian monks. Afterward, they scraped the flesh from her bones with broken pieces of tile and threw her limbs to the flames.

Despite her brutal murder, Hypatia's legend inspired retellings of her exquisite beauty, remarkable intelligence, and strength of character. An incident, recorded by the Platonic philosopher Damascius, born in Alexandria in A.D. 450, pivots around an amorous student who could not comprehend her words. Lecturing on Plotinus's concept of beauty, Hypatia directed her comments his way:

> When a man sees the beauty in a woman's body, he must not seek to conquer her with his lust, but realize instead that her beauty is but an image of what real beauty is. By sinking to the lowest depths of his animal nature, he is not contemplating the true essence of beauty, but in his blindness is actually consorting with the illusive shadows of Hades.

(DAMASCIUS, FRAG. 102, p. 77, lines 15–17 [Zintzen])

With the concept of beauty at hand, the student approached her after class and confessed his love for her. With Stoic calm, Hypatia reached into her bag, withdrew the Alexandrian version of a sanitary napkin, and said to the young man, "This is what you love. You do not really love beauty."

Although Hypatia's response seems crude, she succeeded in turning the young man's mind away from the flesh to the inner dimension of beauty. Like Plotinus, she taught her students that wisdom alone was not enough to gain union with perfection. Mere knowledge is mired in mortality and only recognizes beauty through human eyes.

Since Constantine the Great had officially decreed Christianity to be compulsory for everyone in the empire, Cyril and his band of monks took it upon themselves to attack and destroy everything pagan. First to succumb was the magnificent Temple of Serapis. Two years later, the parent Temple of Alexandria was taken down. Its fall was even greater than that of the Serapium, since it involved the destruction of its private library, whose rolls had been stored there for centuries.

The persecution of everything pagan culminated in the murder of Hypatia, and with her, the Greece of the spirit died, the same Greece that had discovered truth and beauty, that had created Alexandria in the person of Alexander the Great.

The ruling monks in Egypt had yet another goal: they became the driving force for a new national movement. Prior to this, patriotism was rare, but under the aegis of religion, ethnic passions arose with such intensity they soon became uncontrollable. Cyril and his monks killed Hypatia not only because she expressed pagan views that were not explicitly Christian, but more importantly, they regarded her as a foreigner. An anti-Greek sentiment overtook Egypt, and its flames even began to devour the cosmopolitan city of Alexandria, culminating in the complete change of language and customs. Beginning with this period the Egyptians were known as Copts, and a new official language was adopted for the whole country. Although the script was Greek, its root was ancient Egyptian, along with six hieroglyph letters.

Occasionally, a new emperor tried to bring the dissenting religious groups together, even making theological concessions to both, but the real differences remained racial and blocked any lasting peace. For this reason, the empire maintained only a small Greek garrison in Alexandria, and consequently, "when the Arabs came, they conquered the city with relative ease."

PART FIVE

The Death

of the City

ONG AFTER THE DEPARTURE of Arius and Athanasius, philosophic and religious quarrels continued to fracture Alexandria's community. While the Monophysites claimed that Christ had only one nature, and although they did not deny Christ's Incarnation and held firm to the belief that His divinity had absorbed the humanity, the Monothelites now moved into a more technical argument, concurring on one hand with the Monophysite position on the single nature of Christ, but adding that He had only one will also, the divine. The orthodox view still maintains that Christ had not only divine and human natures, but two wills as well, both the divine and the human, operating in close unison.

Despite the tension produced by Alexandria's confluence of cultures, the city tended to embrace any new system that entered through its gates—the religion of the Hebrews, the philosophy of Plato, the Christian faith—and on each it left its own indelible impression. Nevertheless, by the seventh Christian century, the physical decay that consumed the city soon turned to a deeper spiritual corrosion. The Arabs, who had already overtaken most of Egypt, avoided Alexandria because to them its cosmopolitan and cultural reputation also betrayed signs of corruption and temptation.

Despite the tacit boycott, some Arabian travelers were intent on visiting the city. One of them, an anonymous Arabian in the ninth century, wrote:

> The city is all white and bright by night, as well as by day. By reason of the walls and pavements of white marble, the people wear black garments, for it is the glare of the marble that makes the monks wear black. So too it is painful to go out by night, since a tailor can see to thread his

needle without a lamp. No one enters the city without a covering over his eyes.

Scores of the world's most renowned scholars, scientists, theologians, writers, and philosophers continued to flow into Alexandria as the centuries rolled on. It still rivaled both Athens and Rome, at times outpacing them as a cultural, political, and intellectual mecca. But the founders' dream would be shattered by the emperor Heraclius (A.D. 575–642), who had won the imperial throne in Constantinople and now was about to give Egypt to the Persians without resistance.

Heraclius was determined to put an end to the religious disputes that had wracked Egypt since the advent of Christianity, and to solve this bitter problem once and for all, he pronounced Monothelitism the official religion, appointing Cyrus to carry out the decree as patriarch and imperial viceroy. It was an irreparable blunder; Cyrus was the worst man for this kind of job. He came to Alexandria in the Christian year 631 and, without bothering to mollify the warring religious factions, he began persecuting the Copts, and even tried to kill the Coptic patriarch.

Emperor Heraclius had no idea what was transpiring in Egypt because Cyrus, in his dispatches, never told him the truth. Earlier, Heraclius had assembled a Greek garrison of soldiers in Alexandria and another near Memphis, at a fort called Babylon. He also had a few military units scattered around the Nile Delta. But by this time, the people of Alexandria were seething: he had paid little attention to their problems and through Cyrus had aggravated the situation by making the city vulnerable to the Persians.

Since the Persians had no fleet, the city at least seemed safe from attack from the sea, and her fortified walls provided equal security by land. Circumventing Alexandria from the Western Harbor, and passing under a bridge at Canopic Way, was a canal. The Persians didn't know the canal was unguarded at the harbor end until they were informed by a foreign student named Peter. A dozen select soldiers were quickly chosen, and in the disguise of fishermen they rowed into the canal from the harbor side, walked down Canopic Way, and unlocked the Moon Gate so the main Persian army could enter.

Under the rule of the Persians, the people were allowed most of their usual privileges. Heraclius, who up to now had done nothing about the foreign invaders, suddenly took interest, launched an attack against the

Persian armies in Asia, and routed them. Egypt was free once again, but not for long.

A greater danger now emerged from the east. Cyrus never bothered to consider it, let alone confront it. Far worse, the emperor Heraclius did not send one ship to Egypt's assistance. In truth, he never anticipated the threat of Mohammedanism (later known as Islam). Syria and the Holy Land were the first to fall to the Arabs, and in the Christian year 641, ten years after the death of the prophet Mohammed, the country was seized by an army of 4,000 cavalry under the command of the Arab general Amru, who was not only a superb military genius, but a man of wit and intelligence. When he was not leading his armies into battle, he sat in his tent and composed poetry.

Amru entered Egypt along the coastal route, then moved quickly up the Nile, seizing the imperial fortress at Heliopolis and taking control of the Babylon citadel where Cyrus hid. As Christianity lost its tenuous foothold on Egyptian soil, Cyrus betrayed his own weakness by negotiating a hasty peace with General Amru and by abandoning the rest of Egypt, with the exception of Alexandria, to the Arabs, as a last ditch attempt to protect the remaining Alexandrian Christians.

For a while at least, the city was not in danger. With its impregnable walls, it was well fortified and protected from the south, and the Arabs had no navy to attack it from the sea. Although General Amru lacked artillery, his cavalry more than made up for it.

The Arabs finally decided to approach Alexandria from the southeast. The patriarch Cyrus had already arrived from the fortress of Babylon and was conducting a liturgy in the Caesarium. Emperor Heraclius's imperial army had already evacuated the city and returned to Constantinople, leaving Alexandria defenseless.

General Amru entered Alexandria through the Sun Gate. His army did the usual looting and raping, but they did not destroy any of the city's edifices. In fact, it is said that they were deeply impressed with the marble colonnades running along both sides of Canopic Way and the Street of the Soma. They also marveled at the Temple of Serapis, the Caesarium, the Mouseion and Library, the University, the two gigantic obelisks overlooking the Great Harbor near Antirrhodus, the Mausoleum of Alexander the Great, and, of course, Pharos Lighthouse.

General Amru treated the people mercifully. Those who wished to leave were permitted to do so, while those choosing to remain could worship as they pleased as long as they paid a tribute. With reserved pride, he then sent the following dispatch to the caliph Omar at Cairo (the new name for Memphis): "I have taken a city which contains 4,000 palaces, 4,000 baths, 400 theaters, 1,200 greengrocers, and 40,000 Jews who pay tribute."

The caliph was unimpressed. Nodding quickly to the messenger, he rewarded him with a loaf of bread, a vial of olive oil, and a few dates.

For almost a thousand years, the Arabs would never realize the value of their prize, except to acknowledge that Allah had granted them a large and powerful city. It meant little to them that Alexandria had remained unrivaled in the world for centuries, that the genius of Greek wisdom had created it, and that it was the intellectual birthplace of Christianity.

History laid the full blame of the destruction of Alexandria's Great Library on the Arabs, but in truth, many of the precious volumes had already been destroyed by the same fanatical Christian monks who killed Hypatia.

⌒ⲚⲚⳑↃ

True to its nature, Alexandria could never accept complete obeisance to anyone or anything. Supported by an intact imperial fleet, it eventually revolted against the Arab rule, and General Amru was dispatched there once again to subdue the riots. There was a general massacre, and by Amru's order, what remained of the Library was totally destroyed. The priceless manuscripts and papyrus rolls were carted off and used as fuel for heating all the baths of the city. The English historian Edward Gibbon wrote that enough hot water was supplied to last six months for four thousand baths. The palm-leaf manuscripts were used to ignite the flames.

During this time, an Arab sheikh visited the emperor Heraclius in Constantinople and suggested that the emperor should adopt the new religion sweeping the East and call it Islam, or Peace. Heraclius politely dismissed both the sheikh and his idea. The sheikh then sent his envoys to the imperial viceroy at Alexandria, who also acted in a polite manner and summarily dispatched some gifts to the sheikh: a donkey, a mule, a bag of gold sovereigns, several goatskins laden with butter and honey, and two beautiful Alexandrian maidens, one of whom became the sheikh's favorite concubine.

Meanwhile, for weeks the new patriarch, John, tried to prevent Amru from destroying the priceless scrolls at the Mother Library. The two had long been good friends, and only recently, while he was occupying Syria, Amru had summoned John to his headquarters and asked him endless questions concerning the Holy Scriptures. Did Christ, for example, govern the world as God, even when he was in Mary's womb? The discussions delighted Amru as well as the patriarch, and they often lasted well into the night. As a Muslim, Amru had a high regard for Holy Scripture, but he sternly informed the patriarch that nowhere in the Pentateuch was there even a passing reference to a Trinity:

> "God has no children," he stated flatly. "If He had a son, I would be the first to worship him. Please, do not tell me there is a Trinity in God. He is one, and one only!"

According to the Christian writer Bar-Hebraeus (A.D. 1226–1286), the patriarch finally got around to asking Amru something he did not dare bring up during their daily conversations:

> "You have sealed up every warehouse in Alexandria, and you rightly lay claim to all the goods in our city. To this, I do not object, but there are certain things which are of use neither to you nor to your soldiers, and I would like to ask you to leave them here."
>
> "What exactly are these things?" Amru inquired.
>
> "The books in our Mother Library. You must understand that when Ptolemy Philadelphus succeeded to the throne of Egypt he became a seeker after knowledge and a man of some learning. He searched for books everywhere, regardless of expense, offering booksellers and collectors the very best terms in order to persuade them to bring their wares here. Before long, some fifty-four thousand books were acquired, but Ptolemy did not stop here. He knew that there were other important books in all corners of the world: India, Persia, Georgia, Armenia, Babylon, Judaea. He instructed his agent Demetrius to seek them out at all costs. And this was Ptolemy's policy until he died. These valuable books have graced our Mother Library for centuries, and we beg you not to destroy them."

Amru was taken by the patriarch's sincere plea, and after a long moment he replied:

> "On the matter of these books, I cannot act without the permission of the Caliph. However I can write to him and inform him about the extraordinary things you have just now related."

The caliph's answer came after a delay of many weeks:

> "The contents of these books are either in accordance with the teaching of the Koran, or they are opposed to it. If in accord, then they are useless, since the Koran itself is sufficient; and if in opposition, they are pernicious and must be destroyed."

Only a few manuscripts of Euclid and Ptolemy were saved; also an invaluable treatise by Pappus, in which he collated, examined, and criticized the best-known works of the two mathematicians. With the death of the Library, Alexandria seemed to lose its soul. Centuries would pass before it could function again, a shadow of its former greatness.

After the Arab conquest, Alexandria's physical decay was quickly followed by a spiritual decay. Amru and his Arabs instinctively kept away from Alexandria and, instead, founded near Cairo a new cultural center of their own. The thousand-year interval between the Arab conquest of Egypt and its fall to Napoleon was marked more by geography than politics. If Alexander the Great had returned at any time during these years he never would have recognized the city he founded. The greatest change occurred in the twelfth century, when the Canopic mouth of the Nile silted up, blocking the flow of fresh water into Lake Mareotis and making the lake unnavigable. Consequently, Alexandria was cut off from the entire river system of Egypt and was unable to trade as easily as before, hindering its continued growth as either a trade or cultural locus. There was also a drastic change in the shape of the city: the Heptastadion, which was built by the Ptolemies to connect the mainland with the island of Pharos, fell into disrepair. It eventually became a broad spit of land that, in turn, caught so much of the Nile's silt and mud that Pharos Island was ultimately joined to the mainland, becoming the present Ras-el-Tin.

Although the Arabs neglected the city, they continued to admire it and even tried to adapt it to their needs, converting the huge Church of St. Theonas into the colossal Mosque of a Thousand Columns, and the Cathedral of St. Athanasius into the Attarine Mosque. A third mosque, that of the prophet Daniel, was built directly over the site of the Mausoleum. But the Caesarium, the Mouseion, the Pharos Light, the Ptolemaic palaces—all lay in ruins. So did the walls. And though the Arabs built new walls in A.D. 828, their course was so short (they enclosed but a fragment of the ancient city), they vividly show the decline of the town and of the population.

Tradition says that soon after the new walls were built, the Venetians stole from Alexandria the true body of St. Mark, concealing it first in a tub of pickled pork in order to divert the attentions of the Muslim officials on the quay. "For the Alexandrians, it wasn't a catastrophic loss, but it brought much satisfaction to Venice."

Toward the end of the Arab rule, the Mameluke sultan of Cairo, Kait Bey, constructed on the ruins of Pharos Light the powerful fort that still bears his name. Not part of a city rejuvenation effort, the fort was instead built to defend the city against the growing naval power of the Turks. It proved to be of no avail, and in 1517 the Turks conquered Egypt and began another sad chapter in the history of Alexandria.

Under the Turks, the city's population continued to shrink, and on the neck of land that was formerly the Heptastadion, a new settlement sprung up, known as the Turkish Town, which still exists. "It is but a small strip of ramshackle houses scattered between tired worn-out mosques," reported the English captain John Foxe in 1577. After having been caught by Turkish corsairs in Alexandria and imprisoned with his crew, Captain Foxe organized a mutiny with the help of a friendly Spaniard and succeeded in recapturing his ship. Under the heavy fire of Turkish guns stationed at Fort Kait Bey, Foxe managed to work his ship out of the Eastern Harbor and safely into the Mediterranean.

On his visit to Alexandria in 1610, the English author George Sandys lamented the city's decline:

> Such was this Queen of Cities and Metropolis who now hath nothing left her but ruins; and those ill witnesses of her perished beauties; declaring rather that towns as well as men are vanished by the ages. Sundry mountains were raised of the ruins, by Christians not to be mounted, lest they take too exact a survey of the city, in which are often found (especially after a shower) rich stones and medals engraven with their Gods and men with such perfection of Art as these now cut seem lame and unlively counterfeits.

EPILOGUE

ON JULY 1, 1798, the 4,000 inhabitants of Alexandria looked out over the harbor and saw it filled with a huge fleet. Men disembarked all night from the ships, and by noon of the next day 5,000 French soldiers under Napoleon had occupied Alexandria. They were but a small part of a larger force that had come to Egypt to presumably assist Turkey in putting down a revolt by the Egyptians. Napoleon was a general at this time, and, Egypt, particularly Alexandria, had captivated him so much that in his battles with the English he envisioned himself as a revived Alexander the Great, conquering the exotic empires of the East, pursuing the same dreams as Caesar and Mark Antony.

He did not linger in Alexandria. Leaving Admiral Brueys to dispose the fleet as safely as possible, with Lord Nelson in pursuit, he led his army into Cairo and won the Battle of the Pyramids. Meanwhile, Brueys attempted to negotiate his fleet into the Western Harbor, but the entrance was tight and the shallow water, although capable of accepting the smaller transports, prevented the huge men-of-war from passing through. Brueys impatiently swung his fleet around to another anchorage in the Bay of Aboukir, but Nelson detected the movement of the French ships, attacked them by surprise, and destroyed them. This famous engagement, the Battle of the Nile, proved disastrous to Napoleon, and although he succeeded in taking Cairo, he had now lost total command of the sea. As a result, his conquering land forces were unable to receive reinforcements or supplies and they began suffering from both disease and hunger.

Turkey seized this opportunity to declare war on the French, and, supported by Nelson's victorious fleet, a large Turkish force landed at Aboukir in July of 1799. Napoleon led his troops to a brilliant victory, but the loss of his fleet had shattered his grandiose dream of ruling the East, and like Mark Antony, he deserted his army and fled back home.

In March 1801, Sir Ralph Abercrombie landed at Aboukir with a contingent of 1,500 men. His plan was not to conquer Egypt, but to compel the remaining French army to evacuate it. Staying close to the sea, he marched westward toward Alexandria, advancing as far as Mandurah with his left flank supported by Lake Aboukir. The French forces out-flanked him at Ramleh, near Mareotis, whose freshwater lake had now completely dried up, and as a result, Abercrombie's army suffered heavy losses. He himself was wounded by a musket shot and had to abandon his command. British sailors carried him into a boat, but before they could get him to a hospital ship, he was dead.

His successor, General Hutchinson, acted swiftly and, at the advice of his engineers, cut the dike that separated Lake Aboukir from Lake Mareotis. To the delight of the British soldiers, the salt water rushed in and, in a few days, thousands of acres had been flooded, isolating Alexandria from the rest of Egypt. Later that same year, a second British force landed west of Alexandria, at Marabout, and the French, caught between two fires, were obliged to surrender. They were given easy terms and allowed to leave Egypt with all the honors of war. Then, with their goal accomplished, the British left the country to the Turks.

Today Alexandria is more closely connected with the rest of Egypt than ever in the past. Yet the old influences remain, and it is the oldest of them, the Hellenistic ideals of Alexander the Great, to which it still clings. In 1922, E. M. Forster wrote:

> Her future like that of other commercial cities is dubious; and neither the Pharos of Sostratus nor the Idylls of Theocritus nor the Enneads of Plotinus are likely to be rivaled again. Only the climate, only the north wind and the sea remain as pure as when Menelaus, the first visitor, landed on Pharos three thousand years ago; and at night, the constellation of Berenice's hair still shines as brightly as when it caught the attention of Conon the astronomer.

Alexandria has suffered. Travelers approaching the city by air or by ship are often overwhelmed by the decay of this legendary, once-great metropolis. Thus far, excavations have revealed much of the ancient city's rich history, but two contrasting forces acting on modern Alexandria and its coastline confront further attempts to resurrect the past: the building-up of the present city and the erosion of the coast by the sea. With new buildings under construction or standing above potential archeological sites, it is nearly impossible to find a space in which to dig. Other sites are either already submerged or being submerged by the onslaught of the Mediterranean, making it difficult for diving expeditions to find Alexandrian relics in the silt-churned waters.

Yet, for the generations that knew, adored, and lived in the city, for those who made the intellectual pilgrimage to absorb Alexandria's wisdom, and even for those who will one day look upon the extraordinary antiquities unearthed from the Egyptian sand or dredged from the Mediterranean, it is clear that Alexandria's influence is extensive. Like the reach of Alexander the Great's empire during its peak, Alexandria has not only helped to determine present-day political geography, but has also fostered a wide range of western thought, from philosophy to religion and how the West perceives itself in the span of world history.

BIBLIOGRAPHY

CHIEF ANCIENT SOURCES

Appian. *Roman History.* Written in Greek; translated by H. White. London: Bohn's Classical Library, 1899.

Arrian, *Anabasis of Alexander.* Written in Greek; translated by Rooke. London, 1812.

Diodorus Siculus, *Library of History.* Cambridge: Loeb Classical Library, 1939.

Eusebius, *Church History,* in Migne, *Patrologia Graeca.* Paris, 1856.

Plutarch. *Parallel Lives.* Dryden translation, revised by Arthur Hugh Clough. Boston, 1897.

OTHER ANCIENT SOURCES

Aristophanes, Aristotle, Athenaeus, Julius Caesar, Cicero, Clement, Dio Cassius, Euripides, *The Greek Anthology,* Herodotus, Homer, Jerome, Marcus Aurelius, Origen, Ovid, Pausanias, Plato, Pliny, Plotinus, Polybius, Strabo, Thucydides.

MODERN SOURCES

Balanos, Demetrios. *Patrologia* (in Greek). Athens, 1930.

Bentwich, N. *Philo Judaeus of Alexandria.* Philadelphia: Jewish Publication Society, 1910.

Bernhardy, G. *Eratosthenes.* Berlin, 1822.

Bigg, C. *The Christian Platonists of Alexandria.* London: Oxford University Press, 1886.

Bradford, E. *Cleopatra.* London: Hodder & Stoughton, 1971.

Cavafy, C. P. *Poems* (in Greek). Athens, 1950.

Chadwick, Henry. *Early Christian Thought and the Classical Tradition: Studies in Justin, Clement, and Origen*. London: Oxford University Press, 1966.

deLubac, Henri, *Origen on First Principles*. London, 1936.

Karl Wilhelm Dindorf (1802–1883) was a classical scholar and professor of literary history at the University of Leipzig. He later edited books on Athenaeus and the Greek dramatists and poets, all of which he combined into his *Poetae Scenici Graeci* (1880). My quote is from his *Sophocles*.

Dzielska, Maria. *Hypatia of Alexandria*. Cambridge, Mass.: Harvard University Press, 1995.

Forster, E. M. *Alexandria: A History and a Guide*. London: M. Hagg, 1938.

Fraser, P. M. *Ptolemaic Alexandria*. London: Clarendon Press, 1972.

Gibbon, Edward. *The History of the Decline and Fall of the Roman Empire*. London, 1862.

Gorringe, H. *Egyptian Obelisks*. New York: Privately printed, 1882.

Heath, T. L. *Aristarchus of Samos*. London: Oxford University Press, 1913.

Library of the Greek Fathers (in Greek, *Bibliothiki Ellinon Pateron*). Vols. 9 and 10. Athens, 1956.

Merton, Thomas. *Clement of Alexandria*. Verona, 1962.

Migne, *Patrologia Graeca*. Paris, 1856.

Milne-Edwards, Henry (1800–1885), *Natural History (Histoire Naturelle)*. Paris, 1837.

Origen. "Against Celsus," in Migne, *Patrologia Graeca*. Vol. XI. Paris, 1856–1864.

Pearson, L. *The Lost Histories of Alexander the Great*. Historia, 1960.

Plotinus. *The Enneads*. Translated by Thomas Taylor. London: Bohn's Classical Library, 1895.

Rufus, Quintus Curtius. *History of Alexander*. Translated by P. Pratt. London, 1821.

Smith, T. *Euclid, His Life and System*. Edinburgh: T. Clarke, 1902.

Tarn, Sir William W. *Alexander the Great*. London: Cambridge University Press, 1948.

Thévet, André. *Portraits and Lives of Illustrious Men*. Paris, 1584.

Volkmann, H. *Cleopatra*. Translated by T. J. Cadoux. London, 1958.

Vrettos, Theodore. *Origen*. New York, 1978.

Weigall, Arthur. *The Life and Times of Cleopatra*. London, 1914.

NOTES

14 "The Hellespont would blush": Ibid., 18: 2.

15 "Alexander, the son of Philip": Plutarch, IV, 179.

17 "Let me wash off": Ibid., 184.

17 "This indeed is what it means": Ibid.

18 "as though they were": Ibid., 185.

18 "these Persian women": Arrian, VII, 13.3.

18 "to put them to death": Plutarch, IV, 186.

18 "I have never seen": Ibid.

19 "Our great conquests": Arrian, III, 18.

19 "Alexander, you have now": Diodorus Siculus, XVII, 92: 1f.

20 "It is the fate of a king": Plutarch, IV, 195.

21 "I will not steal a victory": Ibid., 200.

21 "Now that we no longer": Ibid., 201.

24 "as if struck through the liver": Ibid., 253.

24 "The last days": Arrian, VII, 27–28.

27 "Do not settle him here": F. Jacoby, *Rhein. Mus.* (1903), 461f.

28 "As for the exact thoughts": Arrian, VII, 30; Tarn, II, 325.

PART TWO—THE MIND OF THE CITY

34 "Think of it": Herodes, Papyrus Ms. British Museum (135); Milne, *Catalogue 96,* 66.

34 "There it towered": Milne, 66.

35 "This unique establishment": A. Hamilton, *Roman Journals of Ferdinand Gregovorius* (London, 1907).

38 "During an evening symposium": Aulus Gellius, *Noctes Atticae.*

43 "There is no royal road": Quotation preserved by Proclus, the chief representative of the later Neoplatonists, on a reply made by Euclid to King Ptolemy.

47 "And so," he later wrote: Cicero, *Tusc. Disp.,* V.C.23.

55 "A mild old age": *Greek Anthology,* VII, Epigram 78.

58 "drawn there": Strabo, XVII, 6.

58 "sailors cannot perceive lights": Ibid., 31f.

60 "I know that I am mortal": Ptolemaeus, *Almagest,* IV, 9.

62 "As I know you will be rejoiced": R. H. Major, *Select Letters of Christopher Columbus* (London, 1847).

67 "The king, extremely surprised": Plutarch, V, 135–137.

72 "Indeed, love flitted through the literature": Forster, *Alexandria,* 33.

72 "Someone told me, Heracleitus": William Cory, *Ionica* (London: Smith, Elder & Co., 1858), 7.

PART THREE—THE POWER OF THE CITY

77 "The people of Alexandria": From a letter dated A.D. 134, written in Alexandria by Hadrian, in Plutarch, V, 170.

79 "She was a brilliant linguist": Ibid., 179–180.

79 "a slave to her lusts": Josephus, *Against Apion,* II, 56–58.

80 "arriving from Ptolemy himself": Diodorus Siculus, I, 83: 1–9.

81 "A person who refused a bribe": Theodor Mommsen, in Bradford, 35–36.

83 "If an Egyptian king": Ibid., 40.

87 "It was a tragic situation": Plutarch, IV, 147.

87 "He that enters at a tyrant's door": Sophocles, from a lost and unknown play, Frag. Incert. 54, in Dindorf, 711.

87 "Surely, I may be mistaken": Plutarch, IV, 149.

90 "All the Gauls did Caesar vanquish": Bradford, 65.

90 "Home we bring the bald adulterer": Ibid.

95 "came flocking along both sides": Ibid., 81.

97 "was the deep black lustre": Ibid., 12.

98 "I detest the queen": Cicero, "Letter to Atticus," VII, 11.

[98] "The drip of water": J. W. Mackail, in Bradford, 103.

[99] "On this day": Cicero, *Philippics*, II, 14.

[100] "no war could be successful": Ibid., 24.

[100] "I don't understand": Dio Cassius, XLIV, 10f.

[102] "You see, the Ides of March": Plutarch, IV, 320.

[102] "I wish you luck": Dio Cassius, XLIV, 18f.

[103] "And you too, my child!": Ibid., 19.

[104] "I bequeath to every Roman": Plutarch, IV, 325.

[109] "Give them games, bread, wine": Cicero, *Philippics*, VII, 7.

[111] "Fly?" he exclaimed: Appian, II, 117f.

[112] "The barge she sat in": Shakespeare, *Antony and Cleopatra*, Act II, Scene 3, 196–209.

[114] "If you would return": Socrates of Rhodes, *Civil War*, bk. 3.

[115] "It would be tedious": Plutarch, V, 180.

[115] "We only have a small party": Pliny, IX, 58 (117–122).

[116] "General," she taunted: Plutarch, V, 182.

[118] "There, for this is the only": Ibid., 185.

[118] "Shall I cut the cables?": Ibid.

[119] "Let nobody henceforth": Ibid., 186–189.

[124] "He who had eaten": Dio Cassius, XLIX, 33.

[130] "and at their command, a Queen": Ibid., 150.

[132] "Octavian was no more than": Bradford, 201.

[132] "To the Romans": Ibid., 203.

[140] "You see," she said: Suetonius, in Plutarch, V, 213.

[141] "Let Antony give up": Ibid., 217.

[142] "General, look at these wounds!": Dio Cassius, I, 25.

[143] "In her bitter anger": Plutarch, V, 217.

[145] "Who is this that follows Antony?": Ibid., 220.

[145] "It is surprising": Ibid., 220f.

[151] "She has betrayed me!": Dio Cassius, LI, 2f.

[151] "Now, Antony": Plutarch, V, 228.

[152] "Well done, Eros!": Ibid., 230.

[153] "the gold Alexandrian sunlight": Bradford, 259.

[154] "a Caesar too many": A parody on Homer's "too many leaders are not well" (*Iliad*, II, 204).

[154] "I will not be exhibited": Plutarch, V, 236.

[155] "You know very well": Ibid., 235.

[157] "So, here it is!": Volkmann, 193; Dio Cassius, LI, 16f.

[157] "This is a fine deed, Charmion!": Dio Cassius, LI, 16f.

PART FOUR—THE SOUL OF THE CITY

[164] "Wisdom is more moving": Forster, 66.

[165] "There was once a time": Philo, "On the Unchangeableness of God," Loeb Classical Library, III, 1–6.

[166] "take reason along": Ibid., 7f.

[166] "In nature": Philo, "On the Special Laws," VII, 283.

[166] "A woman may and should": Ibid., 301f.

[166] "Men seek pleasure": Ibid., 302f.

[168] "Where was my body": Philo, "On the Cherubim," II, 75.

[169] "The character of Gaius": Philo, "Embassy to Gaius," X, 346.

[170] "The descent of my soul": Porphyry, "Plotinus," Loeb Classical Library, I, 9.

[171] "This is the man I've been seeking": Ibid., 9f.

[174] "The gods ought to come to me": Ibid.

[174] "This is the thief": Ibid., 37.

[176] "Clement's wisdom": Merton, *Clement of Alexandria*, 6.

[176] "In Clement, there is no shadow": Ibid., 9.

[177] "Zeus Is Dead": Ibid., 19.

[179] "The Old Testament": Chadwick, 43.

[179] "Plato, Aristotle, and the Stoics": Ibid., 43f.

[179] "who made man": Ibid., 59.

[183] "Christ should not be the object": Henri deLubac, *Origen on First Principles,* IV, 313f.

[183] "Which of us": Jerome, "Epistle," 33.4.

[184] "From this day on": Vrettos, *Origen,* 206.

[185] "And who saw your *Messiah*": Origen, "The True Word," in Migne, *Patrologia Graeca,* XI, 641.

[185] "The story of his divine parentage": *Library of the Greek Fathers,* IX, 121: 38.

[186] "Furthermore, God would never": Ibid., 127: 32–40.

[186] "Who are you": Ibid., 256: 30f.

[187] "they should be aware": Ibid., 194: 34–195.

[187] "Put away your vain illusions": Ibid., 247: 41f.

[188] "You audaciously believe": Ibid., 289: 20f.

[188] "Ye men of Israel": Acts of the Apostles, V, 35.

[188] "the highest speculations": Migne, *Patrologia Graeca,* XI, 1187.

[191] "You want to cast away": Vrettos, *Origen,* 289.

[193] "for God is a God of love": Origen, *On First Principles,* II, 10.

[194] "It is a thing equally deplorable": Hilary of Poitiers, in Gibbon, I, 684–690.

[197] ". . . a terror arising": Socrates, *Ecclesiastical History,* I, 26.

[200] "the people ran in crowds": Athanasius, "Defense of his Flight," 1.

[201] "I was seated upon my chair": Athanasius, "Against the Arians," 81f.

[203] "from the eye of suspicion": Gibbon, II, 810.

PART FIVE—THE DEATH OF THE CITY

211 "The city is all white": Forster, 85.

214 "I have taken a city": Luciano Canfora, *The Vanished Library* (Berkeley: University of California Press, 1989), 83.

215 "God has no children": Ibid., 86.

215 "You have sealed up": Ibid., 87–90.

220 "Her future like that of other commercial cities is dubious": Forster, 103–104.

Index

About the Author

Theodore Vrettos studied at Holy Cross Greek Theological School, Tufts University, and Harvard. He has taught at Northeastern University, State College of Massachusetts at Salem, and Simmons College and now devotes his time entirely to writing. He lives in Massachusetts with his wife.